ECDL

Advanced Word Processing

Brendan Munnelly
and Paul Holden

ECDL Advanced Approved
Courseware Syllabus AM3 Version 1.0

PEARSON
Prentice
Hall

Harlow, England • London • New York • Boston • San Francisco • Toronto • Sydney • Singapore • Hong Kong
Tokyo • Seoul • Taipei • New Delhi • Cape Town • Madrid • Mexico City • Amsterdam • Munich • Paris • Milan

PEARSON EDUCATION LIMITED

Head Office:
Edinburgh Gate
Harlow CM20 2JE
Tel: +44 (0)1279 623623
Fax: +44 (0)1279 431059

Website: www.it-minds.com

First published in Great Britain in 2002

© Rédacteurs Limited 2002

ISBN 0-130-98984-3

British Library Cataloguing in Publication Data
A catalogue record for this book is available from the British Library

'European Computer Driving Licence' and ECDL and Stars device are registered trademarks of the European Computer Driving Licence Foundation Limited in Ireland and other countries.

ECDL Advanced Word Processing may be used in assisting students to prepare for the European Computer Driving Licence Advanced Word Processing Examination. The author makes no warrant that the use of this book will ensure passing the relevant examination.

Use of the ECDL-F approved courseware Logo on this product signifies that it has been independently reviewed and approved in complying with the following standards:

Acceptable coverage of all courseware content related to ECDL Advanced Syllabus AM3 Version 1.0. This courseware has not been reviewed for technical accuracy and does not guarantee that the end use will pass the associated ECDL (Advanced) Examinations.

Any and all assessment tests and/or performance-based exercises contained in *ECDL Advanced Word Processing* relate solely to this book and do not constitute, or imply, certification by the European Driving Licence Foundation in respect of any ECDL examinations. For details on sitting ECDL examinations in your country, please contact the local ECDL licensee or visit the European Computer Driving Licence Foundation Limited website at www.ecdl.com.

References to the European Computer Driving Licence (ECDL) include the International Computer Driving Licence (ICDL).

ECDL Advanced Word Processing Syllabus Version 1.0 is published as the official syllabus for use within the European Computer Driving Licence (ECDL) and International Computer Driving Licence (ICDL) certification programme.

Rédacteurs Limited is at www.redact.ie

Brendan Munnelly is at www.munnelly.com

10 9 8 7 6 5 4 3
07 06 05 04 03

Typeset by Pantek Arts Ltd, Maidstone, Kent.
Printed and bound in Great Britain by Ashford Colour Press, Gosport, Hampshire.

The Publishers' policy is to use paper manufactured from sustainable forests.

Preface

What is ECDL?

ECDL, or the European Computer Driving Licence, is an internationally recognized qualification in Information Technology skills. It is accepted by businesses internationally as a verification of competence and proficiency in computer skills.

The ECDL syllabus is neither operating system nor software specific.

For more information about ECDL, and to see the syllabus for *ECDL Module 4, Word Processing, Advanced Level*, visit the official ECDL website at www.ecdl.com.

About this book

This book covers the ECDL Advanced Word Processing syllabus Version 1.0, using Microsoft Word 2000 to complete all the required tasks. It is assumed that you have already completed the word processing module of ECDL 3 using Microsoft Word, or have an equivalent knowledge of the product.

The chapters in this book are intended to be read sequentially. Each chapter assumes that you have read and understood the information in the preceding chapter.

Every chapter contains the following elements:

- **Learning objectives:** This sets out the skills and concepts that you will learn in the chapter.

- **New words:** A list of the key terms introduced and defined in the chapter.

- **Syllabus reference:** A list the items from the ECDL Advanced Word Processing Syllabus that are covered in the chapter.

- **Exercises:** Practical, step-by-step tasks to build your skills.

- **Tasks summary:** A list of the key procedures covered in the chapter.

- **Concepts summary:** A brief guide to the key ideas in the chapter.

- **Quick quiz:** A series of multiple-choice questions to test your knowledge of the material contained in the chapter.

Exercises files

Almost all chapters are accompanied by 'before' and 'after' exercises files. Use the 'before' files as directed. You can check the correctness of your work by comparing them against the 'after' files.

Hardware and software requirements

Your PC should meet the following specifications:

- Pentium 75MHz or higher processor

- Windows 98 ME, NT, 2000 or XP

- 64MB RAM

- Word 2000

- Excel 2000

Typographic conventions

The following typographic conventions are used in this book:

- **Bold face text** is used to denote the names of Microsoft Word menus and commands, buttons on toolbars, tabs and buttons in dialog boxes, and keyboard keys.

- *Italicized text* is used to denote the names of Microsoft Word dialog boxes, and lists, options and checkboxes within dialog boxes.

Good luck with your ECDL studies and test. And remember: 'What one fool can learn, so can another'.

Contents

Chapter 3: Recycle content and formatting: templates

Chapter 4: Separating content from format: templates and styles

Chapter 5: Here's one I prepared earlier: AutoText

Chapter 6: Word checks your documents: AutoCorrect

Chapter 7: Word typesets your documents: AutoFormat As You Type

Chapter 8: Word updates your documents: fields

Chapter 9: Word does everything: macros

Chapter 10: 'Are you sure about this?': comments and document protection

Chapter 11: Displaying, accepting and rejecting revisions: change tracking

Chapter 12: Many subdocuments, one document: master documents

Chapter 13: 'Please complete and return': Word forms

Chapter 14: Tables: merging, splitting, sorting and totalling

Chapter 15: Spreadsheets in Word

Chapter 16: Charts in Word

Chapter 17: Footnotes and endnotes

Chapter 18: Bookmarks and cross-references

Chapter 19: Tables of contents

Chapter 20: Captions

Chapter 21: Indexes

Chapter 22: Font and paragraph effects

Chapter 23: Text boxes and text orientation

Chapter 24: Graphics in Word

Chapter 25: Many columns, one document

Chapter 26: Many sections, one document

Chapter 27: Mail merge

1 Finishing faster by beginning differently: outlines

Objectives

In this chapter you will learn how to:

- Use Outline view to enter headings for a new document
- Display an existing document in Outline view
- Promote and demote headings in Outline view
- Move headings within a document in Outline view
- Control the display of headings and text in Outline view

New words

In this chapter you will meet the following terms:

- Heading level
- Outline
- Outline view
- Outline numbering

Exercise files

In this chapter you will work with the following Word files:

- Chapter1_Exercise_1-1_Before.doc
- Chapter1_Exercise_1-2_Before.doc
- Chapter1_Exercise_1-3_Before.doc
- Chapter1_Exercise_1-4_Before.doc

Syllabus reference

In this chapter you will cover the following item of the ECDL Advanced Word Processing Syllabus:

- **AM3.1.2.6**: Use outline options.

Getting past page 1

When writing a new document, which do you find more difficult: writing the first page or two, or getting beyond the first few pages?

Typically, it's the second step. Why? Because you fall into the trap of trying to perfect your first pages before moving on to the remainder of your document.

Here's the solution: *start differently*.

- Don't begin by focusing on your first sentence, paragraph or page.

- Do begin by considering your entire document.

This method is called *outlining*. It means asking yourself – and perhaps your colleagues – questions such as 'How many sections will be needed?' and 'What subsections will be in each section?'

Only when you have completed your outline, and agreed it with your colleagues, do you write the content of the document.

Outlines: what do they look like?

An outline is a list of a document's headings. Most documents are unlikely to need more than three heading types or *heading levels*: main headings, subheadings and sub-subheadings.

In Word, main headings are called level-1 headings, subheadings are level-2 headings, and so on.

In the following example, you can see five level-1 headings. Of these, only the second ('Codes of Conduct') and fifth ('Help Us To Help You') contain level-2 headings.

> Mission Statement
> Codes of Conduct
> > Standards of Individual Behaviour
> > Consultant-based Services
> > Nursing Services
> Standards of Service
> Teaching and Research
> Help Us To Help You
> > Keeping Us Informed
> > Submitting Feedback
> > Making a Complaint

Heading Level

The relative importance of a heading in a document. Typically, two or three heading levels are sufficient: main headings (level-1 headings), subheadings (level-2 headings) and sub-subheadings (level-3 headings).

In outlines, lower-level headings are indented ('moved in') progressively from the left margin. Indents in an outline have one purpose only: to show the relative importance of the various headings. The indents do *not* affect how the document appears when printed.

> **Outline**
>
> *A list of the headings in a document, with indentation used to represent the level of each heading.*

Promoting and demoting

In an outline, the act of changing a heading from a lower to a higher level is called *promoting* the heading. Conversely, changing a heading from a higher to a lower level is called *demoting* the heading.

Outlining: the benefits to you

With outlines, you can:

- **Agree structure before writing content**. Will other people be reviewing your document? If so, it makes sense to write the main content only *after* you have secured agreement on the overall structure.

  Otherwise, the document you write, although excellent in many ways, may not be the one that your colleagues and superiors actually want – an example of climbing to the top of a ladder only to discover that it is leaning against the wrong wall.

- **Begin with what's easy**. You can begin by writing those parts you feel more confident about – the middle of section three, for example, or the first four subsections of section two.

  Sections that you find more difficult or awkward can be left until the end. You will feel more confident about tackling these when your document is 80–90% complete.

- **Identify problem areas quickly**. Some sections of your document may need information that you do not have to hand.

  You are more likely to meet your deadline if you identify these sections at the start of the project than in the middle or towards the end.

- **Delegate content tasks**. If you are managing a document-creation project, you can delegate different sections of the outline to other contributors.

Outlines in Word

In Word, an outline is one of four available views of a document. (The other views are Normal, Print Layout and Web Layout.) If you have a document currently open, you can see its outline by choosing **View | Outline**.

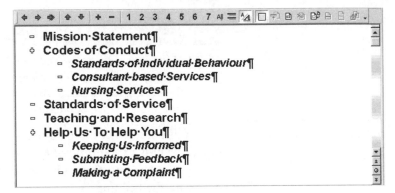

Outlines and styles

Outline heading levels are tied to Word's built-in heading styles, as shown below. (You will learn more about built-in heading styles in Chapter 2.)

Outline heading level	Paragraph style
Level-1 heading	Heading 1
Level-2 heading	Heading 2
Level-3 heading (etc.)	Heading 3 (etc.)
Body text	Normal

You can use styles other than heading styles in your outlines, but it's cumbersome and the methods are not covered in this book.

If a document contains only a single style such as Normal, it displays in Outline view without any organization or structure.

> **Outline view**
>
> *A view in Word that displays a document outline. Outline view provides options to change headings levels, reorder headings, and control which heading levels and other paragraphs are displayed.*

The Outlining toolbar

By default, Word's Outline view contains an Outlining toolbar with buttons for promoting and demoting headings, moving headings (and associated text) within the document, and controlling how many heading levels are displayed.

`←  ⇒  ⇨  ⬆  ⬇  ✛  —   1  2  3  4  5  6  7  All  ≡`

You will learn the purpose of each Outlining toolbar button as you use it in the exercises. A list of buttons and their functions is included at the end of this chapter for easy reference.

Working with outlines: the four tasks

Here are the four tasks that you need to be able to perform with outlines in Word:

- **Create a new document in outline view**. When you begin a new document by creating the document outline, you gain all the benefits associated with outlines and document creation. Exercise 1.1 provides an example.

- **Reorganize an already-written document in Outline view**. As Exercise 1.2 shows, you can quickly and easily restructure the content of an existing document by manipulating its outline.

- **Apply paragraph numbering in Outline view**. In Outline view, you can apply sequential numbering to paragraphs with a single mouse click. You may find this feature useful when working with legal and other highly-structured documents. See Exercise 1.3.

- **Exploit automatic paragraph renumbering**. If you rearrange numbered paragraphs in Outline view, Word automatically renumbers the paragraphs for you. Exercise 1.4 takes you through the steps.

Working with outlines of new documents

As you will see in Exercise 1.1, creating an outline can be the first step in writing a new document. After typing your headings and applying the correct heading levels to them, you then can switch from Outline to Normal or Print Layout view, and type the body text of your document.

Following this method provides you with two benefits:

- Your document is structured correctly from the start.

- Your headings are formatted automatically with the appropriate built-in heading styles.

Exercise 1.1: Creating a document in Outline view

In your first exercise, you will use Word's outline features to help you create a patients' charter for a fictitious organization, the Elmsworth Health Trust.

1) Open Word. If a new, blank document is not created by default, create one.

2) Choose **View | Outline**. Alternatively, click the **Outline View** button at the lower left of the Word window.

Outline View button

3) Type the following lines of text, pressing the **Enter** key after every line except the last one:

```
Codes of Conduct
Individual Standards of Behaviour
Courtesy
Privacy
Religious Beliefs
Consultant-based Services
Nursing Services
```

By default, Word positions your paragraphs as main (level-1) headings.

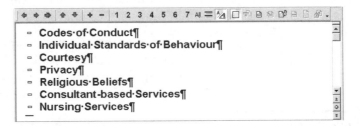

Demote button

4) Click anywhere in the second paragraph, and click the **Demote** button on the Outlining toolbar. The paragraph is now a level-2 heading and looks like this:

  ◇ **Codes·of·Conduct**¶
     □ *Individual·Standards·of·Behaviour*¶
  □ **Courtesy**¶

(Another way to demote a heading is to click anywhere in the paragraph and press the **Tab** key.)

5) Drag the mouse over paragraphs three to seven to select them, and click the **Demote** button twice. Your selected paragraphs are now level-3 headings. Click anywhere outside the five paragraphs to deselect them.

```
    ⟩ Codes·of·Conduct¶
         ⟡ Individual·Standards·of·Behaviour¶
              ▫ Courtesy¶
              ▫ Privacy¶
              ▫ Religious·Beliefs¶
              ▫ Consultant-based·Services¶
              ▫ Nursing·Services¶
         _
```

Promote button

6) Select the last two paragraphs, and click the **Promote** button to make them level-2 headings. Click anywhere outside the two paragraphs to deselect them.

```
    ⟡ Codes·of·Conduct¶
         ⟡ Individual·Standards·of·Behaviour¶
              ▫ Courtesy¶
              ▫ Privacy¶
              ▫ Religious·Beliefs¶
         ▫ Consultant-based·Services¶
         ▫ Nursing·Services¶
```

(Another way to promote a paragraph is to click anywhere in the paragraph and press the **Shift+Tab** keys.)

7) Choose **View | Print Layout**. You can see that your outline heading levels now appear as paragraph styles.

8) Save your sample document with the following name:

Chapter1_Exercise_1-1_After_*Your_Name*.doc

Then close the sample document.

Working with outlines of already-written documents

As you will discover in Exercise 1.2, you can open an existing document, display it in Outline view, and, as you need

- **Change heading levels**. For example, you can demote a level 1 heading to a level-2 heading, or promote a level-3 heading to a level-2 heading, and so on.

- **Reorder content**. You can move content within documents simply by moving the relevant headings in the outline.

   That's right – when you move a heading in Outline view, all subordinate content, both lower-level headings and body text, moves with it.

Reorganizing a lengthy document in Outline view with just a few mouse clicks is faster and less likely to lead to errors than the alternative: working in Normal or Print Layout view, and scrolling repeatedly through pages to perform multiple cut-and-paste operations.

Exercise 1.2: Reorganizing a document in Outline view

In this exercise, you will use Word's outline features to reorder the content of a document, the patients' charter of Elmsworth Health Trust.

1) Open the following file:

    Chapter1_Exercise_1-2_Before.doc

2) Choose **View | Outline**.

3) Click the **Show Heading 3** button on the Outlining toolbar.

    This displays only heading levels 1, 2 and 3. Any lower-level headings and text in Normal style are not shown.

4) Click anywhere in the level-3 heading, 'Waiting Times During Appointments'.

5) Click the **Move Down** button twice. Click anywhere outside the heading to deselect it.

    ◇ **Appointments**¶
        ◇ Waiting·Times·During·Appointments¶
        ◇ Routine·Appointments¶
        ◇ Urgent·Appointments¶

    Before

    ◇ **Appointments**¶
        ◇ Routine·Appointments¶
        ◇ Urgent·Appointments¶
        ◇ Waiting·Times·During·Appointments¶

    After

6) Select the level-2 heading 'Appointments' and the three level-3 headings beneath it.

    ◇ **Appointments**¶
        ◇ Waiting·Times·During·Appointments¶
        ◇ Routine·Appointments¶
        ◇ Urgent·Appointments¶

7) Click the **Move Up** button four times. Click anywhere outside the headings to deselect them. Word reorders the selected headings like this:

    ◇ **Admissions·to·Hospital**¶
        ◇ Urgent·Treatment¶
        ◇ Planned·Treatment¶
        ◇ Emergency·Treatment¶
    ◇ **Appointments**¶
        ◇ Waiting·Times·During·Appointments¶
        ◇ Routine·Appointments¶
        ◇ Urgent·Appointments¶

    Before

    ◇ **Appointments**¶
        ◇ Waiting·Times·During·Appointments¶
        ◇ Routine·Appointments¶
        ◇ Urgent·Appointments¶
    ◇ **Admissions·to·Hospital**¶
        ◇ Urgent·Treatment¶
        ◇ Planned·Treatment¶
        ◇ Emergency·Treatment¶

    After

8) In the final part of this exercise, you will move the heading 'Help Us To Help You' and its subordinate headings so that they are at the end of the document.

    One way is to select the four relevant headings as shown, and then click the **Move Down** button repeatedly.

Show Heading 3 button

Move down button

Move up button

ECDL Advanced Word Processing

◊ **Help·Us·To·Help·You**¶
  ◊ *Keeping·Us·Informed*¶
  ◊ *Submitting·Feedback*¶
  ◊ *Making·a·Complaint*¶

1

*Show Heading 1
button*

Let's try another approach. Click the **Show Heading 1** button on the Outlining toolbar, so that only level-1 headings are shown.

◊ **Elmsworth·Health·Trust:·Patient's·Charter**¶
◊ **Mission·Statement**¶
◊ **Codes·of·Conduct**¶
◊ **Standards·of·Service**¶
◊ **Teaching·and·Research**¶
◊ **Help·Us·To·Help·You**¶
◊ **Information·and·Records**¶

Click anywhere in the heading 'Help Us To Help You', and click the **Move Down** button. Click anywhere outside the heading to deselect it.

9) Let's check if moving the selected level-1 heading also moved the subordinate level-2 headings.

2

*Show Heading 2
button*

Click the **Show Heading 2** button on the Outlining toolbar, so that Word displays both level 1 and level 2 headings.

As you can see, Word automatically moved the subordinate level-2 headings.

◊ **Help·Us·To·Help·You**¶
  ◊ *Keeping·Us·Informed*¶
  ◊ *Submitting·Feedback*¶
  ◊ *Making·a·Complaint*¶
◊ **Information·and·Records**¶
  ◊ *Delays·and·Postponements*¶
  ◊ *Identity·of·Staff*¶
  ◊ *Medical·Information*¶

◊ **Information·and·Records**¶
  ◊ *Delays·and·Postponements*¶
  ◊ *Identity·of·Staff*¶
  ◊ *Medical·Information*¶
◊ **Help·Us·To·Help·You**¶
  ◊ *Keeping·Us·Informed*¶
  ◊ *Submitting·Feedback*¶
  ◊ *Making·a·Complaint*¶

Before   After

10) Save your sample document with the following name:

    Chapter1_Exercise_1-2_After_*Your_Name*.doc

You can close the document.

Did you notice the grey lines under the headings in this exercise? In Outline view, a grey line under a heading indicates that the heading contains undisplayed lower-level headings and/or body text.

Working with outlines and outline numbering

Many engineering, legal and other highly-structured documents contain numbered headings, such as:

■ 'According to section 4.5, that window should be on the other wall.'

■ 'I refer the court's attention to subsection 4.29.'

When documents have multiple heading levels, lower-level headings *inherit* their leading numbers (or letters) from the relevant higher ones as shown below:

5. A level-1 heading   8.3. A level-2 heading
   5.1. A level-2 heading   8.3. (a) A level-3 heading
   5.2. Another level-2 heading   8.3. (b) Another level-3 heading

In Word, the sequential numbering (or alphabetizing) of headings is called *outline numbering*. You can apply outline numbering to a document's headings in Print Layout, Outline or Normal view. It is better to apply outline numbering through styles (using the **Format | Style** command) than by direct formatting (the **Format | Bullets and Numbering** command).

Outline Numbering

The application of sequential numbering to headings of a document. Lower-level headings inherit their leading numbers from higher-level headings.

When you reorder numbered headings in Outline view, Word renumbers the headings to take account of their new location in the document. This automatic renumbering is a huge time-saver: you can imagine the effort needed to renumber headings manually.

Exercise 1.3: Applying outline numbering to a document

In this exercise, you will apply outline numbering to the headings of a document.

1) Open the following file:

   ```
   Chapter1_Exercise_1-3_Before.doc
   ```

   If you are not viewing the document in Print Layout view, choose **View | Print Layout**.

2) Click in any heading in the Heading 1 style – for example, the document title 'Elmsworth Health Trust: Patients' Charter'.

3) Choose **Format | Style** and click the **Modify** button.

4) In the *Modify Style* dialog box, click the **Format** button and choose **Numbering** from the menu displayed.

5) Click the **Outline Numbered** tab of the dialog box displayed.

   You must select a sample numbering format that contains the word 'heading'. Click the format selected below, and then click **OK**, **OK** and **Apply** to close the box.

Word applies the outline numbering to your document.

3

Show Heading 3 button

6) Choose **View | Outline**, and click the **Show Heading 3** button on the Outlining toolbar to verify that Word has applied outline numbering to all three heading levels in your document, as in the following example:

```
◇ 1→Elmsworth·Health·Trust:··Patient's·Charter¶
◇ 2→Mission·Statement¶
◇ 3→Codes·of·Conduct¶
     ◇ 3.1 → Individual·Standards·of·Behaviour¶
          ◇ 3.1.1 → Courtesy¶
          ◇ 3.1.2 → Privacy¶
          ◇ 3.1.3 → Confidentiality¶
          ◇ 3.1.4 → Religious·Beliefs¶
     ◇ 3.2 → Consultant-based·Services¶
     ◇ 3.3 → Nursing·Services¶
◇ 4·Standards·of·Service¶
     ◇ 4.1 → Appointments¶
          ◇ 4.1.1 → Routine·Appointments¶
```

7) Close and save your sample document with the following name:

    Chapter1_Exercise_1-3_After_*Your_Name*.doc

Exercise 1.4: Reordering numbered headings in Outline view

In this exercise, you will change the order of sequentially numbered headings.

1) Open the following file:

    Chapter1_Exercise_1-4_Before.doc

2) Choose **View | Outline**.

3) Click anywhere in the level-1 heading called 'Teaching and Research'.

4) Click the **Move Down** button four times. Click anywhere outside the heading to deselect it.

```
◇ 5→Information·and·Records¶
     ◇ 5.1 → Delays·and·Postponements¶
     ◇ 5.2 → Identity·of·Staff¶
     ◇ 5.3 → Medical·Information¶
◇ 6→Help·Us·To·Help·You¶
     ◇ 6.1 → Keeping·Us·Informed¶
     ◇ 6.2 → Submitting·Feedback¶
     ◇ 6.3 → Making·a·Complaint¶
◇ 7→Teaching·and·Research¶
```

Notice that Word automatically renumbers the headings that you moved.

5) Close and save your sample document with the following name:

   `Chapter1_Exercise_1-4_After_Your_Name.doc`

You have now completed the four exercises in this chapter.

Chapter 1: quick reference

Outlining toolbar:
Promote *and* **Demote**
buttons

Button	Description
←	Promotes a paragraph to a higher heading level.
→	Demotes a paragraph to a lower heading level.
⇒	Demotes a paragraph to body text (Normal style).

Outlining toolbar: **Move
Up** *and* **Move Down**
buttons

Button	Description
↑	Moves a paragraph up above the preceding paragraph.
↓	Move a paragraph down after the following paragraph..

Outlining toolbar: **Show
Heading** *buttons*

Button	Description
1	Displays level-1 headings only.
2	Displays level-1 and level-2 headings only.
3	Displays level-1, level-2 and level-3 headings only.
=	Displays all heading levels and the first line only of body text paragraphs.
All	Displays the entire document, both headings and body text.

Shortcut keys

Keys	Description
Tab	Demotes the paragraph in which the insertion point is located.
Shift+Tab	Promotes the paragraph in which the insertion point is located.

Tasks summary

Task	Procedure
Display Outline view of the active document.	Choose **View | Outline**.
Promote or demote a heading.	Click anywhere in the heading and click the **Promote** or **Demote** button on the Outlining toolbar.
Move a heading (and subordinate content).	Select the heading and click the **Move Up** or **Move Down** button on the Outlining toolbar.
Control which headings are displayed.	Click the relevant **Show Heading** button on the Outlining toolbar.
Apply outline numbering to headings.	Click in any level-1 heading and choose **Format | Style**. Click **Modify**, **Format**, **Numbering**. Click the **Outline Numbered** tab, select a style that contains the word 'heading', and click **OK**, **OK** and **Apply**.

Concepts summary

In general, an *outline* is a list of the headings in a document. A *heading level* indicates the importance of a heading in relation to other headings. Outlines use indentation to represent the level of each heading, with lower-level headings indented further than higher-level ones.

In Word, an outline is a view of document. The outline heading levels shown are tied to the *built-in heading styles* applied in the document. Outline view includes the *Outlining toolbar*, which provides options for changing heading levels and reordering the headings.

For a new document, working in Outline view enables you to focus on the entire document and gain agreement from colleagues on its overall structure before you write the main content.

When working on an already-written document, Outline view allows you to restructure the document's content quickly and easily by manipulating the outline headings. This is because moving a heading in Outline view also moves all subordinate content, both lower-level headings and body text.

For legal and technical documents, you can apply sequential *outline numbering* to headings. If you move headings that are sequentially numbered, Word automatically renumbers them to take account of their new location in the document.

Chapter 1: quick quiz

Circle the correct answer to each of the following multiple-choice questions about outlines in Word.

Q1	A document outline is ...
A.	A list of the styles and fonts used in a document.
B.	A list of a document's headings, with lower-level headings indented progressively to reflect their relative importance.
C.	A list of the first lines of each paragraph in a document, arranged vertically in a single-column table.
D.	A first draft of a document that has not been checked for spelling or grammar, and that does not include a table of contents.

Q2	A Word outline cannot help you perform which of the following tasks?
A.	Gain agreement from colleagues about the overall structure of a document before the content is written.
B.	Begin writing the body of the document with the headings already formatted in the appropriate heading style.
C.	Identify sections of a document for delegation to colleagues.
D.	Display the readability statistics of a document.

Q3	You want to display the active document in Word's Outline view. Which action do you perform?
A.	Choose **File | Outline View**, select the *Outlining* checkbox, and click **OK**.
B.	Choose **Format | Views | Outlining**.
C.	Choose **View | Outline**.
D.	Choose **Tools | Document**, select the **Outline view only** option, and click **Apply**.

Q4	In Word, which of the following statements about outlines and styles is true?
A.	Heading levels in the outline are tied to heading styles in the document.
B.	A document can have heading styles or outline heading levels, but it cannot have both.
C.	Only the styles Outline 1, Outline 2 and Outline 3 can be used in a document outline.
D.	Text in Normal style cannot be displayed in a Word outline.

Q5	When creating a new Word document in Outline view, which of the following tasks are you most likely to perform?
A.	Create a single-column Word table for storing the names of people who will review your document.
B.	Specify the page margins for your new document
C.	Select the default folder for storing your document's template.
D.	Type your document's headings and arrange them in the appropriate order.

Q6	You are working on an already-written Word document in Outline view. Which of the following tasks are you most likely to perform?
A.	Move headings and subordinate content up and down in a document.
B.	Change the attributes of numbered bullets.
C.	Edit the body text, and check for errors in spelling and grammar.
D.	Check that the correct language setting is selected.

Q7	In a Word outline, what happens to numbered headings when you move them up or down in the document?
A.	Word displays an error message, telling you that numbered headings cannot be moved in Outline view.
B.	Word removes the numbers from the headings that you move.
C.	Word automatically renumbers the headings in the document to reflect their new location.
D.	The headings are preserved but not renumbered – you need to renumber them manually.

Q8	In Word Outline view, which toolbar button do you click to display level-1 and level-2 headings only?
A.	➡
B.	2
C.	=
D.	1

Q9	In Word Outline view, which toolbar button do you click to promote a selected paragraph to a higher level?
A.	All
B.	1
C.	⬅
D.	⬆

Q10	In Word outline view, which toolbar button do you click to demote a selected heading to body text (Normal style)?
A.	⇨
B.	⬇
C.	⇒
D.	═

Q11	In Word outline view, which toolbar button do you click to move a heading up in the document?
A.	1
B.	⬇
C.	⇒
D.	⬆

Q12	In Word Outline view, what is the effect of pressing the key combination Shift+Tab?
A.	Word displays the entire document, and not just the document's headings.
B.	The paragraph that contains the insertion point is moved forward in the document.
C.	Only levels-1 and level-2 headings are displayed. Other headings and body text are hidden.
D.	The paragraph that contains the insertion point is promoted one level.

Answers

1: B, **2:** D, **3:** C, **4:** A, **5:** D, **6:** A, **7:** C, **8:** B, **9:** C, **10:** A, **11:** D, **12:** D.

2 Do once what you used to do every day: styles

Objectives	In this chapter you will learn how to:
	■ View the styles available to a document
	■ Identify the styles that are used in a document
	■ Create new paragraph and character styles
	■ Modify existing paragraph and character styles
New words	In this chapter you will meet the following terms:
	■ Heading styles
	■ Character styles
	■ Style Area
	■ Paragraph styles
	■ Style Box
	■ Direct formatting
Exercise files	In this chapter you will work with the following Word files:
	■ Chapter2_Exercise_2-1_Before.doc
	■ Chapter2_Exercise_2-2_Before.doc
	■ Chapter2_Exercise_2-3_Before.doc
	■ Chapter2_Exercise_2-4_Before.doc
	■ Chapter2_Exercise_2-5_Before.doc
Syllabus reference	In this chapter you will cover the following items from the ECDL Advanced Word Processing Syllabus:
	■ **AM3.1.2.4**: Create new character or paragraph styles.
	■ **AM3.1.2.5**: Modify existing character or paragraph styles.

Styles in Word: one click does it all

A style is a named set or ensemble of attributes that can be created, saved and then applied to items within documents.

Styles save you significant formatting effort and time, perhaps up to 80% with longer documents. Why? Because by applying a style, you can apply a wide range of attributes in a single operation. That's so much faster than applying each attribute individually.

An example of a style at work:

1. You select the text:

   Word Styles: The Benefits
   A style is a named set of multiple attributes that can be created, saved and applied to selected text, tables or other objects. I've known long-time Microsoft Word users who have

2. You select the style that you want from the Style Box:

3. Word applies the style's various attributes, such as font, indent and borders, in a single action.

   Word Styles: The Benefits
   A style is a named set of multiple attributes that can be created, saved and applied to selected text, tables or other objects. I've known long-time Microsoft Word users who have

Word's built-in styles

Word contains approximately 100 built-in, ready-to-use styles. The ones that you are likely to use most often are listed below, together with their default values.

Built-in style name	Font	Weight	Font size (points)	Additional spacing (points)
Heading 1	Arial	Bold	16	12 before, 3 after
Heading 2	Arial	Bold	14	12 before, 3 after
Heading 3	Arial	Bold	13	12 before, 3 after
Normal	Times New Roman	Normal	12	None

Although somewhat plain, Word's built-in styles are adequate for many documents.

Word's styles are of two types:

- **Paragraph styles**. These can control all aspects of a paragraph's appearance. You can apply a paragraph style only to entire paragraphs – not to selected text within a paragraph.

- **Character Styles**. These contain font, border and language attributes. You can apply character styles to an entire paragraph or to selected text within a paragraph.

Both paragraph and character styles are covered by the ECDL syllabus. Typically, you will use paragraph styles much more frequently than character styles. For this reason, the exercise for character style is located at the end of this chapter.

Paragraph style
A named set of formatting, positioning and other attributes that can be applied to paragraphs.

The styles Heading 1, Heading 2, etc., are called heading styles. By default, Word uses these styles for displaying outlines and generating tables of contents.

You don't have to use these styles for headings in your documents, but you will find it easier to exploit other Word features if you do.

Heading styles
The styles named Heading 1, Heading 2, and so on. By default, Word uses these in outlines and tables of contents.

Direct formatting is an alternative to using styles. You select text and change its attributes with menu commands or toolbar buttons. Direct formatting overrides the attributes applied with styles.

Direct formatting
*Formatting applied by means other than by styles. Typically, formatting or alignment applied with buttons on the Formatting toolbar, or with the **Format	Font**, **Format	Paragraph** and **Format	Borders and Shading** commands.*

Styles: how you benefit

Styles, as you have learnt, enable you to apply a wide range of attributes in a single operation. Here are some other benefits provided by styles in Word:

- **Consistency**. Documents formatted with styles have a consistent, professional appearance.

- **Ease of updating**. You can change the appearance of all headings in a document simply by amending the relevant styles.

- **Automation and organization**. Styles enable you to take advantage of time-saving features in Word, such as outlines, AutoFormat, table-of-contents generation and master documents.

- **Faster operation**. Word has to work harder at displaying and managing files that contain a lot of direct formatting. Documents formatted with styles are smaller in file size and display on screen more quickly.

- **Document exporting**. If you need to export a Word document to a file format used by desktop publishing (DTP) software or to the web, you'll be glad that you used styles.

Most DTP software can recognize and work with Word styles, and Word styles can be incorporated within cascading style sheets (CSS) in Hypertext Mark-up Language (HTML) documents.

Styles and templates

Styles are related to another Word feature: templates. The relationship between styles and templates is less than straightforward, and is covered in Chapter 4.

Styles: the five tasks

Here are the five tasks that you need to be able to perform with styles:

- **View styles available to a document**. You can use the Style Box on the Formatting toolbar to display the styles available to your current document. Exercise 2.1 shows you how.

- **Identify styles used in a document**. Word offers two convenient features to help you identify the styles applied to text in any document. You will discover how to use them in Exercise 2.2.

- **Amend the attributes of an existing style**. You can amend the attributes of any style, whether it is a built-in Word style or a user-created style. See Exercise 2.3.

- **Create a new style**. In Exercise 2.4, you learn how to create a new style and define its attributes.

- **Work with character styles**. Exercise 2.5 takes you through the steps of creating, amending and deleting a character style.

Displaying style information

In the first two exercises of this chapter, you will work with paragraph styles that already exist: you will begin by displaying a list of the styles available to a document, and then view the styles that are already applied within the document.

Exercise 2.1: Viewing the styles available to a document

1) Start Word and open the following file:

       Chapter2_Exercise_2-1_Before.doc

2) On the Formatting toolbar, click the **Style Box** drop-down arrow.

Word displays an abbreviated list of the styles that are available to your current document. Each style is formatted, so that you can see what it looks like before you apply it.

Click anywhere in the document to close the drop-down list.

3) Hold down the **Shift** key and click the **Style Box** drop-down arrow. Word now shows all available styles, not just the main ones.

Click anywhere in the document to close the drop-down list.

Then close the sample document.

Style Box

A box on the Formatting toolbar that can display a drop-down list of the styles available to a document. The styles are formatted, so that you can see what they look like before you apply them.

Exercise 2.2: Viewing styles used in a document

Ever wonder what styles are used in a particular Word document? In this exercise you discover how to find out, using two Word features – What's This? and the Style Area.

1) Open the following file:

       Chapter2_Exercise_2-2_Before.doc

2) Choose **Help | What's This**. Notice how Word displays a question mark beside the cursor.

3) Click on any text for Word to display a pop-up window containing the relevant style details.

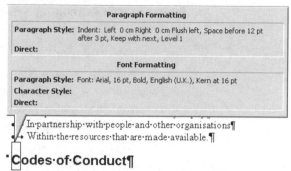

Paragraph Formatting	
Paragraph Style: Indent: Left 0 cm Right 0 cm Flush left, Space before 12 pt after 3 pt, Keep with next, Level 1	
Direct:	
Font Formatting	
Paragraph Style: Font: Arial, 16 pt, Bold, English (U.K.), Kern at 16 pt	
Character Style:	
Direct:	

In·partnership·with·people·and·other·organisations¶
Within·the·resources·that·are·made·available.¶

Codes·of·Conduct¶

Our·staff·will·introduce·themselves·to·you·and·explain·how·they·can·help.·All·staff·

You can continue clicking on text throughout your document to view the relevant style details.

When finished, press **Esc** to close the pop-up window.

4) Switch to Normal view.

5) Choose **Tools | Options**, and click the **View** tab in the dialog box displayed.

6) Enter a Style Area width of 2.5 cm.

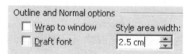

Outline and Normal options
☐ Wrap to window   Style area width:
☐ Draft font   2.5 cm

7) Click **OK**. Your current document now looks as shown in the next example. Notice the Style Area at the left of the Word window. You can use the mouse to resize the Style Area.

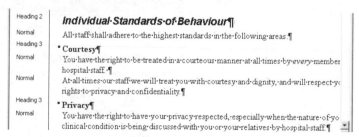

Heading 2	***Individual·Standards·of·Behaviour¶***
Normal	All·staff·shall·adhere·to·the·highest·standards·in·the·following·areas.¶
Heading 3	**Courtesy¶**
Normal	You·have·the·right·to·be·treated·in·a·courteous·manner·at·all·times·by·*every*·member hospital·staff.¶
Normal	At·all·times·our·staff·we·will·treat·you·with·courtesy·and·dignity,·and·will·respect·yo rights·to·privacy·and·confidentiality.¶
Heading 3	**Privacy¶**
Normal	You·have·the·right·to·have·your·privacy·respected,·especially·when·the·nature·of·yo clinical·condition·is·being·discussed·with·you·or·your·relatives·by·hospital·staff.¶

8) When you have finished, close your document.

Style Area

A resizable pane that can be displayed in Normal or Outline view to show the styles used throughout a document.

Working with existing styles

In Exercise 2.3, you will open a sample document, amend attributes of the Body Text and Heading 1 built-in styles, and then save the document.

Exercise 2.3: Amending existing styles

1) Open the following file:

   `Chapter2_Exercise_2-3_Before.doc`

2) Click in any paragraph that is in the Normal style. (When modifying paragraph styles, you don't need to select an entire paragraph. By definition, paragraph styles apply to paragraphs, so it's enough just to position the insertion point in a paragraph whose style you want to modify.)

3) Choose **Format | Style**, and click the **Modify** button.

4) In the *Modify Style* dialog box, click the **Format** button, and then click the **Font** option.

5) Select Garamond, Regular style, 12 point, and click **OK**.

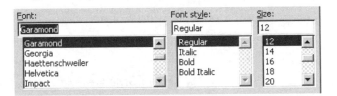

6) You are returned to the *Modify Style* dialog box. Click the **Format** button, and then the **Paragraph** option.

   In the *Spacing* area, enter 6 pt in the *After* box. Click OK.

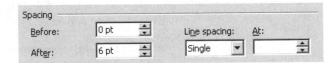

7) You are returned to the *Modify Style* dialog box. Ensure that the *Add to template* and *Automatically update* checkboxes are deselected.

   Click **OK**. You are returned to the *Style* dialog box. Click **Apply**.

   Notice that *all* paragraphs in the Normal style are amended.

8) Click in any paragraph that is in the Heading 1 style, choose **Format | Style**, and click the **Modify** button.

9) In the *Modify Style* dialog box, click the **Format** button, and then the **Border** option.

10) Select a 1-point top border. Click **OK**.

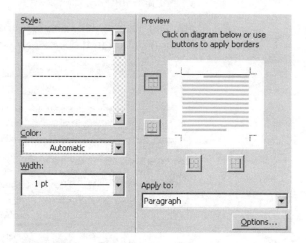

11) You are returned to the *Modify Style* dialog box. Click the **Format** button, and then the **Paragraph** option.

12) In the *Spacing* area, increase the value in the *Before* box to 24 pt. Click **OK**.

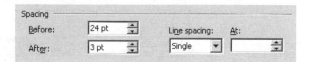

13) You are returned to the *Modify Style* dialog box. Ensure that the *Add to template* and *Automatically update* checkboxes are deselected.

Click **OK**. You are returned to the *Style* dialog box. Click **Apply**.

Notice that *all* paragraphs in the Heading 1 style are amended.

14) Close and save your sample document with the following name:

Chapter2_Exercise_2-3_After_*Your_Name*.doc

Working with new styles

Through the **Format | Style** command, Word gives you complete control over every aspect of a new paragraph style that you create. Style attributes are available in the seven categories:

- Font
- Paragraph
- Tabs
- Border

- Language
- Frame
- Numbering

You can access each category of attributes by clicking the **Format** button in the *New Style* dialog box.

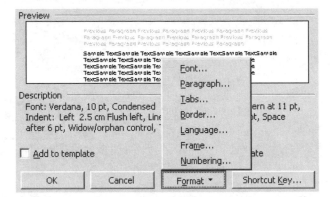

In addition to these various attributes, there are six other important fields available in the *New Style* dialog box:

Field name	Description
Name: My New Style1	You must give a unique name to each new style that you create. You can rename styles as often as you want.
Style type: Paragraph Paragraph Character	You must choose either *Paragraph* or *Character*. You cannot change the style type at a later stage.
Based on: ¶ Normal	Optionally, you can select an existing style on which your new style will be based. Except where you specify otherwise, your new style takes on the attributes of the selected Based on style. If you do not select a Based on style, ensure that you set a language for your new style, otherwise the default will be No proofing. You can add, remove or change the Based on style at a later stage.

Field name	Description
Style for following paragraph: ¶ Normal ▼	You must specify the style that Word will apply to a paragraph created by pressing **Enter** after a paragraph in your new style. For both headings and body text, your typical choice for this field will be the Normal style. You can change the style for the following paragraph at a later stage.
☐ Add to template	If you select this checkbox, your new style is saved to the document template, not just to the document. It is then available to all other documents based on the same template.
☐ Automatically update	If you select this checkbox, Word will redefine the style to reflect any changes you make with direct formatting.

Based on style

A style that supplies default attributes to one or more other styles. If the Based on style changes, so do all the attributes that the dependent styles share with the Based on style – that is, those that were specified explicitly by the user.

Style shortcut keys

Another option provided by the *New Style* dialog box is the ability to associate a shortcut key with a new style. If you plan to use a style frequently, it makes sense to give it a shortcut key. You can also assign keyboard shortcuts to existing styles.

You access this option by clicking the **Shortcut Key** button in the *New Style* (or *Modify Style*) dialog box.

Do not assign styles to keyboard shortcuts already used for common Word tasks, such as applying bold (**Ctrl+B**) or italics (**Ctrl+I**), or saving (**Ctrl+S**) and printing (**Ctrl+P**).

Exercise 2.4: Creating a new style

In this exercise, you will create a new style and explore how direct formatting can affect a style's attributes.

1) Open the following file:

        Chapter2_Exercise_2-4_Before.doc

2) Click in any paragraph that is in the Heading 1 style.

3) Choose **Format | Style**, and in the dialog box displayed, click the **New** button.

4) In the *Name* box, enter 'Heading 1 *Your Name*', select a *Style type* of 'Paragraph', a *Based on* style of 'Heading 1', and a *Style for following paragraph* of 'Normal'. The following example shows how Ken Bloggs might fill in the details.

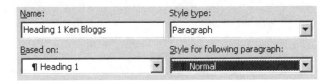

Click the **Format** button, click **Font**, change the *Color* to red, and click **OK**.

5) Click the **Shortcut Key** button. With the insertion point in the *Press new shortcut key* box, type the combination of keys that you want to assign to your new style. For example, **Ctrl+Shift+F1**.

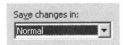

If the keyboard shortcut you entered is already assigned to another style or to another Word feature, Word displays a message beneath the box. You can override any previous keyboard shortcut.

6) Click the drop-down arrow to the right of the *Save changes in* box, and select the template Normal (Normal.dot) as the location in which you want to store your keyboard shortcut.

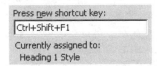

When finished, click **Assign**, and then click **Close**.

7) You are returned to the *New Style* dialog box. Leave the *Add to template* checkbox deselected. Select the *Automatically update* checkbox.

8) Click **OK** to close the *New Style* dialog box, then click **Apply** to close the *Style* dialog box. You are returned to your document.

Notice that Word applies the new style to the paragraph in which the insertion point is located.

9) Choose **Edit | Replace**, and replace all occurrences of the Heading 1 style with your new Heading 1 Your Name style.

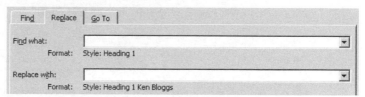

10) Select any paragraph in the Heading 1 *Your Name* style, choose **Format | Font**, and change the font to Arial Narrow.

Notice that Word changes all other paragraphs in the Heading 1 *Your Name* style to Arial Narrow. This is because you selected the *Automatically update* checkbox when creating the new style.

11) Click in any paragraph in the Heading 1 Your Name style. Choose **Format | Style**, click **Modify**, deselect the *Automatically update* checkbox, click **OK** and click **Apply**. This prevents further direct formatting from affecting the attributes of your new style.

12) Close and save your sample document with the following name:

Chapter2_Exercise_2-4_After_*Your_Name*.doc

Reapplying styles after direct formatting changes

Direct formatting, applied using the Formatting toolbar or with commands such as **Format | Font** and **Format | Paragraph**, overrides the style-based attributes that are applied to the relevant paragraphs.

Sometimes, after a paragraph has been formatted directly, you will want to change the paragraph's attributes back to those of its style. In other words, you want to reapply the style.

Reapplying a style means applying a style to a paragraph that meets the following conditions:

■ The paragraph has direct formatting applied to it.

■ The paragraph is already in the style you are about to apply, but it looks different from other paragraphs in the same style because of the direct formatting.

When using the Style Box you reapply a style to such a paragraph, Word displays a *Modify Style* dialog box similar to this:

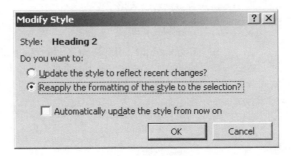

Typically, you will select the second option, *Reapply the formatting of the style to the selection*, because you will not want the relevant style definition to be amended.

If you select the first option, *Update the style to reflect recent changes*, Word redefines the style so that it has the attributes of the directly formatted paragraph. It has the same effect as selecting the *Automatically update* checkbox displayed when creating or modifying the style with the **Format | Style** command.

Working with character styles

Earlier in this chapter, you learnt about character styles that contain only font, border and language attributes. Unlike paragraph styles that apply to entire paragraphs, you can apply character styles to a paragraph or to selected text within a paragraph.

Take a look at the styles in the drop-down Style Box list. Notice that only paragraph styles have the paragraph mark symbol (¶) beside their style name.

A paragraph style   *A character style*

> **Character style**
>
> *A named set of font, border and language attributes that can be saved and applied to selected text or paragraphs.*

In Exercise 2.5, you will create and amend a character style.

Exercise 2.5: Creating and amending a character style
1) Open the following file:

        Chapter2_Exercise_2-5_Before.doc

2) Choose **Format | Style**, and in the dialog box displayed, click the **New** button.

3) In the *Name* box, enter 'Char Style *Your Name*', select a *Style type* of Character, and a *Based on* style of Default Paragraph Font.

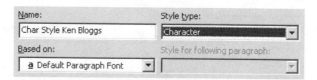

Character styles do not offer a *Style for following paragraph* option.

4) Click the **Format** button, click **Font**, select Arial, Regular, 10 pt, and click **OK**.

5) You are returned to the *New Style* dialog box. Leave the *Add to template* check box deselected. The *Update automatically* checkbox is not available for character styles.

   Click **OK** to close the *New Style* dialog box, and then click **Apply** to close the *Style* dialog box. You are returned to your document.

6) In the sample document, select the text 'Elmsworth Health Trust' in the first paragraph under the heading 'Elmsworth Health Trust: Patients' Charter', click the Style Box drop-down arrow, and select your new character style. Click anywhere else in the document to deselect the text.

   Elmsworth Health Trust: Patients' Charter

   At Elmsworth Health Trust, we are committed to delivering a world-class service. standards apply whether you are:

7) Your next step is to modify your character style.

   Click anywhere in the text that you selected in Step 6, and choose **Format | Style**. In the dialog box displayed, select the new style from the *Styles* list and click the **Modify** button.

8) Click the **Format** button, click **Font**, select Arial Narrow, Regular, 10 pt, and click **OK**.

9) You are returned to the *New Style* dialog box. Leave the *Add to template* checkbox deselected.

   Click **OK** to close the *New Style* dialog box, and then click **Apply** to close the *Style* dialog box. You are returned to your document.

   Notice that Word applies the style change to the selected text.

   Close and save your sample document with the following name:

   `Chapter2_Exercise_2-5_After_Your_Name.doc`

Chapter 2: quick reference

Tasks summary

Task	Procedure
To view all available styles for the current document.	Hold down the **Shift** key and click the Style Box drop-down arrow on the Formatting toolbar.
To view the style applied to text.	Choose **Help | What's This?** This and click in the text to display a pop-up information window.
To view styles applied in a document.	In Normal view, choose **Tools | Options**, click the **View** tab, enter a Style Area Width of 2.5 cm, and click **OK**. Word displays the Style Area to the left of the document.
To create a new style.	Choose **Format | Style**, click **New**, define the style attributes, select a *Style for following paragraph* (for paragraph styles only), click **OK** and **Apply**. Optionally, you can define a *Based on* style, and assign a shortcut key for the style.
To amend a style.	Click in an occurrence of the style, choose **Format | Style**, click **Modify**, amend the attributes, click **OK**, and click **Apply**.
To allow style redefinition through direct formatting.	When creating or amending the style, select the *Automatically update* checkbox. Word will redefine the style when you apply direct formatting to any paragraph in that style.

Concepts summary

A *style* is a named set of attributes that can be created, saved and then applied to items within documents. Styles enable you to apply a wide range of attributes in a single operation. And when you change the attributes of a style, all text in that style changes accordingly.

Word contains almost 100 built-in, ready-to-use styles. The ones that you are likely to use most often are *heading styles* (Heading 1, Heading 2, ...) and *Normal* (for body text). You can create new styles, and amend built-in styles and user-created styles.

Word's styles are of two types: *paragraph styles* that can control every aspect of a paragraph's appearance and position, and *character styles* that contain font, border and language attributes only. A *Based on* style is one that supplies default attributes to one or more other styles.

ECDL Advanced Word Processing

Chapter 2: quick quiz

Circle the correct answer to each of the following multiple-choice questions about styles in Word.

Q1	In Word, a style is ...
A.	A named set of attributes that can be saved and then applied to selected items in a document.
B.	A file containing preset formatting and standard content that provides a pattern for individual Word documents.
C.	A list of a document's headings, with lower-level headings indented progressively to reflect their relative importance.
D.	A list of installed Windows fonts that are available for use in Word documents.

Q2	Which of the following is not an advantage of using styles in a Word document?
A.	You will find it easier to export the document to HTML and other non-Word formats.
B.	You are provided with an automatically-created backup in the event of document corruption or loss.
C.	You can change the document's appearance by modifying the relevant style or styles.
D.	Your document has a smaller file size and displays more quickly than a document that has formatting applied manually.

Q3	Which of the following is not a built-in heading style in Word?
A.	Heading 3.
B.	Heading 1.
C.	Word File Heading.
D.	Heading 5.

Q4	Which of the following statements about Word's Style Box is untrue?
A.	The Style Box is located on the Formatting toolbar.
B.	The Style Box is located on the Standard Toolbar.
C.	Holding down the **Shift** key before clicking the **Style Box** drop-down arrow displays the full list of available styles.
D.	Styles listed in the Style Box are formatted, so that you can see what each one looks like before you apply it.

Q5	Which of the following statements about Word's paragraph and character styles is untrue?
A.	Paragraph styles can control every aspect of a paragraph's appearance and position.
B.	Character styles contain only font, border and language attributes.
C.	The *Update automatically* checkbox within the **Format	Style** command is not available for paragraph styles.
D.	Character styles can be applied to paragraphs or to selected text within paragraphs.

Q6	Which of the following methods do you use to display Word's Style Area?
A.	Click anywhere in the document and choose **Help	What's This?**
B.	Click the **Style Area** button beside the Styles Box on the Standard toolbar.
C.	In Print Layout view, choose **Tools	Customize**, select the *Style area* checkbox, and click **OK**.
D.	In Normal view, choose **Tools	Options**, click the **View** tab on the dialog box displayed, enter a non-zero style area width, and click **OK**.

Q.7	When using Word's Format | Style command, which of the following statements best describes the effect of selecting the *Automatically update* checkbox?
A.	It updates the document's table of contents to reflect any changes to the heading styles.
B.	It updates other documents that are based on the same template with the most recent style modifications.
C.	It prevents direct formatting from affecting the style's attributes.
D.	It tells Word to update the style definition whenever direct formatting is applied to a paragraph in that style.

Q.8	Which of the following statements about the *Based on* feature of styles in Word is true?
A.	For any particular style, you can change the *Based on* style chosen at the time that the style was created.
B.	Only Word's collection of approximately 100 built-in styles can be used as *Based on* styles.
C.	You cannot specify a *Based on* style for a character style.
D.	You cannot specify a *Based on* style for a heading style.

Q.9	Which of the following statements about the *Style for following paragraph* feature of styles in Word is true?
A.	For any particular style, you cannot change the *Style for following paragraph* style chosen at the time that the style was created.
B.	Only Word's collection of approximately 100 built-in styles can be selected as *Style for following paragraph* styles.
C.	A typical choice for the *Style for following paragraph* is the Normal style.
D.	The *Style for following paragraph* feature is optional. You need not choose such a style for every new style that you create.

Q10	Which of the following statements about the shortcut key feature of styles in Word is true?
A.	Keyboard shortcuts can be applied only to paragraph styles.
B.	Keyboard shortcuts can be applied to paragraph and character styles.
C.	A keyboard shortcut, once assigned to a style, cannot be changed.
D.	Keyboard shortcuts can be assigned only to Word's collection of approximately 100 built-in styles.

Q11	Directly applied formatting is ...
A.	Formatting applied to selected text or paragraphs in a document through the use of styles.
B.	Formatting applied with the **Format | Font, Format | Paragraph, Format | Borders and Shading** commands, or with the buttons on the Formatting toolbar.
C.	Formatting applied to a template file.
D.	Formatting applied to a document before it is saved.

Q12	What happens when you reapply a style to a paragraph that is already in that style, but that contains directly applied formatting?
A.	Word modifies the style so that it takes on the attributes of the directly applied formatting.
B.	Word gives you the choice of removing the directly applied formatting or of redefining the style to match that formatting.
C.	Word modifies the style but saves the modifications only to the document and not to the associated template.
D.	Word removes the directly applied formatting and restores the attributes of the paragraph back to those of the reapplied style.

Answers

1: A, 2: C, 3: C, 4: B, 5: C, 6: D, 7: D, 8: A, 9: C, 10: A, 11: C, 12: B

3

Recycle content and formatting: templates

Objectives

In this chapter you will learn how to:

- Create a template based on a document
- Create a document based on a user-built template
- Make changes to a template
- Create a new template based on an existing template

New words

In this chapter you will meet the following term:

- Template

Exercise files

In this chapter you will work with the following Word files:

- `Chapter3_Exercise_3-1_Before.doc`
- `Chapter3_Exercise_3-2_Before.doc`
- `Chapter3 Exercise_3-3_Before.dot`
- `Chapter3_Exercise 3-4 Before.dot`

Syllabus reference

In this chapter you will cover the following items from the ECDL Advanced Word Processing Syllabus:

- **AM3.1.3.1**: Change basic formatting and layout options in a template.
- **AM3.1.3.2**: Create a new template based on an existing document or template.

Patterns in document content and structure

If a document begins with the discovery of an unidentified body and concludes with the unmasking of a murderer, the chances are that it's a crime novel.

If it starts with executive summary, contains a competitive analysis and a sales forecast, and ends with pro forma income statements, it's more probably a business-plan document.

When reading any individual document, generally you can tell the category or genre to which it belongs because of the features it shares with other documents in its category:

- **Familiar content**. The same elements tend to reappear in documents of a particular category.

- **Predictable sequence**. The elements tend to be present in the same order as in other documents of that category.

Document patterns and Word templates

Behind every Word document is a pattern or template that can control its appearance and content. Among the things that you can build into templates are page settings, paragraph styles, and standard text and images.

You minimize effort and maximize output by:

- **Categorizing your documents**. Consider the types of documents that you create most frequently. Identify the formatting and content that are common to documents in each category.

- **Building category templates**. Create Word templates for each document type to provide a basis for individual documents.

Examples of business document types that lend themselves to templating are:

- Fax cover sheets

- Letters

- Reports

- Memos

- Press releases

- Business plans

Word comes with almost 30 templates suitable for different document types – CVs, brochures, manuals, and so on. You can customize Word's built-in templates according to your needs. A document is not tied forever to a particular template, and you can change the template associated with a document at any stage. (You will learn more about this in Chapter 4.)

Templates: the benefits to you

The value of templates is simply this: the more standard content and formatting settings that you include in your templates, the less work you need to perform on individual documents.

Working with templates

Here are the four template-related tasks that you need to be able to perform:

- **Create a template based on a document**. Got a document that would be suitable as a template – a company memo, perhaps, or a monthly sales report?

  Exercise 3.1 takes you through the steps of removing all but general-purpose text from such a document, and then saving the document as a template.

  While you can save a document as a template, the reverse is not true: you cannot save a template as a document.

  Word templates end in the file name extension .dot in contrast to .doc for Word documents.

- **Create a document based on a user-built template**. In Exercise 3.2 you use the template that you created in Exercise 2.1 as the basis for a new Word document.

- **Make changes to a template**: You can open, amend and then resave Word templates just as you would Word documents. Exercise 3.3 provides an example.

- **Create a new template based on an existing template**. If you want to create a template that is similar to one you already have, you can open the first template, customize it, and then save the template with a new name. See Exercise 3.4.

Template

A file that provides a pattern for individual Word documents. Template files, which end in .dot, can contain formatting settings and standard text, images and fields.

Exercise 3.1: Creating a new template based on a document

In this exercise, you will use a Word document, an internal company memo, as the basis for a new template.

1) Open Word, and open the following file:

   `Chapter3_Exercise_3-1_Before.doc`

2) In the table beneath the title 'Memo', delete the details specific to this memo. The table should then look like this:

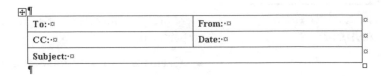

3) Delete the body text of the memo. Leave three paragraph marks beneath the table to facilitate the typing of text in individual memos.

At the bottom of the page you can see a footer with a border along its top. You can leave this footer as it is.

Your memo now contains only standard, general-purpose text, and it is ready to be saved as a template.

4) Choose **File | Save As**. In the dialog box displayed, click the *Save as type* drop-down arrow, and select the *Document Template* option.

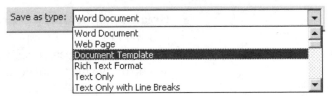

By default, Word prompts you to save templates in the folder named \Templates. Accept this location.

Save in:	Templates		⇐ ⬆ 🔍 ✕ 📂 ▦ ▾ Tools ▾

(You can learn more about the \Templates folder in *'Where are templates stored?'* below.)

5) In the *File name* box, type the following:

Chapter3_Exercise_3-1_After_*Your_Name*

Word automatically adds the file name extension .dot to your new template.

6) Click **Save**. You can close your new template.

Where are templates stored?

You can save a template in any location on your PC, but you can make life easier by storing your templates in the \Templates folder. Where is that? It depends on your version of Windows:

Windows 95, 98, ME

`C:\Windows\Application Data\Microsoft\Templates`

-or-

`C:\Windows\Profiles\`*User_Name*`\Application Data\Microsoft\Templates`

-or-

`C:\Windows\Profiles\`*User_Name*`\Templates`

Windows 2000

`C:\Documents and Settings\`*User_Name*`\Application Data\Microsoft\Templates`

Still can't find your \Templates folder? Use the **Search** command on the **Start** menu to locate it. Document template files that you store in the \Templates folder appear on the *General* tab of the **File | New** dialog box, where they are easy to find when you need them.

If you create a subfolder within \Templates and save your templates in it, your subfolder's name appears as a new tab on the **File | New** dialog box.

Exercise 3.2: Creating a document based on a user-built template

In this Exercise, you will use a memo template as the basis for a new memo document.

1) Choose **File | New** to create a new document.

    In the *New* dialog box, click the *General* tab if it is not displayed already.

2) Click the following template:

    `Chapter3_Exercise_3-2_Before.dot`

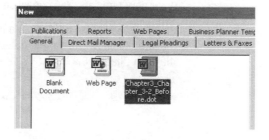

3) Select the *Create New Document* option, and click **OK**.

4) Type some text in the memo, and save the document with the following name:

    Chapter2_Exercise_3-2_After_*Your_Name*.doc

5) Save and close the sample memo document.

Exercise 3.3: Making changes to a template

In this exercise, you will amend some aspects of the template similar to the one you created in Exercise 3.1 and used as the basis for a document in Exercise 3.2.

1) Open the following file:

    Chapter3_Exercise_3-3_Before.dot

2) Click to the right of the heading 'Date:'. Press the Spacebar so that the insertion point is one empty space to the right of the colon.

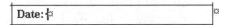

3) Choose **Insert | Field**. In the *Categories* list, select *Date and Time*. In the *Field names* list, select *Date*.

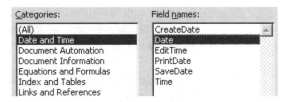

4) Click **OK**.

5) Choose **File | Save As**. By default, Word prompts you to save the amended template in the folder named \Templates. Accept this location.

    In the *File name* box, type the following:

    Chapter3_Exercise_3-3_After_Your_Name

6) Click **Save**. Word automatically adds the file name extension .dot to your new template. You can close the template file.

    In future, whenever the template is opened, the date field will be updated to show the current date. You will learn more about Word fields in Chapter 8.

Exercise 3.4: Creating a new template based on an existing template

In this exercise, you will open a memo template similar to the one that you worked on in Exercise 3.3 and use it to create a template for a fax cover sheet.

1) Open the following file:

    `Lesson3_Exercise_3-4_Before.dot`

2) Replace the title 'Memo' with the new title 'Fax Message'.

3) Click anywhere in the table cell containing the word 'From:', choose **Table | Select | Cell**, and then select **Edit | Cut**.

4) Drag across the two cells in the top row of the table, and choose **Table | Merge Cells**. The top row should now look like this:

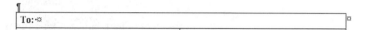

5) Click anywhere in the table cell containing 'CC:', choose **Table | Select | Cell**, and then **Select Edit | Cut**.

6) Drag across the two cells in the second row of the table and choose **Table | Merge Cells**.

7) Choose **View | Header and Footer**, delete the footer text 'Company Confidential', and click **Close** on the Header and Footer toolbar.

8) Choose **File | Save As**. In the dialog box displayed, click the *Save as type* drop-down arrow, and select the *Document Template* option.

    By default, Word prompts you to save templates in the folder named \Templates. Accept this location.

    In the *File name* box, type the following:

    `Chapter3_Exercise_3-4_After_Your_Name`

9) Click Save. Word automatically adds the file name extension .dot to your new template. You can close the template file.

Chapter 3: quick reference

Task	Procedure
Create a new template based on a document.	Remove all but general-purpose text from the document. Choose **File	Save As**, select *Save as type* as *Document Template*, and click **Save**.
Create a document based on a particular template.	Choose **File	New**, select your required template from the dialog box, select the *Create New Document* option, and click **OK**.
Amend a template.	Open the template, make the required changes, and resave it.
Create a new template based on an existing template.	Open the template, make the required changes, and save it under a new name.

Concepts summary

A template is a pattern for documents that can hold preset formatting and standard content, including text, images and fields. The more content and formatting that you include in your templates, the less work you need to perform on individual documents.

Examples of business document types that lend themselves to templating include fax cover sheets, company memos, letters, press releases, reports and business plans.

To create a new template from an existing document, remove all but general-purpose text from the document and then save it as a template. You can open, amend and then resave Word templates just as you would Word documents. You cannot save a template as a document.

By default, Word prompts you to save templates in the folder named \Templates. Templates stored in the \Templates folder appear on the *General* tab of the **File | New** dialog box, where they are easy to find when you need them.

Word templates end in the file name extension .dot in contrast to .doc for Word documents.

Chapter 3: quick quiz

Circle the correct answer to each of the following multiple-choice questions about templates in Word.

Q1	A Word template is …
A.	A free upgrade program supplied by Microsoft to registered Word users.
B.	A file containing preset formatting and standard content that provides a pattern for individual Word documents.
C.	A list of a document's headings, with lower-level headings indented progressively to reflect the relative importance.
D.	An automatically created back-up version of a document.

Q2	Which of the following is a benefit provided by templates?
A.	Documents based on built-in Word templates load and display more quickly.
B.	Creating templates for commonly-used document types reduces effort because individual documents based on the templates will already contain standard formatting and content.
C.	Templates provide automatic back-ups in the event of file corruption or loss.
D.	Templates make it easier to convert documents to outlines.

Q3	Which of the following files is a Word template?
A.	Template.doc
B.	Update.dot.doc
C.	Template_fax.wrd
D.	Report.dot

Q4	Which of the following statements about Word templates is untrue?
A.	A template can be saved as a document.
B.	A document can be saved as a template.
C.	A built-in Word template (such as Fax.dot) can be modified and saved under a new template name (such as Fax2.dot).
D.	A template can be deleted.

Q5	Which of the following statements about Word's \Templates folder is untrue?
A.	The \Templates folder may store both built-in and user-created templates.
B.	The \Templates folder is the default location for storing files with a file type of document template (.dot).
C.	Templates saved in the \Templates folder appear on the **General** tab of the **File	Open** dialog box.
D.	Templates must be stored in the \Templates folder.

Q6	You want to base a new Word document on a template that you have created. Which of the following actions do you take?
A.	Click the **New** button on the Standard toolbar.
B.	Choose **File	New** and select the required template from the *Template options* drop-down list.
C.	Remove Normal.dot from the \Templates folder.
D.	Choose **File	New**, select the required template from the dialog box displayed, and click **OK**.

Answers

1: B, **2:** B, **3:** D, **4:** A, **5:** D, **6:** D.

Separating content from format: templates and styles

Objectives

In this chapter you will learn how to:

- Save a style and a style modification in a template
- Base a new document on a selected template
- Change the template on which a document is based
- Apply Word's AutoFormat feature to a plain, unformatted document

New words

In this chapter you will meet the following terms:

- Template-based formatting
- AutoFormat

Exercise files

In this chapter you will work with the following Word files:

- Chapter4_Exercise_4-1_Before.doc
- Chapter4_Exercise_4-1_Template1.dot
- Chapter4_Exercise_4-1_Template2.dot
- Chapter4_Exercise_4-2_Doc1.doc
- Chapter4_Exercise_4-2_Doc2.doc
- Chapter4_Exercise_4-2_Template1.dot
- Chapter4_Exercise_4-2_Template2.dot
- Chapter4_Exercise_4-3_Before.doc

Syllabus reference

In this chapter you cover the following items from the ECDL Advanced Word Processing Syllabus:

- **AM3.1.2.5**: Modify existing character or paragraph styles.
- **AM3.1.3.1**: Change basic formatting and layout options in a template.
- **AM3.1.1.4**: Apply automatic text formatting options.

Styles and templates: a review

You covered Word's styles in Chapter 2 and templates in Chapter 3. Let's begin this chapter by summarizing what you know:

- **Style.** A named *set of attributes* that can be created, saved and then applied to items within documents. When you change the attributes of a style, all text in that style changes accordingly.

- **Template.** A pattern for documents that can hold *preset formatting* and *standard content*, including text, images and fields.

In this chapter you will explore the *relationship* between templates and styles, and discover how that relationship affects the documents that you work with.

Style location: document or template?

Ask yourself the question, where is style stored? Unlike a document or a template, a style is not a separate file. Yet each style must be stored somewhere – but where?

You can store a new style that you create in either of two locations: in the current document, or in the current template (that is, the template on which the current document is based).

- **Current document.** A style stored in the current document is available in that document only.

  This is the sensible choice for one-off styles that you create for use only in a single document and are unlikely to ever need again.

- **Template.** A style stored in a template is available to all other documents that are also based on that template.

  When you want to reuse a style in multiple documents – for example, all fax cover sheets or all sales reports – but the best place to store the style is in the template.

The Add to template checkbox

What controls where a new style is stored? Answer: the settings of the *Add to template* checkbox, which appears in the *New Style* dialogue box within the **Format | Style** command.

When you select *Add to template*, you are telling Word: 'This is a style that I may want to use in other documents. So store my new style in the current template.'

When you leave the *Add to template* checkbox deselected (its default value), Word stores your new style in the current document only.

Select this checkbox to save a new style in the current template.

If this checkbox is deselected, the style is stored only in the current document.

New Style

Name: My Heading

Style type: Paragraph

Based on: ¶ Heading 1

Style for following paragraph: ¶ Normal

Preview

Mission Statement

Description
Heading 1 + Level 1

☑ Add to template   ☐ Automatically update

OK   Cancel   Format ▾   Shortcut Key...

Separating content from format: the benefits

When you store styles in a template, you take away control of the document's format from the document itself and pass that control to another file: the template file.

This approach to formatting a document with styles saved in a template is called template-based formatting or style-sheet-based formatting. (The terms *template* and *style sheet* are often used interchangeably.) This approach offers the following advantages:

- **Consistency across multiple documents**. You can ensure that multiple documents share the same appearance simply by basing them on a common template.

- **Multiple document reformatting**. You can change the appearance of multiple documents simply by amending a *single* file, the template file. All documents based on that template, whether they number 10 or 10,000, change accordingly.

Template-based formatting

An approach in which documents are formatted by applying styles saved in a common template. It enables the formatting of multiple documents to be managed from a single template file.

Templates and documents: how they are first connected

New button

Every Word document is based on a template. The association between a document and its underlying template is made in one of two ways:

- **Word chooses the template**. If you create a document by clicking the **New** button on the Standard toolbar, Word associates your document with the so-called Normal template, also known as Normal.dot.

- **You choose the template**. If you create a document by choosing **File | New**, Word displays a dialog box and prompts you to select your required template.

When you click on a template icon, select the *Create New Document* option, and click **OK**, Word creates a new document based on the template that you have selected.

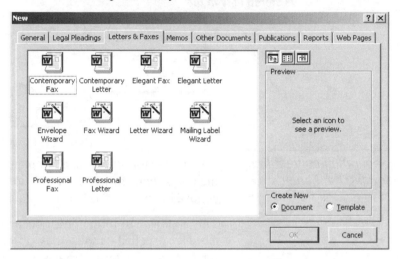

Changing the template on which a document is based

A document is not tied forever to the template chosen at the time it was created. You can change a document's template as often as you wish.

Exercise 4.1: Attach a new template to a document

In this exercise, you open a document containing text, attach a new template to it, and discover how the new template affects the document's appearance.

1) Open Word, and open the following file:

    `Chapter4_Exercise_4-1_Before.doc`

    A sample from the document is shown below.

> **˙|The·New·Era·of·e-Business:·Part·1¶**
>
> ***Introduction¶***
>
> By·transforming·the·way·that·people·and·businesses·communicate·and·interact,·the·Internet·has·dramatically·changed·the·face·of·business.¶
>
> Impressed·by·the·Internet's·rising·popularity,·many·businesses·have·established·an·online·presence.·A·rich·variety·of·business·information—from·product·and·service·catalogues·to·press·releases·to·company·contacts—is·now·available·to·Internet·users.¶
>
> Today,·many·businesses·realise·that,·in·order·to·compete·successfully,·they·need·to·sell·their·goods·and·services·directly·to·consumers·or·other·businesses·over·the·Internet.¶

Formatting is applied to the document using Word's built-in Heading 1, Heading 2, Normal and List Bullet styles.

2) Choose **Tools | Templates** and **Add-Ins**.

3) Click **Attach** to display the templates located in your \Templates folder, click the following template to select it, and then click **Open**:

   `Chapter4_Exercise_4-1_Template1.dot`

   You are returned to the *Templates and Add-ins* dialog box.

4) Select the *Automatically update document styles* checkbox. The dialog box should now look similar to this:

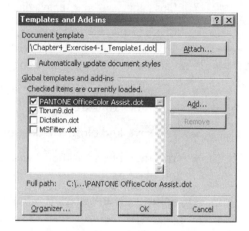

5) Click **OK** to close the dialog box and attach the selected template to your selected document.

   Notice how your sample document has changed appearance. This is because the style definitions for Heading 1, Heading 2, Normal and List Bullet in the new template are different to those of the document's original template, Normal.dot.

> ·   The·New·Era·of·e-Business:·Part·1¶
>
> ·   Introduction¶
>
>   By·transforming·the·way·that·people·and·businesses·communicate·and· interact,·the·Internet·has·dramatically·changed·the·face·of·business.¶
>
>   Impressed·by·the·Internet's·rising·popularity,·many·businesses·have· established·an·online·presence.·A·rich·variety·of·business·information —from· product·and·service·catalogues·to·press·releases·to·company·contacts —is· now·available·to·Internet·users.¶
>
>   Today,·many·businesses·realise·that,·in·order·to·compete·successfully,· they·need·to·sell·their·goods·and·services·directly·to·consumers·or·other· businesses·over·the·Internet.¶

6) Repeat steps 2 to 4, but this time select the following template:

   `Chapter4_Exercise_4-1_Template2.dot`

Notice again how your sample document has changed appearance.

> ### ·The·New·Era·of·e-Business:·Part·1¶
>
> ·
>
> **Introduction¶**
>
> By·transforming·the·way·that·people·and·businesses·communicate·and·
> interact,·the·Internet·has·dramatically·changed·the·face·of·business.¶
>
> Impressed·by·the·Internet's·rising·popularity,·many·businesses·have·
> established·an·online·presence.·A·rich·variety·of·business·information·–·from·
> product·and·service·catalogues·to·press·releases·to·company·contacts·–·is·
> now·available·to·Internet·users.¶
>
> Today,·many·businesses·realise·that,·in·order·to·compete·successfully,·they·
> need·to·sell·their·goods·and·services·directly·to·consumers·or·other·
> businesses·over·the·Internet.¶

7) Close and save your sample document with the following name:

Chapter4_Exercise_4-1_After_*Your_Name*.doc

Style modifications and templates

Consider the following sequence of events:

- When working with a particular document, you modify the attributes of a style.

- You save and close the document.

- You then open another document that is based on the same template as the first.

Does the style modification that you made in the first document affect the format of the second document? The answer is that it depends.

Everything that you have learnt so far about styles and templates also applies to style modifications and templates. When you modify a style – that is, change its attributes in some way – you can store the modification in the current document or template.

- **Style in template, modification in document**. It is possible to store a style in a template, and to store a modification to the same style in a document.

  In this case, the original style is available to all documents based on the template, but the newer, modified style is available only to the current document.

- **Style in document, modification in template**. You can create a new style and store it in the current document only. Later, you can amend the style's attributes in some way and save the modified version of the style in the current template.

  In this case, the original style is available to the current document only, but the modified style is available to all documents based on the relevant template.

As with new styles, the storage location of a style modification depends on the setting of the *Add to template* checkbox. This checkbox, which appears in the *New Style* dialog box, also appears within the *Modify Style* dialog box. Both dialog boxes are available through the **Format | Style** command.

Exercise 4.2: Modifying a style stored in a template

In this exercise, you work with two documents that are based on the same template. You will redefine a style in one document, and discover the effects of the style modification on the other document.

1) Open the following file:

   Chapter4_Exercise_4-2_Doc1.doc

2) Choose **Tools | Templates and Add-Ins**. Click **Attach** to display the templates located in your \Templates folder, click the following template, and then click **Open**:

   Chapter4_Exercise_4-2_Template2.dot

   You are returned to the *Templates and Add-ins* dialogue box.

   Select the *Automatically update document styles* checkbox.

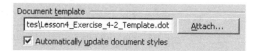

3) Click **OK** to close the dialog box and attach the selected template to your sample document. Notice how your sample document has changed appearance. Leave this document open.

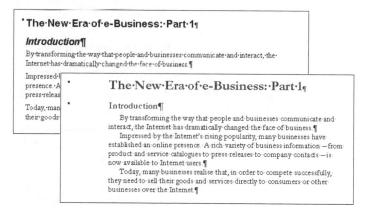

4) Open the second file:

   Chapter4_Exercise_4-2_Doc2.doc

5) Choose **Tools | Templates and Add-Ins**, click **Attach** to attach the following template, and then click **Open**:

   Chapter4_Exercise_4-2_Template.dot

Select the *Automatically update document styles* checkbox, and click **OK** to close the *Templates and Add-ins* dialog box.

Leave this second document open. You now have two documents based on the same template.

6) In your first sample document, click anywhere in the main heading, 'The New Era of e-Business: Part 1'. It is in the Heading 1 style.

7) Choose **Format | Style**, click **Modify**, **Format**, **Font**, change the *Color* to a different colour, and click **OK**.

You are returned to the *Modify Style* dialog box. Select the *Add to template* checkbox, click **OK**, and then click **Apply** to close the dialog box. The document's main heading is now shown in your selected new colour.

8) Close your first sample document by clicking the **Close** box or by choosing **File | Close**. Word displays the following message box:

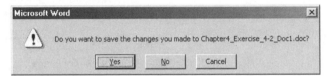

Click **Yes** to save the change to your document.

9) Word next displays a second dialog box, asking you if you want to save the change to the template.

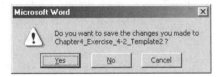

Click **Yes** to save the change to your template.

Only your second sample document is now open on your screen.

10) Look at the colour of the main heading in the second sample document. You can see that it has not been effected by the colour change that you made in step 8. For the style modification to take effect, you need to *reattach* the template containing the amended style to the document.

11) Choose **Tools | Templates and Add-Ins**, click **Attach** to attach the following template, and click **Open**:

    Chapter4_Exercise_4-2_Template2.dot

Do not select the *Automatically update document styles* checkbox. Click **OK** to close the *Templates and Add-ins* dialog box.

You can see that the main heading is still in its original colour.

12) Choose **Tools | Templates and Add-Ins**, click **Attach** to attach the following template, and click **Open**:

    Chapter4_Exercise_4-2_Template2.dot

13) This time, select the *Automatically update document styles* checkbox. Click **OK** to close the *Templates and Add-ins* dialog box.

14) Now you can see that the main heading is in the new colour, reflecting the modification to the Heading 1 style saved in the document's template.

15) Choose **Format | Style**, click **Modify**, **Format**, **Font**, change the *Color* to its original colour, and click **OK**.

    You are returned to the *Modify Style* dialog box. Select the *Add to template* checkbox, click **OK**, and then click **Apply** to close the dialog box. The document's main heading is now in its original colour.

16) You can close and save your second sample document, saving the change to its template as you do.

17) Reopen Chapter4_Exercise_4-2_Doc1.doc and Chapter4_Exercise_4-2_Doc2.doc, reattach them to the Chapter4_Exercise_4-2_Template1.dot template, and close and save them.

The Automatically update document styles *checkbox*

Available within the **Tools | Templates and Add-Ins** command, the setting of this checkbox determines whether style modifications, saved in the document's template, affect the format of a document:

- **Checkbox selected**. The document is affected by the latest style modifications that are saved in the document's template.

- **Checkbox deselected**. The document is unaffected by style modifications saved in the template since the connection between the document and template was last made.

Select this checkbox to ensure that a document contains the latest template-based style modifications.

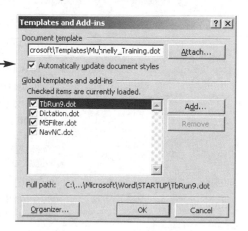

In summary, if you create a new style or modify an existing one, and you want the new or modified style to be available to other documents based on the same template, you must:

- When using the **Format | Style** command to create or modify a style, select the *Add to template* checkbox.

- When closing the document that was open when you created or modified the style, save the changes to the template when prompted.

- Reattach the template to other documents, using the **Tools | Templates and Add-Ins** command, and ensure that you select the *Automatically update document styles* checkbox.

Applying styles with AutoFormat

If you need to apply styles to an unformatted document – for example, a plain-text, ASCII file imported from a non-Word source – you will find the AutoFormat feature a great time-saver.

AutoFormat works by examining factors such as line length (shorter lines are probably headings) and detecting the presence of special characters (a line beginning with an asterisk (*) and followed by a space or a tab is probably a bullet). It then applies appropriate heading and other styles to the document.

AutoFormat is, in effect, automated guesswork by Word. Its choices may not always be correct, but it is a valuable aid nonetheless.

AutoFormat also offers a number of other features that help tidy up a document, as does a related Word feature called AutoFormat As You Type. You will learn more about these features in Chapter 7.

You have two options when applying AutoFormat to all or selected parts of a document:

- **AutoFormat now**. This automatically formats the document or selected paragraphs based on your chosen settings.

- **AutoFormat and review each change**. This prompts you every time AutoFormat detects something in the document that it thinks it should reformat, and asks you whether you want to apply or ignore its suggested formatting.

AutoFormat

A Word feature that automatically applies appropriate heading, list and other styles to an unformatted or partly-formatted document based on an analysis of that document's structure.

The main AutoFormat options relating to styles are shown in the following table. You access these options by choosing **Format | AutoFormat**, and clicking the **Options** button.

AutoFormat option	Effect on document
Headings	Paragraphs identified as headings are converted to the appropriate heading style – Heading 1, Heading 2, etc.
Lists	Paragraphs identified as items in a bulleted or numbered list are converted to the appropriate paragraph styles – List Bullet or List.
Automatic bulleted lists	Paragraphs identified as items in a bulleted or numbered list are converted to the Normal style, but bulleted or numbering formatting is applied to them within that style.
	If you select both the *Lists* and the *Automatic bulleted lists* options, the *Lists* option takes preference.
Other paragraphs	Paragraphs identified as body text are converted to the Normal style.
Preserve styles	Any paragraph styles already applied to text in the document are unchanged by AutoFormat. The exception is Plain Text style (Word default style for plain-text, unformatted documents).

Exercise 4.3: Applying styles with AutoFormat

In this exercise, you will apply AutoFormat to an unformatted document.

1) Open the following file:

   Chapter4_Exercise_4-3_Before.doc

   Notice that the entire document is in Plain Text style, Word's default style for plain-text, unformatted documents.

   There are no heading styles, and the asterisk character (*) is used to indicate items in a bulleted list.

2) Choose **Format | AutoFormat**, and click **Options**. Select the options shown below and click **OK**.

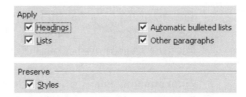

3) You now have two options: you can run AutoFormat in a single pass, or you can ask Word to prompt you for confirmation before it makes any changes. Click the *AutoFormat and review each change* option.

Select a document type to guide Word's formatting operation: *General document* (your current template), *Letter* or *Email*. In this case, select the *General document* option.

4) Click **OK**.

(If you had selected the *AutoFormat now* option in step 3, Word would now apply the formatting changes. If you are unhappy with the changes made, you can choose **Edit | Undo** to reverse them.)

5) AutoFormat applies the changes to the sample document, which you can see on your screen. You can use the scrollbar or navigation keys to move through your document to inspect how well Word has formatted your document.

6) In the foreground, you can see the following dialog box:

If you approve of the changes, click **Accept All**.

If the changes suggested are not at all what you want, click **Reject All**.

Selecting either option ends the AutoFormat procedure and returns you to the document.

7) If you want to accept some changes but not others, click **Review Changes**.

Word now highlights each suggested formatting change on screen. Insertions are marked in blue and deletions in red. All changes are indicated by a vertical bar in the page margin.

A new dialog box, shown below, appears in the foreground. Click the **Hide Marks** button if you do not want Word to display the revision marks.

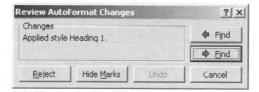

8) To inspect each formatting change, click **-> Find**. Word displays a dialog box indicating the first suggested formatting change.

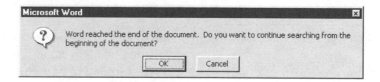

Click **Reject** to reject the suggested change. Click **-> Find** to accept the suggested change and display the next one.

9) Repeat step 8 until you have moved through all the suggested changes. You now see the following dialog box:

Click **Cancel**.

10) Word again shows the *Review AutoFormat Changes* dialog box. Click **Cancel**.

11) You are now shown the AutoFormat dialog box. Click **Accept All**. This implements only those changes that you have accepted by clicking the **-> Find** button in Steps 8 and 9, and not any changes that you did not accept by clicking the **Reject** button.

You have now completed the AutoFormat procedure.

12) Choose **File | Save As**, and save your document with the following name:

```
Chapter4_Exercise_4-3_After_Your_Name.doc
```

You can now close your document.

Chapter 4: quick reference

Tasks summary

Task	Procedure
Base a new document on a template other than the Normal template.	Choose **File	New**, click on a template icon from the dialog box, select the *Create New Document option*, and click **OK**.
Attach a different template to a new document.	Choose **Tools	Templates and Add-Ins**, click **Attach**, select the new template, select the *Automatically update document styles* checkbox, and click **OK**.
Save a style or a style modification in a template.	Within the **Format	Style** dialog box, select the *Add to template* checkbox, and save the template when prompted as you close the document.
Update a document's format to reflect the latest style modifications saved in the document's template.	Reattach the document template: choose **Tools	Templates and Add-Ins**, click **Attach**, select the current template, select the *Automatically update document styles* checkbox, and click **OK**.

Concepts summary

Template-based formatting is an approach in which documents are formatted by applying styles saved in a common template. It enables the formatting of multiple documents to be managed from a single template file.

ECDL Advanced Word Processing

An advantage of this approach is that is enables you to enforce a common format across multiple documents by basing the documents on the same template. In addition, you can change the appearance of multiple documents simply by amending their template file.

To apply the template-based formatting approach in Word, styles – and style modifications – must be saved in a template rather than in individual documents. When styles are added or modified, the template must be saved when the document is closed. Also, individual documents must be reattached to their template so that they reflect the latest updates to styles that are saved in the templates.

Chapter 4: quick quiz

Circle the correct answer to each of the following multiple-choice questions about templates, styles and AutoFormat in Word.

Q1	You want to base a new Word document on a template other than the Normal template. Do you...
A.	Click the **New** button on the Standard toolbar?
B.	Choose **File	New**, and select the required template from the *Template Options* drop-down list?
C.	Remove Normal.dot from the \Templates folder?
D.	Choose **File	New**, select the required template from the dialogue box displayed, and click **OK**?

Q2	Which of the following statements about styles and templates in Word is untrue?
A.	A style can be stored only in the Normal.dot template.
B.	A style can be stored in a template or a document.
C.	A style can be stored in a template, while a modification to the same style can be stored in a document.
D.	Two documents with the same styles can look very different.

Q3	When using Word's Format | Style command, what is the effect of selecting the *Add to template* checkbox?
A.	It ensures that the style is saved to the Normal.dot template.
B.	It merges the styles in your current template to the Normal.dot template.
C.	It makes the style or style modification available to the current template and not just to the current document.
D.	It converts all character styles to paragraph styles.

Q4	Two Word documents share the same template and styles but look different. Which of the following is a possible reason for this?
A.	The user modified a style when working on the second document but saved the style changes only to the second document, and not to the template.
B.	Both documents are based on the Normal template.
C.	Neither document is based on the Normal template.
D.	The template is not located in the \Templates folder.

Q5	What happens when you apply AutoFormat to an unformatted Word document?
A.	Word automatically applies the AutoFormat template (AutoFormat.dot) to the document.
B.	Word examines the document's structure and applies appropriate headings and other styles accordingly.
C.	Word runs a built-in macro on the document that corrects automatically any spelling and grammar errors.
D.	Word makes a back-up copy of the document and applies style-based formatting to the back-up copy. The original document is unaffected.

Answers

1: D, **2:** A, **3:** C, **4:** A, **5:** B.

ECDL Advanced Word Processing

5

Here's one I prepared earlier: AutoText

Objectives	In this chapter you will learn how to: ■ Add a new text, table and image entries to AutoText ■ Insert an AutoText entry in a document ■ Amend an AutoText entry ■ Delete an AutoText entry
New words	In this chapter you will meet the following term: ■ AutoText
Exercise files	In this chapter you will work with the following Word files: ■ `Chapter5_Exercise_5-1.doc` ■ `Chapter5_Exercise_5-2_Before.dot`
Syllabus reference	In this chapter you will cover the following item from the ECDL Advanced Word Processing Syllabus: ■ **AM3.1.1.5**: Use automatic text entry options.
About AutoText	AutoText is a Word feature for storing and inserting commonly-used text, graphics, tables and fields.
Two kinds of AutoText entries	Items stored in AutoText are called *AutoText entries*. There are two kinds: those supplied with Word, and those you add yourself. ■ **Built-in entries**. Word offers a categorized range of supplied AutoText entries. Most are simple text entries relevant to letter-writing. Others are items suitable for insertion in document headers or footers.

- **User-created entries**. You can add your own AutoText entries. For example, your organization's name and contact details, formatted tables, and standard paragraphs such as disclaimers.

  You can also add images to AutoText, such as a scanned image of your signature.

An example of AutoText At work
1. Position the insertion point. 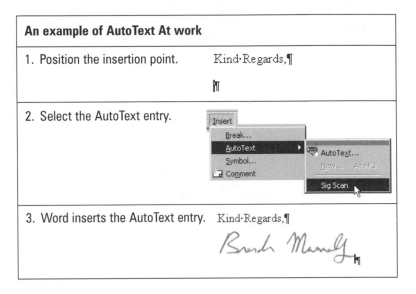
2. Select the AutoText entry.
3. Word inserts the AutoText entry.

*The **AutoText** tab*

To display your current AutoText entries, choose **Tools | AutoCorrect**. Click the **AutoText** tab, and scroll through the entries. When finished, click **OK**.

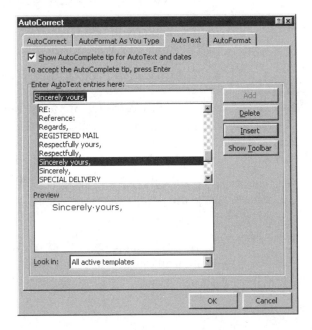

How much information can you store in an AutoText entry? Answer: it depends on the size of your PC's memory.

AutoText

A Word feature that stores frequently used text, tables and graphics, and enables users to insert these items as needed in individual documents.

AutoText: the benefits to you

A template, as you learned in Chapter 3, can store standard content – text, tables, graphics and fields – or automatic inclusion in any individual document based on that template. So what does AutoText offer that templates do not?

AutoText is valuable for:

- **Content that appears frequently but not always.** Like templates, AutoText can store ready-made content. But unlike templates, AutoText gives you the option of inserting or not inserting the content.

- **Content that appears across different document types**. Templates work best with narrowly categorized documents. AutoText entries can be applied more widely across many different document types – from one-page letters to lengthy reports.

Both templates and AutoText offer common benefits. They:

- **Save time**. AutoText can help eliminate a lot of repetitive typing.

- **Reduce errors**. Less typing results in documents with fewer misspellings and other errors.

Working with AutoText: the four tasks

Here are the four tasks you need to be able to perform with AutoText in Word:

- **Create new AutoText entries**. Exercise 5.1 takes you through the steps of creating new AutoText entries for a text paragraph, a table and an image.

- **Insert AutoText entries in a document**. In Exercise 5.2, you discover how to insert AutoText entries in a document.

- **Amend an AutoText entry**. Sometimes, you may want to modify an AutoText entry. Exercise 5.3 shows you how.

- **Delete an AutoText entry**. Finally, in Exercise 5.4, you learn how to delete an entry from AutoText.

Working with new AutoText entries

Two topics you need to understand before you create new AutoText entries are storage location and formatting.

AutoText and templates

Built-in AutoText entries are stored in the Normal template, from where they are available to every document that you work on.

User-created AutoText entries, however, are stored in the Word template associated with the document that was open when you created the entry. If this was Normal.dot, then your AutoText entry is available to all documents. If it was another template – say, Fax.dot – the entry is available only to documents based on that template.

AutoText and formatting

Typically, you create AutoText entries by selecting existing text, tables or graphics, and then storing them in AutoText. How does AutoText deal with formatting? The rules are straightforward:

- **Character formatting**. AutoText entries retain their character formatting (font, bold, italic, etc.).

  If you do not want a new AutoText entry to include paragraph formatting, select the paragraph without its paragraph mark.

- **Paragraph formatting**. If you want an AutoText entry to retain its paragraph formatting (alignment, indents, borders, tabs, etc.), include the paragraph mark when you select the entry.

Exercise 5.1: Creating AutoText entries

In this exercise, you will create three new AutoText entries: a text paragraph, a table, and a scanned image of a signature.

1) Open the following file:

   Chapter5_Exercise_5-1.doc

2) Select the following text paragraph, including the paragraph mark at the end.

3) Choose **Insert | AutoText | New**.

   (This option is available only if you have selected either text or a graphic within the document.)

4) In the *Create AutoText* dialog box, type a short, descriptive name for the entry. AutoText names can include spaces. In this example, type the name 'Slogan'.

Click **OK**.

5) Click anywhere in the Monthly Sales Report table, choose **Table | Select Table**.

6) Choose **Insert | AutoText | New**. In the *Create AutoText* dialog box, type the name 'Monthly Sales Report Table' and click **OK**.

7) Click on the image of the scanned signature to select it.

8) Choose **Insert | AutoText | New**. In the *Create AutoText* dialog box, type the name 'BM Sig Scan' and click **OK**.

9) You can close the sample document without saving it.

   Your work – the addition of three new AutoText entries – is contained in the template, not in the document.

Working with existing AutoText entries

The best way to gain an appreciation of AutoText is to use this feature in creating a document.

Exercise 5.2: Inserting AutoText entries in a document

In this exercise, you will insert the AutoText entries that you created in Exercise 5.1, together with two built-in Word AutoText entries.

1) Choose **File | New** and select the following template from the **General** tab:

   `Chapter5_Exercise_5-2_Before.dot`

   Click **OK**.

   Word now displays a new document based on the selected template.

2) Position the insertion point before the paragraph mark that is above the word 'Memo'.

Memo¶

3) Choose **Insert | AutoText | Normal | Slogan**.

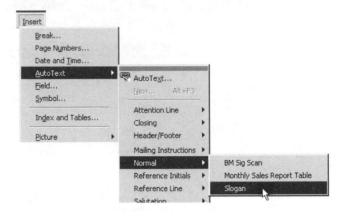

Word inserts the AutoText entry as shown.

4) Position the insertion point at the third paragraph mark beneath the table.

5) Choose **Insert | AutoText | Salutation | To Whom It May Concern**. Word inserts the AutoText entry.

6) Press **Enter** three times.

7) Choose **Insert | AutoText | Normal | Monthly Sales Report Table**. Word inserts the AutoText entry.

8) Press **Enter** three times.

9) Choose **Insert | AutoText | Closing | Best Regards**. Word inserts the AutoText entry.

10) Press **Enter** twice.

11) Choose **Insert | AutoText | Normal | BM Sig Scan**. Word inserts the AutoText entry.

12) Save your sample document with the following name, and close it:

Chapter5_Exercise_5-2_After_*Your_Name*.doc

Can you amend an AutoText entry? Not directly. But you can insert an entry in a document, modify the entry in the document, and then resave the entry in AutoText under the same name. The amended AutoText entry then overwrites the original entry.

Exercise 5.3: Amend an AutoText entry

In this exercise, you will modify an AutoText entry by amending it in a document and then resaving it to AutoText.

1) Click the **New** button on the Standard toolbar to create a new, blank document.

2) Choose **Insert | AutoText | Normal | Monthly Sales Report Table**. Word inserts the AutoText entry.

3) Select the text 'Monthly Sales Report'.

4) Choose **Format | Font**, change the font colour to light grey, and click **OK**.

5) Click anywhere in the Monthly Sales Report table, and choose **Table | Select Table**.

6) Choose **Insert | AutoText | New**. In the *Create AutoText* dialog box, type the name 'Monthly Sales Report Table' and click **OK**.

7) Word prompts you like this:

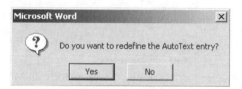

Click **Yes**. The named AutoText entry is now amended.

You can close the document without saving it. Your work – the modification of an AutoText entry – is contained in the template, not in the document.

Exercise 5.4: Deleting an AutoText entry

Removing an entry from AutoText is a simple task, as this exercise demonstrates.

1) Choose **Tools | AutoCorrect**, and click the **AutoText** tab.

2) Scroll through the list of AutoText entries to find an entry that you want to delete.

3) When you see the entry you want to delete, click to select it.

4) Click the **Delete** button.

5) Repeat steps 2 to 4 to remove any other AutoText entries you don't want.

6) When finished, click **OK** to close the dialog box.

Chapter 5: quick reference

Task	Procedure
Save selected item as an AutoText entry.	Select the item, choose **Insert	AutoText	New**, type a short name for the entry, and click **OK**.
	To include the item's paragraph formatting, select the paragraph mark at the end of the item.
Insert an AutoText item in the current document.	Position the insertion point, choose **Insert	AutoText**, and click the required entry on the submenu.
Amend an AutoText entry.	In a document, type the amended entry, choose **Insert	AutoText	New**, and type the short name for the entry you want to amend. When prompted to redefine the entry, click **Yes**.
Delete an AutoText entry.	Choose **Tools	AutoCorrect**, click the **AutoText** tab, select the entry for deletion, click **Delete**, and click **OK**.

Concepts summary

AutoText is a Word feature that stores frequently-used content, and enables users to insert these items as needed in individual documents. Items stored in AutoText can include text, tables, graphics and fields.

Like templates, AutoText can store ready-made content. But unlike templates, AutoText gives you the option of inserting or not inserting the content.

Word includes a categorized range of *built-in AutoText entries*. Most are simple text entries relevant to letter-writing. Others are items suitable for insertion in document headers or footers.

You can add your own AutoText entries, such as your organization's name, contact details and logo. AutoText entries retain their character formatting (bold, italic, etc.) and, optionally, their paragraph formatting (alignment, indents, etc.).

User-created AutoText entries are stored in the Word template associated with the document that was open when the entry was created.

Items suitable for inclusion in AutoText are those that are relevant across many different document types – from one-page letters to lengthy reports.

Chapter 5: quick quiz

Circle the correct answer to each of the following multiple choice questions about AutoText in Word.

Q1	Which of the following statements best describes the AutoText feature in Word?
A.	AutoText checks a document's readability statistics and automatically makes such improvements as are necessary.
B.	AutoText generates document outlines automatically, based on the document's headings and subheadings.
C.	AutoText applies paragraph styles to a document based on factors such as line length and presence of bullet characters and numbers at the beginning of paragraphs.
D.	AutoText stores frequently-used text, tables, graphics and fields, and enables users to insert these items as needed in individual documents.

Q2	Which of the following is not an advantage of using AutoText in Word documents?
A.	Reduced likelihood of spelling errors as commonly-used text items can be retrieved from AutoText and inserted as needed in individual documents.
B.	Availability of automatically-created back-ups in the event of document corruption or loss.
C.	Documents look more professional, as logos and other standard graphics can be retrieved quickly from AutoText and inserted in individual documents.
D.	Faster production of documents containing sales figures and other numerical data, as highly-formatted tables can be retrieved from AutoText and inserted in individual documents.

Q3	Which of the following items can you not store as an AutoText entry in Word?
A.	Multiple paragraphs of text.
B.	A colour image.
C.	A template.
D.	A date field.

Q4	Which of the following factors determines the maximum size of the entries that you can store in AutoText?
A.	Your version of Word.
B.	The size of your PC's memory.
C.	The speed of your internal network connection.
D.	None of the above – entries may not exceed 256 characters.

Q5	Which of the following commands do you choose to create an AutoText entry from a selected item in a Word document?
A.	Insert	AutoText	New.
B.	Tools	AutoText	Add.
C.	Insert	Add	AutoText.
D.	Format	AutoCorrect	AutoText	New.

Q6	Which of the following commands do you choose to insert an AutoText entry in an open Word document?
A.	Insert	AutoText	New.
B.	Insert	AutoText	<Submenu Name>	<AutoText Entry Name>.
C.	Format	Add	<AutoText Entry Name>.
D.	Format	AutoCorrect	AutoText	<Submenu Name>	<AutoText Entry Name>.

Q7	You want to include an item's paragraph formatting attributes when adding it as an AutoText entry in Word. Do you...
A.	Exclude the item's paragraph mark when selecting it?
B.	Hold down the **Shift** key when selecting the item?
C.	Include the item's paragraph mark when selecting it?
D.	Hold down the **Ctrl** key when selecting the item?

Q8	Which of the following statements about amending AutoText entries is correct?
A.	Only user-created, not built-in, AutoCorrect entries can be amended.
B.	An entry can be amended directly in the *AutoText* dialog box.
C.	An entry can be amended only by saving a modified version of the entry with the same name as the entry you want to amend.
D.	Only text entries, not tables, can be amended.

Answers

1: D, **2:** B, **3:** D, **4:** B, **5:** A, **6:** D, **7:** C, **8:** C.

Word checks Your documents: AutoCorrect

Objectives

In this chapter you will learn how to:

- Turn AutoCorrect on and off
- Apply AutoCorrect options selectively
- Include and exclude the Office 2000 spellchecker in AutoCorrect
- Add a new AutoCorrect entry
- Amend an AutoCorrect entry
- Delete an AutoCorrect entry
- Use AutoCorrect exceptions.

New words

In this chapter you will meet the following term:

- AutoCorrect

Syllabus reference

In this chapter you will cover the following item of the ECDL Advanced Word Processing Syllabus:

- **AM3.1.1.3**: Use automatic text correction options.

About AutoCorrect

AutoCorrect is a Word feature that can improve your documents by automatically detecting and correcting:

- **Misspelled words**. For example, 'teh' instead of 'the', and 'calulated' instead of 'calculated'.
- **Grammatical errors**. For example, 'might of had' instead of 'might have had'.
- **Missing interword spaces**. For example, 'aboutit' instead of 'about it'.

- **Incorrect capitalization**. For example, 'tuesday' instead of 'Tuesday'.

- **Unformatted symbols**. For example, '(c)' instead of the copyright symbol '©'.

By default, AutoCorrect runs interactively in the background as you type and edit text. Whenever you type anything that it regards as an error, AutoCorrect fixes your entry as soon as you press the **Spacebar** or **Enter** key.

An example of AutoCorrect at work	
1. You mistype a word.	and·then·teh¶
2. You press the **Spacebar**.	
3. AutoCorrect fixes your error.	and·then·the·¶

A lot of the time, you may not even notice AutoCorrect making its corrections.

Two kinds of AutoCorrect entries

Items stored in AutoCorrect are called *AutoCorrect entries*. There are two kinds:

- **Built-in entries**. AutoCorrect contains almost 1000 common errors and solutions.

- **User-created entries**. You can add your own AutoText entries. These may be spelling mistakes that you make most often, or the full form of abbreviations that you commonly use.

For example, you could create an AutoCorrect entry that replaces 'asap' with 'as soon as possible', or 'spec' with 'specifications'.

The AutoCorrect *dialog box*

To view the AutoCorrect entries available to your current document, choose **Tools | AutoCorrect**, click the **AutoCorrect** tab, and scroll through the entries in the lower half of the dialog box. When finished, click **Cancel**.

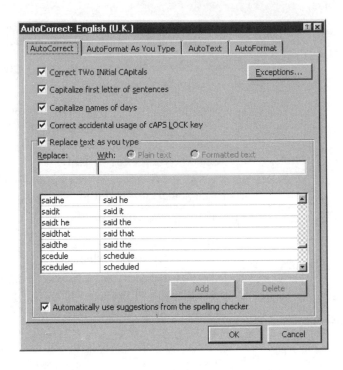

AutoCorrect and the
Office 2000 spellchecker

By default, AutoCorrect also draws on the many thousands of errors and their replacements contained in the Microsoft Office 2000 spelling dictionary.

AutoCorrect, when working with the Office 2000 spellchecker, does not replace every suspect word you type. AutoCorrect replaces a typed word only if it decides that what you have typed is an error. You many find this feature either helpful or annoying, and therefore choose to either leave it on or switch it off.

In effect, AutoCorrect offers not one but two options for detecting and correcting misspellings: one based on AutoCorrect entries, and a second based on the Office 2000 spellchecker.

The two options are independent of each other. You can decide to activate one, both, or neither.

AutoCorrect

A Word feature that automatically detects and corrects various errors as you type. AutoCorrect can fix misspellings, incorrect capitalization, missing interword spaces, and unformatted symbols, and can draw on the errors and replacements contained in the Office 2000 spelling dictionary.

Working with AutoCorrect

Here are the tasks that you need to be able to perform with AutoCorrect:

- **Switch AutoCorrect on and off**. Exercise 6.1 shows you how.

- **Apply AutoCorrect options selectively**. Sometimes, you may want to use some AutoCorrect options but not others. Follow Exercise 6.2 to discover how to apply AutoCorrect selectively.

- **Using the Office 2000 spellchecker in AutoCorrect**. You can decide to include or exclude automatic spell checking and replacement within AutoCorrect. Exercise 6.3 takes you through the steps.

- **Add new AutoText entries**. You are not limited to using only Word's AutoCorrect built-in entries.

  Exercises 6.4 and 6.5 show you how to add unformatted and formatted entries of your own.

- **Amend and delete existing AutoCorrect entries**. You can modify and delete both built-in and user-created entries in AutoText. Exercise 6.6 takes you through the steps.

- **Work with AutoCorrect exceptions**. Imagine that your organization is named *Teh Limited* or *Taht Enterprises*, for example. You would not want Word 'correcting' your name every time you typed it. See Exercise 6.7.

Working with AutoCorrect settings

In the first three exercises, you will explore various settings within AutoCorrect.

Exercise 6.1: Switching AutoCorrect off and on

Before performing this exercise, start Word and open a new, blank document. The **Tools | AutoCorrect** menu command is available only when you have at least one document open.

1) Choose **Tools | AutoCorrect**, and click the **AutoCorrect** tab of the dialog box displayed.

2) Deselect or select the *Replace text as you type* checkbox, as appropriate.

☑ Replace text as you type

Deselecting this checkbox disables the four AutoCorrect options above this check box, regardless of whether the checkboxes are selected.

Selecting or deselecting this checkbox does not affect the *Automatically use suggestions from the spelling checker* checkbox.

It is possible to disable AutoCorrect entries yet still use AutoCorrect to implement spelling corrections automatically from the Office 2000 Spellchecker.

3) Click **OK**.

Word saves your AutoCorrect settings. You can close the sample document without saving it.

Exercise 6.2: Applying AutoCorrect options selectively

Before performing this exercise, first open a new, blank Word document. The **Tools | AutoCorrect** menu command is available only when you have at least one document open.

1) Choose **Tools | AutoCorrect**, and click the **AutoCorrec**t tab of the dialog box displayed.

Ensure that the *Replace text as you type* checkbox is selected. This check box must remain selected through all the steps in this exercise.

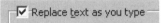

2) Select the first of the four AutoCorrect checkboxes, deselect the other three as shown, and click **OK**.

☑ Correct TWo INitial CApitals

☐ Capitalize first letter of sentences

☐ Capitalize names of days

☐ Correct accidental usage of cAPS LOCK key

3) Type the following text and press **Enter** twice:

THe lazy brown fox

Notice how AutoCorrect corrects your typing error.

4) Choose **Tools | AutoCorrect**, click the **AutoCorrect** tab, select the second of the four AutoCorrect checkboxes, deselect the other three, and click **OK**.

5) Type the following text and press **Enter** twice.

the lazy brown fox

Notice how AutoCorrect corrects your typing error.

6) Choose **Tools | AutoCorrect**, click the **AutoCorrect** tab, select the third of the four AutoCorrect checkboxes, deselect the other three, and click **OK**.

7) Type the following text and press Enter twice:

the lazy brown fox on friday

Notice how AutoCorrect corrects your typing error.

8) Choose **Tools | AutoCorrect**, click the **AutoCorrect** tab, select the fourth of the four AutoCorrect checkboxes, deselect the other three, and click **OK**.

9) Type the following text:

    The lazy br

10) Press the **Caps Lock** key

11) Type the following text and press **Enter** twice:

    OWN fox

Notice how AutoCorrect corrects your typing error. This correction option applies only to the use of the **Caps Lock** key, not the **Shift** key.

You can close the sample document without saving it.

Exercise 6.3: Using the Office 2000 spellchecker in AutoCorrect

Before performing this exercise, first open a new, blank Word document. The **Tools | AutoCorrect** menu command is available only when you have at least one document open.

1) Choose **Tools | Options**, click the **Spelling & Grammar** tab, and select the *Check spelling as you type* checkbox if it is not selected already.

Click **OK** to close the dialog box. You must select this option if you want to use the Office 2000 spellcheck feature within AutoCorrect.

2) Choose **Tools | AutoCorrect**, and click the **AutoCorrect** tab of the dialog box displayed.

Ensure that the *Replace text as you type* checkbox is selected.

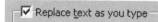

3) Select the *Automatically use suggestions from the spelling checker* checkbox.

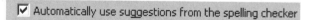

4) Click **OK** to close the dialog box.

5) Type the following text and press **Enter**:

    The greene carrrot

6) Notice that Word replaces 'carrrot' with 'carrot', but not 'greene' with 'green'. This is because Word decided that only 'carrrot' was a definitely a misspelling.

You can close the sample document without saving it.

If you prefer not to use the Office 2000 spellchecker option within AutoCorrect, choose **Tools | AutoCorrect**, click the **AutoCorrect** tab, deselect the *Automatically use suggestions from the spelling checke*r checkbox. and click **OK**.

Working with new AutoCorrect entries

When adding an AutoCorrect entry, you can choose whether to include paragraph formatting with the entry by selecting the paragraph mark immediately after it.

Exercise 6.4: Adding an unformatted AutoCorrect entry

In this Exercise you will add an unformatted entry to AutoText. Unformatted entries may be up to 256 characters in length.

1) Open a new, blank Word document, type the following text, and press **Enter** twice:

   No pizza is complete without plenty of chese

2) Select the item in the currently open document that you want AutoCorrect to replace. In this instance, select the word 'chese'.

   > No·pizza·is·complete·without·plenty·of·chese¶

   (If the item is a complete paragraph, or if if is text at the end of a paragraph, do not include the paragraph mark in your selection. Including the paragraph mark in your selection has the effect of including the formatting of your selected item. See Exercise 6.5.)

3) Choose **Tools | AutoCorrect**, and click the **AutoCorrect** tab of the dialog box displayed.

4) In the *Replace* and *With* boxes, type your text items.

   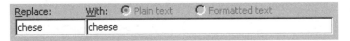

Replace:	With:	⦿ Plain text	○ Formatted text
chese	cheese		

   (Because you began this procedure by selecting text, the *Replace* box already contains your selected text.)

5) Click **Add** to add your entry to AutoCorrect.

   You can repeat steps 3 and 4 to add further entries.

6) When finished, click **OK** to close the dialog box.

   You have now added an unformatted entry to AutoCorrect.

7) As a test, on a new line type the following word and press **Space**:

   Chese

   Notice how AutoCorrect corrects your misspelling.

   You can close the sample document without saving it.

ECDL Advanced Word Processing

Exercise 6.5: Adding a formatted AutoCorrect entry

In this exercise, you will add a formatted entry to AutoText. Word does not place a limit on the size of formatted AutoCorrect entries.

1) Open a new, blank Word document, type the following text, and press **Enter** twice:

    ABC Training Services

2) Select your typed text, choose **Format | Font**, select Arial for *Font*, 14 point for *Size*, change the colour to red, and click **OK**.

3) With your text still selected, click the **Center** button on the Formatting toolbar.

4) Select the item that you want AutoCorrect to insert in your document – not the item you want AutoCorrect to replace.

    In this instance, select 'ABC Training Services'.

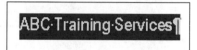

   If the item is a complete paragraph, or if it is text at the end of a paragraph, include the paragraph mark in your selection. You do this because you want the AutoText entry to include both paragraph and character attributes.

5) Choose **Tools | AutoCorrect**, and click the **AutoCorrect** tab of the dialog box displayed.

6) The *With* box contains your selected text. By default, the *Formatted text* checkbox is selected.

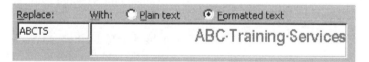

   In the *Replace* box, type the text you want AutoCorrect to replace.

   In this instance, type the following:

    ABCTS

7) Click **Add** to add your entry to AutoCorrect, and click **OK** to close the dialog box.

8) As a test, on a new line type the following text and press **Enter**:

    ABCTS

   Notice how AutoCorrect replaces your typed abbreviation with the formatted AutoCorrect entry.

   You can close the sample document without saving it.

AutoCorrect entries and templates

When you create an AutoCorrect entry, Word stores the entry in the current document's template. The AutoCorrect entry is then available to all new documents that are also based on that template.

Working with existing AutoCorrect entries

Word allows you to modify and delete AutoCorrect entries, whether they are Word's built-in entries or those added you have added yourself.

Exercise 6.6: Amending or deleting an AutoCorrect entry

This exercise takes you through the steps of modifying and deleting AutoCorrect entries.

1) Choose **Tools | AutoCorrect**, and click the **AutoCorrect** tab of the dialog box displayed.

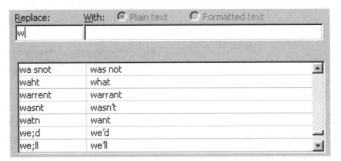

2) Scroll down through the list to locate the relevant entry.

When you find the relevant entry, click it to select it.

3) Word displays the entry in the *Replace* and *With* boxes.

4) To amend the selected entry, edit the text in the *With* box and click **Amend**.

If the AutoText entry contains formatted text (as indicated by an asterisk), you can amend only the *Replace* box and not the *With* box. To amend such an entry completely, recreate it, overwriting and original entry.

To remove the selected entry, click **Delete**.

5) Repeat steps 2 to 4 to amend or delete further AutoCorrect entries.

6) When finished, click **OK** to close the dialog box.

Working with AutoCorrect exceptions

You may want to take advantage of AutoCorrect's helpful features when working on your documents – but there may be some words or abbreviations that you do not want AutoCorrect to replace automatically.

AutoCorrect allows you to enter *exceptions* in three categories:

ECDL Advanced Word Processing

- **First letter after full stop exceptions**. Use this option to override the *Capitalize first letter of sentences* option in specified instances.

  A number of built-in exceptions of this type are supplied with Word. For example, 'approx.' and 'dept.' and 'subj.'. You can remove or modify these, or add new ones of your own.

- **Initial capitals exceptions**. If your organization is named 'Global EBusiness Incorporated', you can prevent AutoCorrrect from changing this to 'Global Ebusiness Incorporated'.

- **Other exceptions**. This is a miscellaneous category. If your organization is named 'Teh Limited' or TAHT.COM', for example, you would enter the exception in this category.

Exercise 6.7: Working with AutoCorrect exceptions

How do you add or modify AutoCorrect exceptions? How do exceptions affect what you type? Follow this exercise to find out.

1) Open a new, blank Word document, type the following text, and press **Enter** twice:

   `Please deliver a qty. of 10 pallets.`

2) Choose **Tools | AutoCorrect**, click the **AutoCorrect** tab of the dialog box displayed, and click the **Exceptions** button.

3) Click the **First Letter** tab, and locate the 'qty.' entry.

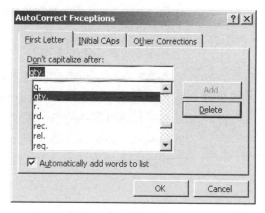

4) Click the **Delete** button to remove the exception. Click **OK** to close the *AutoCorrect Exceptions* dialog box, and click **OK** again to close the *AutoCorrect* dialog box.

5) On a new line of your sample document, type the following text and press *Enter* twice:

   `Please deliver a qty. of 10 pallets.`

Notice that this time, AutoCorrect changes the first letter after 'qty.' to an upper-case 'O'. This is because Word incorrectly identified the full stop after 'qty' as the end of a sentence.

6) Choose **Tools | AutoCorrect**, click the **AutoCorrect** tab, click the **Exceptions** button, and click the **First Letter** tab.

7) In the *Don't capitalize after* box, type 'qty.', click **Add,** click **OK**, and then click **OK** again. You have re-entered this exception to AutoCorrect.

8) Choose **Tools | AutoCorrect**, click the **AutoCorrect** tab, click the **Exceptions** button, and click the **INitial CAps** tab.

9) In the *Don't correct* box, type 'EBusiness' and click **Add**.

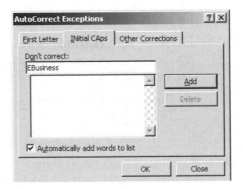

10) Click **OK**, and then click **OK** again.

11) On a new line of your sample document, type the following text and press *Enter* twice:

    Global EBusiness Corporation.

    Notice that AutoCorrect did not change 'EBusiness' to 'Ebusiness'.

12) Remove the 'EBusiness' exception, retype the line that you typed in step 11, and notice what happens.

13) When finished, click **OK** to close the dialog box.

Chapter 6: quick reference

Task	Procedure
Access AutoCorrect options.	Choose **Tools | AutoCorrect** to display the *AutoCorrect* dialog box, select or deselect the relevant checkboxes, and click **OK**.
Switch AutoCorrect on or off.	Select or deselect the *Replace text as you type* checkbox within the *AutoCorrect* dialog box.
Include and exclude the Office 2000 spellchecker in AutoCorrect.	Choose **Tools | Options**, click the **Spelling & Grammar tab**, select the *Check spelling as you type* checkbox, and click **OK**.
	Choose **Tools | AutoCorrect**, select the *Automatically use suggestions from the spelling checker* checkboxes, and click **OK**.
Add an AutoCorrect entry.	Select the item in the current document that you want AutoCorrect to replace, choose **Tools | AutoCorrect**, type the replacement in the *With* box, click **Add** and click **OK**.
	To include paragraph formatting with an entry, include its paragraph mark when selecting it.
Amend an AutoCorrect entry.	Recreate it, overwriting the original entry.
Delete an AutoCorrect entry.	Choose **Tools | AutoCorrect**, select the entry, click **Delete** and click **OK**.

Concepts summary

AutoCorrect can improve your documents by detecting and correcting errors automatically. AutoCorrect contains thousands of common errors and solutions, such as misspelled words, grammatical errors, missing interword spaces, incorrect capitalization, and unformatted symbols.

You can apply AutoCorrect options selectively, amend or delete entries, and add entries of you own. User-created AutoCorrect entries are stored in the Word template associated with the document that was open when the entry was created. The AutoCorrect entry is then available within all new documents based on that template.

Circle the correct answer to each of the following multiple-choice questions about AutoCorrect in Word.

Q1	Which of the following statements about Word's AutoCorrect is untrue?
A.	It can apply built-in heading styles to text typed in a certain way.
B.	It can detect and automatically correct certain grammatical errors.
C.	AutoCorrect entries are stored in the current document template.
D.	You can add your own entries to AutoCorrect.

Q2	Which of the following items can Word's AutoCorrect feature not correct automatically?
A.	Missing interword spaces.
B.	Misspelled words.
C.	Incorrect capitalization.
D.	Two successive hyphens (--) used instead of an en dash (–).

Q3	Which of the following options within the Word' *AutoCorrect* dialog box switches off AutoCorrect?
A.	Automatically use suggestions from spelling checker.
B.	Replace text as you type.
C.	Define styles based on your formatting.
D.	AutoCorrect in use.

Q4	Which of the following options within the *AutoCorrect* dialog box switches on the Office 2000 spellchecker within AutoCorrect?
A.	AutoCorrect in use.
B.	Always suggest corrections.
C.	Automatically use suggestions from spelling checker.
D.	Show spelling errors in this document.

Q5	To include paragraph formatting with a new entry in AutoCorrect, you must …
A.	Include the item's paragraph mark when selecting the item for adding to AutoCorrect.
B.	Hold down the **Shift** key when selecting the item for adding to AutoCorrect.
C.	Hold down the **Ctrl** key when selecting the item for adding to AutoCorrect.
D.	None of the above – you can include only character formatting and not paragraph formatting with AutoCorrect entries.

Answers

1: A, **2**: D, **3**: B, **4**: C, **5**: A.

7

Word typesets your documents: AutoFormat As You Type

Objectives

In this chapter you will learn how to:

- Apply AutoFormat As You Type options selectively.

New words

In this chapter you will meet the following terms:

- AutoFormat As You Type
- Ordinal
- En dash
- Curly quote

Syllabus reference

In this chapter you will cover the following item from the ECDL Advanced Word Processing Syllabus:

- **AM3.1.1.4**: Apply automatic text formatting options.

About AutoFormat As You Type

AutoFormat As You Type is a Word feature that can perform three types of tasks automatically:

- **Character replacement**. Word can replace certain typed characters with their more typographically correct alternatives.

    For example, Word can replace '17th' with '17th' and '3/4' with '¾'.

    Word can also replace straight quotes (" ") with curly quotes (" "), two successive hyphens (--) with a single en dash (–) and three successive hyphens with a column-wide line.

An example of AutoFormat As You Type: character replacement	
1. Type a fraction.	3/4
2. Press the **Spacebar**.	
3. AutoFormat As You Type replaces your typed fraction with the alternative fraction character.	$^3/_4$

- **Bulleted and numbered list conversion**. If you begin a paragraph by typing an asterisk (*) followed by a space, Word can apply the bulleted format when you press **Enter** at the end of the paragraph.

An example of AutoFormat As You Type: lists	
1. Type an asterisk, a space and some text.	*·Item·one¶
2. Press **Enter**.	
3. AutoFormat reformats the line, and the line following it, as bullet points.	•→ Item·one¶ •→ ¶

- **Heading style application**. If you type some text and then press **Enter** twice, Word can apply the Heading 1 style to the text.

As its name suggests, AutoFormat As You Type runs interactively as you enter and edit text. Whenever you type something that it decides to format or replace, AutoFormat As You Type performs the operation as soon as you press the **Spacebar** or the **Enter** key (as appropriate).

AutoFormat As You Type and AutoFormat

In Chapter 4, you met Word's AutoFormat feature, which can apply formatting automatically to already-created documents. You can think of AutoFormat as 'AutoFormat *After* You Type'.

In contrast, AutoFormat As You Type works at the same time as you: it is not a feature that you apply after you have written a document.

Consequently, any change that you make to options within AutoFormat As You Type does not affect text that you have typed previously.

The *AutoFormat As You Type* tab

To view the AutoFormat As You Type options, choose **Tools | AutoCorrect** and click the **AutoFormat As You Type** tab. When finished, click **Cancel**.

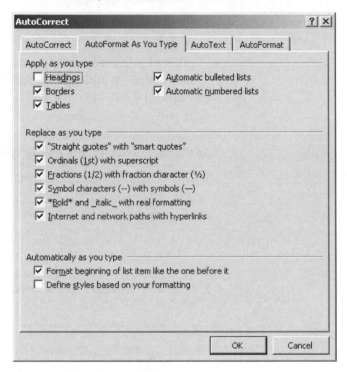

AutoFormat As You Type: the benefits to you

The options within AutoFormat As You Type offer the following benefits:

- **Professional-looking, typeset documents**. Items such as fraction symbols, curly quotes and en dashes give your Word documents the appearance of professionally typeset publications.

  In effect, AutoFormat As You Type provides the features of a typesetting machine within a word processing program.

- **Automatic performance**. AutoFormat As You Type does nothing that you cannot do manually using menu commands and toolbar buttons. For example, you can insert an en dash using the **Insert | Symbol** command.

  With AutoFormat As You Type, however, you can obtain professional typographic effects automatically.

Working with AutoFormat As You Type: the seven tasks

Here are the seven tasks that you need to be able to perform with AutoFormat As You Type:

- **Apply fraction character, ordinal-to-superscript and dash options**. Give your documents a professional appearance with these options. See Exercise 7.1.

- **Apply smart quote options**. Exercise 7.2 shows you how to produce typographically correct quotes and apostrophes automatically.

- **Apply hyperlink options**. Want Word to convert your typed e-mail and web addresses to hyperlinks? Follow Exercise 7.3 to discover how.

- **Apply fast bold and italic options**. Exercise 7.4 shows you how to format text in bold or italics without the usual mouse clicks or keystrokes – a real time-saver.

- **Apply line drawing options**. Exercise 7.5 shows you how to draw three types of line using only the keyboard.

- **Apply automatic list options**. Save effort by enabling Word to generate lists with bulleted and numbered formatting. See Exercises 7.6 and 7.7.

- **Using heading style options**. Exercise 7.8 shows you how Word can automatically apply heading styles to your typed text.

AutoFormat As You Type

AutoFormat As You Type can replace certain typed characters with their more typographically correct alternatives. It can also convert certain paragraphs to bulleted and numbered lists, and apply heading styles to text you enter.

Table options

AutoFormat As You Type can also convert text containing certain patterns of characters to tables. The table option may be useful when applying AutoFormat to ASCII documents (see Chapter 4). It is unlikely, however, that you will ever use the table option when working with AutoFormat As You Type.

Working with fractions, ordinals and dashes

The following three automatic replacement options with AutoFormat As You Type can make a real difference to the quality of your documents:

- **Fractions to fraction characters**. Word can replace three common fractions (1/4, 1/2 and 3/4) with their corresponding fraction characters (¼, ½ and ¾).

  Other fractions – for example, 1/3 or 3/8 – cannot be reformatted automatically. Be careful that this limitation does not lead to inconsistencies in your documents.

- **Ordinals to superscript**. Word can replace ordinals with their superscript alternatives. For example, '1st' and '17th' with '1st' and '17th'.

- **Hyphens to dashes**. Word can replace two successive hyphens (--) with a single en dash (–), and can also insert an en dash when you type a space, a hyphen and a space.

  The use of successive hyphens to create dashes is a throwback to the days of typewriters, which did not have dash keys. If you want to produce a document to publication standard, use dashes instead. See *Dashes: the three types* below for more information about when to use this feature.

Ordinal

A number indicating the place (such as 1st, 2nd, 3rd, etc.) occupied by an item in an ordered sequence.

Exercise 7.1: Automatic fractions, superscript and dashes

Before performing this exercise, start Word. Open a new, blank document. The **Tools | AutoCorrect** command is available only when you have at least one document open.

1) Choose **Tools | AutoCorrect**, and click the **AutoFormat As You Type** tab of the dialog box displayed.

2) Select the three checkboxes shown below, and click **OK**.

> ☑ Ordinals (1st) with superscript
> ☑ Fractions (1/2) with fraction character (½)
> ☑ Symbol characters (--) with symbols (—)

3) Type the following text and press **Enter**:

```
I will finish the first 1/2 of the 3rd
draft of the report on July 14th --
unless my PC crashes again.
```

As you type, notice that Word automatically replaces your fraction, ordinal and single hyphens with their typographic alternatives.

> I will finish the first ½ of the 3rd draft of the report on July 14th – unless my PC crashes again.¶

4) Choose **Tools | AutoCorrect**, click the **AutoFormat As You Type** tab, deselect the three options selected in step 2, and click **OK**.

5) Retype the text you entered in step 3.

Notice that Word does not perform the automatic character replacements this time.

6) Choose **Tools | AutoCorrect**, click the **AutoFormat As You Type** tab, reselect the three options deselected in step 4, and click **OK**.

You can close your sample document without saving it.

Dashes: the three types

Now that you know how to use the automatic hyphen-to-dash replacement option, it's a good idea to learn when to use the different types of dashes.

Fonts contain three kinds of dashes: the hyphen, the en dash and the em dash.

- **Hyphen**. The shortest dash, obtained by pressing the hyphen key once.

Usage	Examples
To hyphenate words.	Pro-am, pre-packed
To separate telephone numbers.	353-1-9876543

- **En dash**. A longer dash. It is the width of a lower-case letter 'n' in the font.

Usage	Dash Examples
To combine words of equal weight.	East–West relations, the Manchester–London flight.
To denote a series of inclusive numbers.	January 4–6, aged 10–12, pages 223–6 of the book.
To set off a parenthetical clause in a sentence.	I think you would look fine wearing either the silk blouse – the one with the blue pattern – or the angora sweater.
To give a special emphasis to the end of a sentence.	Seeing the door slightly ajar, he gave it a push and it opened to reveal Jennifer – in the arms of Steven!

■ **Em dash**: The longest dash. It is the width of a lower-case letter 'm' in the font. The em dash is little used now.

> **En dash**
>
> *A dash that is the width of a lower-case 'n'. Used for separating words of equal weight, denoting series of inclusive numbers, setting off parenthetical clauses, and giving special emphasis to the end of a sentence.*

Working with curly quotes and apostrophes

When typing the abbreviations for inches (") or feet ('), use straight quotes. For quotations or apostrophes, however, use *curly quotes* instead. Curly quotes (also called smart quotes or typographers' quotes) curve towards the text that they enclose.

The difference between curly and straight quotes is more apparent in serif fonts such as Times than sans serif ones such as Arial.

Exercise 7.2: Automatic quotes and apostrophes
Before performing this exercise, open a new, blank document.

1) Choose **Tools | AutoCorrect** and click the **AutoFormat As You Type** tab.

2) Select the *"Straight Quotes"* with *"Smart Quotes"* checkbox, and click **OK**.

    ☑ "Straight quotes" with "smart quotes"

3) Type the following text and press **Enter**:

```
The so-called "Book of Rules" is just a
collection of the author's prejudices.
```

Notice that Word converts your typed double and single quotes to curly quotes.

> The so-called "Book of Rules" is just a collection of the author's prejudices.¶

4) Choose **Tools | AutoCorrect**, click the **AutoFormat As You Type** tab, deselect the checkbox selected in step 2, and click **OK**.

5) Type the following text and press **Enter**:

```
The garden wall is 4' and 6" tall.
```

Notice that Word does not automatically replace your typed quotes with curly quotes.

6) Choose **Tools | AutoCorrect**, click the **AutoFormat As You Type** tab, reselect the option deselected in step 4, and click **OK**.

You can close your sample document without saving it.

Curly quotes

Also called smart or typographers' quotes, these curve towards the text that they enclose (" "). Used for quotations in typeset documents.

Working with hyperlinks

Word can automatically replace e-mail and web addresses that you type with clickable hyperlinks. You will find this feature useful when creating e-mails or documents for publication online. This feature within AutoFormat As You Type is selected by default.

When working with documents that are to be printed on paper, however, you may find this feature a nuisance and want to switch it off.

Exercise 7.3: Automatic hyperlinks

Before performing this exercise, open a new, blank document.

1) Choose **Tools | AutoCorrect** and click the **AutoFormat As You Type** tab.

2) Select the *Internet and network paths with hyperlinks* checkbox and click **OK**.

3) Type the following text and press **Enter**:

> My e-mail address is joe@bloggs.com and my website is at www.bloggs99.com.

Notice that Word converts the e-mail and web addresses to clickable hyperlinks.

> My e-mail address is joe@bloggs.com and my website is at www.bloggs99.com.¶

4) Choose **Tools | AutoCorrect**, click the **AutoFormat As You Type** tab, deselect the checkbox selected in step 2, and click **OK**.

5) Retype the text you entered in step 3.

Notice that Word does not automatically convert your entered addresses to hyperlinks.

Leave this checkbox deselected. You can close your sample document without saving it.

Working with automatic bold and italic formatting

To apply bold or italics to text in a document, you usually select the text and then either click the relevant toolbar button or type the appropriate shortcut keys. AutoFormat As You Type offers alternative methods that do not interrupt your flow of typing:

■ **Bold formatting**. Enclose the text in asterisks (*).

■ **Italic formatting**. Enclose the text in underlines (_).

Exercise 7.4: Automatic bold and italic formatting

Before performing this exercise, open a new, blank document.

1) Choose **Tools | AutoCorrect** and click the **AutoFormat As You Type** tab.

2) Select the following checkbox and click **OK:**

☑ *Bold* and _italic_ with real formatting

3) Type the following text and press **Enter**:

> I think it was *Abraham Lincoln* who said: "I may walk slowly but I _never_ walk backwards."

Notice that Word converts the enclosed words to bold and italics.

> I think it was **Abraham Lincoln** who said: "I may walk slowly but I *never* walk backwards."¶

4) Choose **Tools | AutoCorrect**, click the **AutoFormat As You Type** tab, deselect the checkbox selected in step 2, and click **OK**.

5) Retype the text you entered in step 3.

   Notice that Word does not perform the automatic replacement.

6) Choose **Tools | AutoCorrect**, click the **AutoFormat As You Type** *tab*, reselect the option deselected in step 4, and click **OK**.

   You can close your sample document without saving it.

Working with automatic line drawing

Word can automatically draw column-wide lines whenever you type three or more hyphens (-), underscore characters (_), or equals signs (=) and press **Enter**.

Word draws a thin, thick or double line, respectively. The line – in fact, it is a border – is applied to the paragraph *before* the one in which you type the hyphens, underscores or equals signs. To remove such a border, select the paragraph, choose **Format | Borders and Shading**, choose *None*, and click **OK.**

Exercise 7.5: Automatic line drawing

Before performing this exercise, open a new, blank document.

1) Choose **Tools | AutoCorrect** and click the **AutoFormat As You Type** tab.

2) Select the *Borders* checkbox and click **OK**.

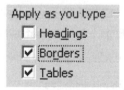

3) Press the hyphen key (-) three times and press **Enter**.

4) Type the following text and press **Enter**:

   Document Heading

5) Press the equals key (=) three times and press **Enter**.

6) Select your typed paragraphs and centre-align them. Your text should look like this:

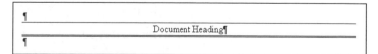

7) Choose **Tools | AutoCorrect**, click the **AutoFormat As You Type** tab, deselect the checkbox selected in step 2, and click **OK**.

8) Repeat steps 3 to 6.

Notice that Word does not draw the column-wide lines.

9) Choose **Tools | AutoCorrect**, click the **AutoFormat As You Type** tab, reselect the option deselected in step 7, and click **OK**.

You can close your sample document without saving it.

Working with automatic lists

Word can automatically format a bulleted list when you begin a paragraph with any of the these three characters, followed by a space or a tab:

- An asterisk (*)

- A closing angle bracket (>)

- A hyphen (-)

When you press **Enter** to add the next paragraph, Word inserts the next bullet automatically. To end the list of bullets, press **Enter** twice, or press **Backspace** to delete the last bullet in the list.

Also, Word can apply numbered list formatting if you type a number or letter, a full stop, and a space or tab at the beginning of a paragraph. When you press **Enter**, Word inserts the next number in the list automatically. To end the list of numbered bullets, press **Enter** twice, or press **Backspace** to delete the last number in the list.

Exercise 7.6: Automatic bulleted and numbered lists

Before performing this exercise, open a new, blank document.

1) Choose **Tools | AutoCorrect** and click the **AutoFormat As You Type** tab.

2) Select the following two checkboxes, and click **OK**:

> ☑ A*u*tomatic bulleted lists
> ☑ Automatic *n*umbered lists

3) Type the four lines of text shown in the left-hand column below. Press **Enter** once after the first three lines, and **Enter** twice after the fourth:

What you type	What Word displays
*John	■ John
Paul	■ Paul
George	■ George
Ringo	■ Ringo

4) Type the four lines of text shown in the left-hand column below. Press **Enter** once after the first three lines, and **Enter** twice after the fourth:

1.John	1. John
Paul	2. Paul
George	3. George
Ringo	4. Ringo
What you type	*What Word displays*

5) Choose **Tools | AutoCorrect**, click the **AutoFormat As You Type** tab, deselect the two checkboxes selected in step 2, and click **OK**.

6) Retype the text you entered in steps 3 and 4.

Notice that Word does not perform the automatic list formatting.

7) Choose **Tools | AutoCorrect**, click the **AutoFormat As You Type** tab, reselect the two options deselected in step 5, and click **OK**.

You can close your sample document without saving it.

Automatic formatting at the beginnings of lists

Sometimes, you will want bold or italic formatting applied to a word or group of words at the beginning of each line in a list.

AutoFormat As You Type gives you the option of formatting only text at the beginning of the first list item, with Word repeating your character formatting for the other list items automatically.

Exercise 7.7: Automatic character formatting at the beginning of a list

Before performing this Exercise, open a new, blank document.

1) Choose **Tools | AutoCorrect** and click the **AutoFormat As You Type** tab.

2) Select the following three checkboxes and click **OK**.

☑ A̲utomatic bulleted lists
☑ Automatic n̲umbered lists

☑ For̲mat beginning of list item like the one before it

3) Type the following line of text, but do not press **Enter** at the end of the line:

    * Kennedy: A US president

4) Select the word 'Kennedy', and apply bold formatting to it.

    *·**Kennedy**:·A·US·president¶

5) Click at the end of the line and press **Enter**. Your screen should look like this:

> •→ **Kennedy**: A US president¶
>
> •→ ¶

6) Click after the bullet point on the second line, type the following text, and press **Enter**:

    Wilson: A British prime minister

Word automatically applies your beginning-of-line formatting as shown:

> •→ **Kennedy**: A US president¶
>
> •→ **Wilson**: A British prime minister¶

7) Choose **Tools | AutoCorrect**, click the **AutoFormat As You Type** tab, deselect the three checkboxes selected in step 2, and click **OK**.

8) Repeat steps 3 to 6.

   Notice that Word does not perform any of the list formatting actions.

9) Choose **Tools | AutoCorrect**, click the **AutoFormat As You Type** tab, reselect the three options deselected in step 7, and click **OK**.

   You can close your sample document without saving it.

Working with automatic heading styles

AutoFormat As You Type can apply Word's built-in heading styles to text that you enter in a certain way.

- **Heading 1 style**. If you type a line of text and press **Enter** twice, Word applies the Heading 1 style.

- **Heading 2 style**. If you press **Tab** on a new line, type some text and press **Enter** twice, Word applies the Heading 2 style.

- **Heading 3 style**. If you press **Tab** twice on a new line, type some text and press **Enter** twice, Word applies the Heading 3 style.

By default, this option is not selected with AutoFormat As You Type. It would be too distracting during normal word processing.

Exercise 7.8 Automatic heading styles
Before performing this exercise, open a new, blank document.

1) Choose **Tools | AutoCorrect** and click the **AutoFormat As You Type** tab.

2) Select the following checkbox and click **OK**:

3) Type the following text and press **Enter** twice:

Heading 1

Notice that Word applies the Heading 1 style to your text. Although you pressed **Enter** twice, the second paragraph mark is not displayed.

"**Heading·1**¶
¶

4) On a new line, press **Tab**, type the following text, and press **Enter** twice:

Heading 2

Notice that Word applies the Heading 2 style to your text. As in step 3, the second paragraph mark is not displayed.

"*Heading·2*¶
¶

5) On a new line, press **Tab** twice, type the following text, and press **Enter** twice:

Heading 3

Notice that Word applies the Heading 3 style to your text. As in steps 3 and 4, the second paragraph mark is not displayed.

▪ **Heading·3**¶
¶

6) Choose **Tools | AutoCorrect**, click the **AutoFormat As You Type** tab, deselect the option selected in step 2, and click **OK**.

7) Repeat steps 3 to 5.

Notice that Word does not apply the heading styles.

Leave this checkbox deselected. You can close your sample document without saving it.

Defining styles based on formatting

At the bottom of the **AutoFormat As You Type** tab of the **Tools | AutoCorrect** dialog box, you can see the following option. By default, it is deselected.

This option, when selected, enables Word to apply heading styles automatically to text that you type, based on how you format and position that text.

For example, if you type a few words on a single line, increase the font size, and centre the line, Word can automatically apply a heading style.

Unfortunately, this option can create more problems than it solves, because it can apply heading styles to lines you never intended as headings, with unwanted effects on outlines and tables of contents. Leave this option deselected – its default value.

Chapter 7: quick reference

Tasks summary

Task	Procedure
To activate or deactivate the various AutoFormat As You Type options.	Choose **Tools	AutoCorrect**, click the **AutoFormat As You Type** tab of the dialog box displayed, select or deselect the relevant checkboxes, and click **OK**.

Concepts summary

AutoFormat As You Type is a Word feature that can perform three types of tasks automatically:

- **Character replacement**. Word can replace certain typed characters with their more typographically correct alternatives. For example, '17th' with '17th' and '3/4' and '¾'. It can also replace straight quotes (" ") with curly quotes (" "), two successive hyphens (--) with a single en dash (–), and three successive hyphens with a column-wide line.

- **Bulleted and numbered list conversion**. If you begin a paragraph by typing an asterisk (*) followed by a space, Word can apply the bulleted format when you press **Enter** at the end of the paragraph.

- **Heading style application**. If you type some text and then press **Enter** twice, Word can apply the Heading 1 style to the text.

AutoFormat As You Type runs interactively as you enter and edit text. Whenever you type something that it decides to format or replace, AutoFormat As You Type performs the operation as soon as you press the relevant **Spacebar** or **Enter** key.

You can apply the various AutoFormat As You Type options selectively.

Chapter 7: quick quiz

Circle the correct answer to each of the following multiple-choice questions about Word's AutoFormat As You Type feature.

Q1	Which of the following statements about Word's AutoFormat As You Type feature is untrue?
A.	It provides the ability to produce typeset-standard documents without the need to insert special characters such as en dashes or fraction symbols manually.
B.	It can apply built-in heading styles to text typed in a certain way.
C.	It allows the user to insert commonly-used text items that are stored in the document template.
D.	It can apply bold and italic formatting to text enclosed in certain characters.

Q2	Which automatic character replacement can AutoFormat As You Type *not* perform?
A.	Tues with Tuesday.
B.	2nd with 2nd.
C.	29th with 29th.
D.	Two hyphens (--) with an en dash (–).

Q3	Which automatic character replacement can AutoFormat As You Type *not* perform?
A.	3/4 with $\frac{3}{4}$.
B.	1/8 with $\frac{1}{8}$.
C.	1/4 with $\frac{1}{4}$.
D.	1/2 with $\frac{1}{2}$.

Q4	**To insert an en dash (–) with Word's AutoFormat As You Type feature, you...**
A.	Use the **Insert	Symbol** menu command.
B.	Type two successive hyphens (--) and press **Enter**.
C.	Type a hyphen (-) while holding down the **Shift** key.
D.	Type a hyphen (-) while holding down the **Ctrl** key.

Q5	**Which checkbox in Word's AutoFormat As You Type feature do you select to replace typed e-mail and web addresses with hyperlinks?**
A.	*Internet and network paths with hyperlinks.*
B.	*Smart addresses active.*
C.	*Replace web addresses with smart hyperlinks.*
D.	*Automatic hyperlink replacement.*

Q6	**Word's AutoFormat As You Type feature can apply bold formatting to text that you enclose in which characters?**
A.	Underscores (_).
B.	Ampersands (&).
C.	Asterisks (*).
D.	Dollar signs ($).

Q7	Word's AutoFormat As You Type feature can apply italic formatting to text that you enclose in which characters?
A.	Dollar signs ($).
B.	Underscores (_).
C.	Ampersands (&).
D.	Asterisks (*).

Q8	In Word's AutoFormat As You Type feature, what is the effect of selecting the *Borders* checkbox?
A.	Word draws a column-wide line when you type three successive hyphens (---) and press **Enter**.
B.	Word applies the currently selected border style to any border that you create.
C.	Word applies a thin border to the header at the top of every page of the document.
D.	Word applies a thin border to the footer at the bottom of every page of the document.

Q9	In Word's AutoFormat As You Type feature, what is the effect of selecting the *Automatic list formatting* checkbox?
A.	Word applies the built-in list style to paragraphs that begin with an asterisk (*) followed by a space or a tab.
B.	Word applies a list style stored in AutoText to paragraphs that begin with an asterisk (*) followed by a space or a tab.
C.	Word applies list formatting when you type a paragraph that begins with an asterisk (*) followed by a space or a tab.
D.	Word applies a list style stored in the Normal template to paragraphs that begin with an asterisk (*) followed by a tab.

Answers

1: C, **2:** A, **3**: B, **4:** B, **5:** A, **6:** C, **7:** B, **8:** A, **9**: C.

8

Word updates your documents: fields

Objectives

In this chapter you will learn how to:

- Insert a field
- Switch between the display of field codes and field values
- Update a field directly
- Lock a field to prevent updating
- Delete a field

New words

In this chapter you will meet the following terms:

- Field
- Field locking

Exercise files

In this chapter you will work with the following Word files:

- Chapter8_Exercise_8-1_Before.doc
- Chapter8_Exercise_8-2_Before.doc
- Chapter8_Exercise_8-3_Before.doc
- Chapter8_Exercise_8-4_Doc1.doc
- Chapter8_Exercise_8-4_Doc2_Before.doc
- Chapter8_Exercise_8-5_Before.doc
- Chapter8_Exercise_8-6_Before.doc
- Chapter8_Exercise_8-7_Before.doc

Syllabus reference

In this chapter you will cover the following items from the ECDL Advanced Word Processing Syllabus:

- **AM3.3.2.1**. Insert a field code.
- **AM3.3.2.2**. Edit or update a field code entry.

- **AM3.3.2.3**. Lock or unlock a field.

- **AM3.3.2.4**. Delete a field code.

Fields: instructions and the results of instructions

In a Word document, fields are *containers* that hold two things: instructions and the results of instructions. Let's look at each more closely:

- **Instructions**. These tell Word to 'show today's date', for example, or to 'show the number of pages in the current document'. A field's instructions remain fixed unless you amend them.

  The set of instructions in a particular field is called a *field code*.

- **Result**. A field also holds the result generated by the field's instructions. This may change with time or as other conditions change.

  For example, a field that instructs Word to show your document's page count will contain changing results as you increase or decrease the number of pages.

  The current result in a particular field is called the *field value*.

In summary, field codes remain fixed while field values may change.

Fields: where do they get their information?

Fields that display text (in this context, 'text' includes numbers and dates) in a document can extract their information from a range of sources, including:

- **System clock**. Some fields can detect the current date and time from your computer's clock.

- **Current document**. Some fields extract information from the document that you are currently working on, including information stored in the tabs of the **File | Properties** dialog box.

- **User information**. Some fields can access the details that you entered when installing Word on your PC.

The Field *dialog box*

You insert fields in your documents with the *Field* dialog box, which you display by choosing the **Insert | Field** command.

The *Field* dialog box contains two lists:

- **Categories**. On the left of the dialog box, you can select a grouping of fields types – Date and Time fields, User Information fields, and so on.

- **Field names**. On the right of the dialog box, you can select an individual field from the field category selected on the left.

If you select the field category of *User Information*, for example, the fields available in this category include *UserName* and *UserInitials*.

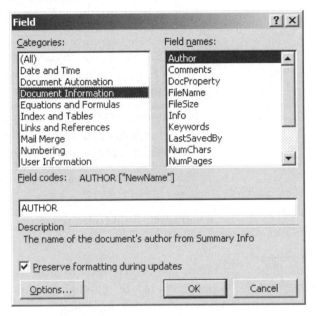

Fields: the benefits to you

Fields offer two main advantages. They:

- **Save time**. Where a suitable field is available, it is generally faster to insert the field than to type the information directly into a document.
- **Reduce errors**. As fields can update automatically over time or with changing conditions, you can be sure that your document contains the most up-to-date, accurate information.

> **Field**
>
> *A container that holds an instruction (**field code**) and the result of the instructions (**field value**). By extracting data from sources such as the current document and the system clock, fields can display continuously updated information.*

Working with fields: the five tasks

Here are the five tasks you need to be able to perform with fields in Word:

- **Insert a field**. Exercise 8.1 takes you through the steps of inserting a field in a Word document. In Exercise 8.2, you will discover how to insert a field from AutoText in a Word document.

- **Change how fields display**. Sometimes, you will want to display the results of fields (the field values). On other occasions, you will prefer to see the instructions that generate the results (the field codes). Exercise 8.3 shows you how to switch between the two views.

- **Update a field directly**. Different types of fields can be updated in different ways or as the result of different conditions. Follow Exercise 8.4 to discover how to update one or all fields in a document directly.

- **Lock a field to prevent updating**. *Locking*, as you will learn in Exercise 8.5, is the act of preventing a particular field from being updated. In Exercise 8.6, you will learn how to unlock a locked field.

- **Delete a field**. Finally, in Exercise 8.7 you learn how to delete a field from a document.

Working with new fields

How are fields placed in a document? Some fields are inserted by Word as the result of running a particular Word feature:

- Word's *tables of contents* and *indexes* require fields for their operation.

- Automatic *page numbering* in headers or footers is based on the use of fields to display updated information.

- *Mail merge* letters contain fields such as *Surname* and *StreetAddress* to indicate the type of details to be extracted from a data source.

In your first field exercise, you will insert a field directly.

Exercise 8.1: Inserting fields in a document

In this exercise, you will insert two fields in a sample document.

1) Open the following file:

```
Chapter8_Exercise_8-1_Before.doc
```

2) Click in the second table cell – the one to the right of the words 'Current Date'.

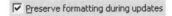

Click here

3) Choose **Insert | Field** to display the *Field* dialog box.

4) On the left of the dialog box, click to select the category of *Date and Time*.

5) On the right of the dialog box, click to select the field name of *Date*.

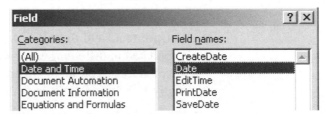

6) Typically, you will leave the *Preserve formatting during updates* checkbox at its selected default value.

☑ Preserve formatting during updates

This means that if you later apply italics or other formatting to your field, Word will not change that formatting whenever it updates the field.

7) Click **OK**. Word inserts the field and closes the dialog box.

8) Click in the fourth table cell – the one to the right of the words 'Current Time'.

9) Choose **Insert | Field** to display the *Field* dialog box.

10) On the left of the dialog box, click to select the category of *Date and Time*.

11) On the right of the dialog box, click to select the field name of *Time*.

12) Again, leave the *Preserve formatting during updates* checkbox at its default value of selected.

13) Click **OK**. Word inserts the field and closes the dialog box.

14) Save the document with the following name:

    Chapter8_Exercise_8-1_After_*Your_Name*.doc

You can now close the document.

Exercise 8.2: Inserting AutoText fields in a document

In this exercise, you will insert two fields in a sample document.

1) Open the following file:

    Chapter8_Exercise_8-2_Before.doc

2) Choose **View | Header and Footer** to display the Header and Footer toolbar.

    By default, Word positions the insertion point in the *Odd Page Header* box.

3) Click the **Insert AutoText** button to display the AutoText fields available.

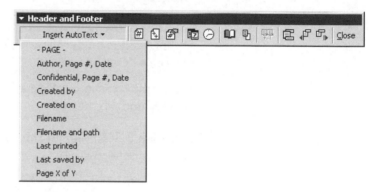

4) Choose the option *Filename and path*. Word inserts the AutoText field.

5) Click the **Show Next** button on the Header and Footer toolbar. Word displays the *Even Page Header* box.

6) Click the **Insert AutoText** button and choose the *Author, Page #, Date* option. Word inserts the AutoText field.

7) Save the document with the following name:

    Chapter8_Exercise_8-2_After_*Your_Name*.doc

    You can now close the document.

Working with existing fields

Typically, what you see in a document is the *result* of a field's instructions, and not the underlying field code. Field results, when clicked, are displayed against a grey background to indicate the presence of a field. The grey background is not shown on print-outs.

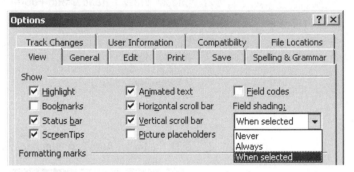

You can control how Word displays field results with the *Field shading* option on the **View** tab of the dialog box displayed with the **Tools | Options** command.

Follow the steps in Exercise 8.3 to view the underlying field code behind a field value.

Exercise 8.3: Changing How Fields Display

1) Open the following file:

    Chapter8_Exercise_8-3_Before.doc

2) Click anywhere in the table cell that contains the date field. Notice how a grey background appears behind the date. This indicates that the date is not regular typed text but a value generated by an underlying field code.

Before selecting the field   *After selecting the field*

3) Right-click on the *Date* field and choose *Toggle field codes* from the pop-up menu displayed. Word replaces the field result with the field code.

4) Repeat step 3 for the *Time* field in the fourth table cell. Both field codes are now displayed.

5) Save the document with the following name:

    Chapter8_Exercise_8-3_After_Your_Name.doc

You can now close the document.

As its name suggests, the *Toggle field codes* command also works in reverse. If you right-click on a field that currently shows the field code, Word replaces the code with the field value.

The shortcut key combination for toggling the display of a selected field is **Shift+F9**. You can toggle the display of *all* fields throughout a document by first selecting all the text in the document and then pressing **Shift+F9**.

To show field codes rather than field values by default, choose **Tools | Options**, click the **View** tab, select the *Field codes* checkbox, and click **OK.**

Working with field updates

Different types of fields are updated in different ways:

- **Automatic page numbering fields**. When you add, remove or reorder pages in a document, Word automatically adjusts the page numbering fields automatically.

- **Date and time fields**. When you open a document that contains date or time fields, Word updates the field results automatically.

- **Updates from printing**. The **Options** button within Word's **File | Print** dialog box offers an *Update fields* checkbox. If this is selected, Word will update all fields in the current document before printing.

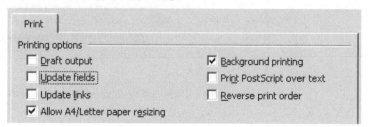

The next exercise takes you through the steps of updating fields directly.

Exercise 8.4: Updating a field directly

1) Open the following file:

```
Chapter8_Exercise_8-4_Doc1.doc
```

2) Do nothing for a couple of minutes. Then right-click anywhere in the table cell that contains the time field and choose *Update field* from the pop-up menu.

    Word updates the field to show the latest time. You can now close the sample document without saving it.

3) Open the following file:

    ```
    Chapter8_Exercise_8-4_Doc2_Before.doc
    ```

4) Choose **File | Save As** and save the file with the following name:

    Chapter8_Exercise_8-4_Doc2_After_*Your_Name*.doc

    Notice that Word does not update the file name displayed in the header automatically. If you close the document and then reopen it, Word will update the file name field for you.

    Instead, let's update the field directly.

5) Choose **View | Header and Footer** to display the Header and Footer toolbar.

6) By default, Word positions the insertion point in the *Odd Page Header* box. The file name field is selected.

7) Right-click anywhere in the field and choose *Update field* from the pop-up menu.

    Word updates the field as shown below:

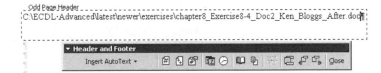

8) Close and save your sample document.

The shortcut key combination for updating a selected field is **F9**. You can update *all* fields throughout a document by first selecting all the text in the document and then pressing **F9**.

Working with locked fields

There may be times when you don't want a particular field to be updated, even when you are updating other fields in the same document.

Word allows you to *lock* a selected field or fields, so that the values remain fixed. You can later unlock the field or fields. Locking a field also prevents it from being amended.

Exercise 8.5: Locking a field to prevent updates

1) Open the following file:

   Chapter8_Exercise_8-5_Before.doc

2) Click anywhere in the table cell that contains the *Time* field and press **CTRL+F11**.

   (There is no menu command for this option: you need to know the keyboard shortcut.)

3) Right-click on the field. Notice that the *Update field* command is not available on the pop-up menu.

4) Save the document with the following name:

   Chapter8_Exercise_8-5_After_Your_Name.doc

   You can now close the document.

Exercise 8.6: Unlocking a field to allow updates

Field locking is a reversible operation. In Exercise 8.6, you will unlock a field similar to the one that you locked in Exercise 8.5.

1) Open the following file:

   Chapter8_Exercise_8-6_Before.doc

2) Click anywhere in the table cell that contains the *Time* field and press **Ctrl+Shift+F11**.

   (There is no menu command for this option: you need to know the keyboard shortcut.)

3) Right-click on the field. Notice that the *Update field* command is again available on the pop-up menu.

4) Save the document with the following name:

   `Chapter8_Exercise_8-6_After_Your_Name.doc`

   You can now close the document.

To lock (or unlock) *all fields* throughout a document, first select the entire document and then press **Ctrl+F11** (or **Ctrl+Shift+F11**).

Locking
Preventing a selected field or fields from being updated. The field values remain fixed after locking. Locked fields can be unlocked at a later stage if required.

Deleting fields

Don't want a particular field in a document any more? Deleting a field is fast and easy.

Exercise 8.7: Deleting a field

1) Open the following file:

   `Chapter8_Exercise_8-7_Before.doc`

2) Drag across the *Time* field to select it and then press the **Delete** key.

   Word removes the selected field from the document.

3) Save the document with the following name:

   `Chapter8_Exercise_8-7_After_Your_Name.doc`

   You can now close the document.

Chapter 8: quick reference

Shortcut keys

Keys	Description
Shift+F9	Toggles the display format of a selected field or fields between field code and field value.
F9	Updates the selected field or fields so that they show the latest value.
Ctrl+F11	Locks a selected field or fields to prevent updates.
Ctrl+Shift+F11	Unlocks a selected field or fields to allow updates.

Task	Procedure
Change how a field is displayed.	Right-click in the field and choose *Toggle field codes*. Or click anywhere in the and press **Shift+F9**.
Update a field so that it shows the latest value.	Right-click in the field and choose *Update field*. Or click anywhere in the field and press **F9**.
Lock a field to prevent it from being updated.	Click anywhere in the field and press **Ctrl+F11**.
Unlock a field to permit updates.	Click anywhere in the field and press **Ctrl+Shift+F11**.

Concepts summary

In a Word document, *fields* are containers for holding instructions (*field codes*) and the results of instructions (*field values*). Field codes remain fixed unless you change them. Field values change over time or as conditions change. You can choose to display field codes or values, as required.

Fields can obtain their information from a range of sources, including the system clock, the current document properties, and the Word user's profile.

Opening a Word document typically updates all field in the document, and Word can also update fields when printing a document. You can *update fields directly*. You can *lock* fields to prevent updates, and *unlock* them later, as required

A number of common Word features, including tables of contents, indexes, automatic page numbering and mail merge rely on fields for their operation.

Chapter 8: quick quiz

Circle the correct answer to each of the following multiple-choice questions about fields in Word.

Q1	Which of the following statements best describes a field in Word?
A.	A named set of attributes that can be saved and then applied to selected items in a document.
B.	A file containing formatting settings and content that provides a pattern for individual Word documents.
C.	A container that holds instructions and the result of the instructions. Field values can change over time or as conditions change.
D.	A list of installed Windows fonts that are available for use in Word documents.

Q2	Which of the following is not a source from which a field may extract information for display in a Word document?
A.	The PC's system clock.
B.	The current Word document.
C.	The current document template.
D.	The details entered by the user when installing Word on the PC.

Q3	Which of the following Word features does not rely on the use of fields for its operation?
A.	Generation of a table of contents.
B.	Automatically updated page numbers in headers or footers.
C.	Mail merge.
D.	Character styles.

Q4	By default, how is a selected field value displayed in a Word document?
A.	In dark blue text.
B.	With a light grey background.
C.	In reverse type (white text against black background).
D.	As a hyperlink.

Q5	Which of the following commands would you choose to insert a new field in a Word document?
A.	Tools | Options | Fields | New.
B.	Insert | Field.
C.	Format | Field Insertion.
D.	Insert | Field | New Field.

Q6	Which of the following shortcut key combinations would you press to toggle between the display of field codes and field values?
A.	Alt+F11.
B.	Shift+F9.
C.	Shift+F11.
D.	F11.

Q7	Which of the following shortcut key combinations would you press to update a field directly?
A.	F9.
B.	F11.
C.	Alt+F9.
D.	Ctrl+Shift+F11.

Q8	Preventing a field in a Word document from being updated is called …
A.	Unlocking.
B.	Linking.
C.	Unlinking.
D.	Locking.

Q9	Which of the following shortcut key combinations would you press to lock a particular field in a Word document?
A.	Alt+F9.
B.	F11.
C.	Shift+F9.
D.	Ctrl+F11.

Q10	Which of the following shortcut key combinations would you press to unlock a particular field in a Word document?
A.	Ctrl+Shift+F11.
B.	Shift+F9.
C.	Ctrl+Shift+F9.
D.	Alt+F9.

Answers

1: C, **2:** C, **3:** D, **4:** B, **5:** B, **6:** B, **7:** A, **8:** D, **9:** D, **10:** A.

9 *Word does everything: macros*

Objectives	In this chapter you will learn how to:

- Record a macro
- Run a macro
- Assign a macro to a keyboard shortcut
- Assign a macro to a toolbar custom button
- Copy a macro between templates

New words

In this chapter you will meet the following terms:

- Macro
- Macro project

Exercise files

In this chapter you will work with the following Word files:

- Chapter9_Exercise_9-1_Before.doc
- Chapter9_Exercise_9-2_Before.doc
- Chapter9_Exercise_9-3_Before.doc
- Chapter9_Exercise_9-5_Before.doc
- Chapter9_Exercise_9-6_Before.doc
- Chapter9_Exercise_9-7_Before.doc

Syllabus reference

In this chapter you will cover the following item of the ECDL Advanced Word Processing Syllabus:

- **AM3.5.2.1**. Record a simple macro (e.g. page set-up changes).
- **AM3.5.2.2**. Copy a macro.
- **AM3.5.2.3**. Run a macro.
- **AM3.5.2.4**. Assign a macro to a custom button on a toolbar.

About macros

Ever feel like you have a million tasks to perform? Or that you are doing the same task a million times over?

Word's macro feature can help you with the second problem. Think of a macro as a tape recorder that records not music or voices but sequences of Word actions and menu commands.

When you have recorded Word actions in a macro, you can then play back the macro as often as you need. In Word, playing back a macro is called *running* a macro.

The Macros dialog box

You perform most macro-related tasks from the *Macros* dialog box, which you access by choosing the **Tools | Macro | Macros** command.

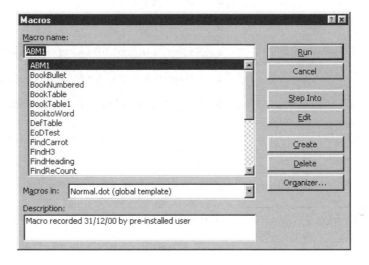

Other automation features in Word

Macros are not the only way of automating tasks in Word. Other automation features include:

- **Templates and styles**. These allow you to apply consistent formatting, standard text and page layout settings across a range of different documents. See Chapter 3.

- **AutoText entries**. These allow you to insert commonly-used text, with or without paragraph formatting, in different documents. See Chapter 5.

Macros are best suited for automating tasks that combine several different Word features. Examples might be combinations of text and paragraph formatting, mail merge operations, and the tidying-up of documents imported from the web or other non-Word sources.

Macros offer two main advantages. They:

- **Save time**. By recording frequently-performed and repetitive tasks in macros, and running the macros as you need them, you can speed up your work greatly.

- **Reduce errors**. As the actions stored in a macro are performed in exactly the same way each time the macro is run, procedures are followed more reliably.

Working with macros: the five tasks

Here are the five macro-related tasks that you need to be able to perform in Word:

- **Record and run a macro**. Exercises 9.1, 9.3, 9.5 and 9.7 provide examples of the macro recording process in Word.

- **Run a macro**. Exercise 9.2 takes you through the steps of running a macro.

- **Assign a macro to a keyboard shortcut**: See Exercises 9.3 and 9.4.

- **Assign a macro to a toolbar button**. See Exercises 9.5 and 9.6.

- **Copy a macro between templates**. A macro, like a style, can be saved in a document or in a template. As Exercise 9.8 shows, you can copy macros between different documents and templates.

Macro

A series of Word actions and menu commands grouped together that when run, perform those actions and commands automatically. Macros are identified by a unique name, and can be stored in a template or document.

Working with simple macros

In the first exercise, you will create a simple macro that opens a new Word document and types some text in it.

Exercise 9.1: Record a simple macro

1) Start Word and open the following document:

```
Chapter9_Exercise_9-1_Before.doc
```

2) Select the first paragraph of body text in the document.

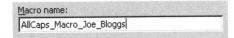

Impressed·by·the·Internet's·rising·popularity,·many·businesses·have·established·an·online·

3) Choose **Tools | Macro | Record New Macro**.

    Alternatively, double-click the **REC** button on the Status Bar along the bottom of the Word window.

    Word displays the *Record Macro* dialog box.

4) In the *Macro name* box, type the following:

    AllCaps_Macro_Your_Name

    Do not enter or change any other details in the dialog box. Click **OK**.

5) Word closes the dialog box and displays the Stop Recording toolbar on your screen.

    This has just two buttons: one to stop recording and another to pause/resume macro recording.

Stop Recording ⟶ 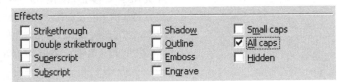 ⟵ *Pause/Resume Recording*

    You will now perform the sequence of actions for your macro to record:

    ■ Choose **Format | Font**.

    ■ Select the *All caps* checkbox.

Effects		
☐ Stri<u>k</u>ethrough	☐ S<u>h</u>adow	☐ S<u>m</u>all caps
☐ Double strikethrough	☐ <u>O</u>utline	☑ A<u>l</u>l caps
☐ Su<u>p</u>erscript	☐ <u>E</u>mboss	☐ <u>H</u>idden
☐ Su<u>b</u>script	☐ En<u>g</u>rave	

    ■ Click **OK**.

    This completes the actions.

7) Click the **Stop Recording** button on the Stop Recording toolbar. Word removes the toolbar from the screen.

    Your macro is now recorded. You can close the sample document without saving it. Your new macro is stored in the Normal template – not in the document.

Were you a little nervous as you recorded your first macro, knowing that Word was remembering your actions? Word does *not* record the speed at which you perform your actions. So you can take the time to think carefully about what steps you want to record.

- **I've made a slight mistake**. Don't panic. Just correct your error and keep going. Word records both your error and your correction as part of the macro, but Word plays back macros so fast that it's unlikely that anyone will notice.

- **I've really messed it up**. Click the **Stop Recording** button, and record the macro again. If you enter the same macro name, Word prompts you to overwrite the original macro. Click **Yes** and perform your actions again.

Running macros

Now that you've recorded your first macro, your next step is to play it back. The procedure in Exercise 9.2 will let you run any available macro. If the relevant macro has not been assigned to a menu, keyboard shortcut or toolbar, this is the *only* way that you can run the macro.

Exercise 9.2: Run a macro

1) Start Word and open the following document:

    Lesson9_Exercise_9-2_Before.doc

2) Select the first paragraph of body text in the document.

    Introduction¶

    > By·transforming·the·way·that·people·and·businesses·communicate·and·interact,·the·Internet·has·dramatically·changed·the·face·of·business.¶

    Impressed·by·the·Internet's·rising·popularity,·many·businesses·have·established·an·online·

3) Choose **Tools | Macro | Macros...** to display the *Macros* dialog box.

4) In the *Macro name* box, select the macro that you recorded in Exercise 9.1.

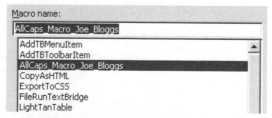

5) Click **Run**. Word runs the macro on the selected text.

    Introduction¶

    > BY·TRANSFORMING·THE·WAY·THAT·PEOPLE·AND·BUSINESSES·COMMUNICATE·AND·INTERACT,·THE·INTERNET·HAS·DRAMATICALLY·CHANGED·THE·FACE·OF·BUSINESS.¶

    Impressed·by·the·Internet's·rising·popularity,·many·businesses·have·established·an·online·

6) Save your sample document with the following name:

Chapter9_Exercise_9-2_After_*Your_Name*.doc

You can close the sample document.

Working with macros and keyboard shortcuts

If you plan to run a macro frequently, you will find it convenient to assign it to a keyboard shortcut. You can then run the macro directly without displaying the *Macros* dialog box. You assign a macro to a keyboard shortcut:

- **When you record the macro**. This is the procedure that you will follow in Exercise 9.3.

- **After the macro has been recorded**. You can assign a keyboard shortcut to a macro that you or another user has already created, or amend a previously assigned shortcut. Exercise 9.4 takes you through the steps.

Do *not* assign macros to keyboard shortcuts already used for common Word tasks, such as applying bold (**Ctrl+B**) or italics (**Ctrl+I**), or saving (**Ctrl+S**) and printing (**Ctrl+P**).

Exercise 9.3: Record a macro and assign it to a keyboard shortcut

In this exercise, you will recreate the macro that you recorded in Exercise 9.1 and assign a keyboard shortcut to it.

1) Open the following document:

Chapter_Exercise_9-3_Before.doc

2) Select the first paragraph of text in the document.

3) Choose **Tools | Macro | Record New Macro** to display the *Record Macro* dialog box.

4) In the *Macro name* box, type the same name as you gave your first macro in Exercise 9.1:

AllCaps_Macro_Your_Name

5) Click the **Keyboard** button. Word prompts you as follows:

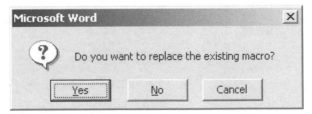

Click **Yes**.

6) Word now displays the *Customize Keyboard* dialog box. Click in the *Press new shortcut key* box, and press **Ctrl+B**.

Word responds by telling you that this keyboard shortcut is already assigned. You could override the current assignment, but that would not be a good idea as this shortcut is for bold formatting.

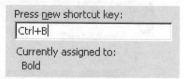

Delete **Ctrl+B** from the box.

7) With the insertion point still in the *Press new shortcut key* box, press the following key combination:

Alt+Ctrl+X

Word responds by telling you that this keyboard shortcut is not assigned to any other action.

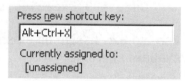

8) Click **Assign** to assign the shortcut key combination, and then click **Close** to close the dialog box.

9) You will now perform the sequence of actions for your macro to record:

- Choose **Format | Font**.

- Select the *All caps* checkbox.

- Click **OK**.

This completes the actions.

10) Click the **Stop Recording** button on the Stop Recording toolbar. Word removes the toolbar from the screen.

11) Your macro is now recorded. You can close the sample document without saving it. Your new macro is stored in the Normal template – not in the document.

12) Let's check that your macro is assigned correctly. Open the following document:

Chapter9_Exercise_9-3_Before.doc

Select the second paragraph of text and press **Alt+Ctrl+X**. Your macro should have the effect shown:

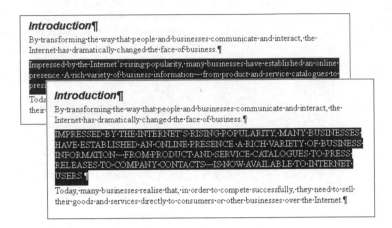

Introduction¶
By·transforming·the·way·that·people·and·businesses·communicate·and·interact,·the·
Internet·has·dramatically·changed·the·face·of·business.¶

IMPRESSED·BY·THE·INTERNET'S·RISING·POPULARITY,·MANY·BUSINESSES·
HAVE·ESTABLISHED·AN·ONLINE·PRESENCE.·A·RICH·VARIETY·OF·BUSINESS·
INFORMATION·—·FROM·PRODUCT·AND·SERVICE·CATALOGUES·TO·PRESS·
RELEASES·TO·COMPANY·CONTACTS·—·IS·NOW·AVAILABLE·TO·INTERNET·
USERS.¶

Today,·many·businesses·realise·that,·in·order·to·compete·successfully,·they·need·to·sell·
their·goods·and·services·directly·to·consumers·or·other·businesses·over·the·Internet.¶

13) Close and save your sample document with the following name:

   Chapter9_Exercise_9-3_After_Your_Name.doc

Exercise 9.4: Assign an existing macro to a keyboard shortcut

In this exercise, you assign a different keyboard shortcut to the macro that you created in Exercise 9.3. You do not need to have a document open to reassign a macro keyboard shortcut – unless the macro is stored in a particular document rather than a template.

1) Right-click any displayed Word toolbar, such as the Standard toolbar, and choose **Customize**.

2) In the *Customize* dialog box, click the **Commands** tab, and click the **Keyboard** button to display the *Customize Keyboard* dialog box.

3) In the *Categories* list, click *Macros*. In the *Macros* list, click the macro that you created in Exercise 9.3.

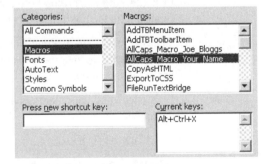

4) Word displays the currently assigned keyboard shortcut for the selected macro. In this case, the keyboard shortcut is **Alt+Ctrl+X**. If no shortcut was assigned to the macro, the *Current keys* box would be empty.

   Your next step is to assign a second shortcut key combination to the macro.

5) Click in the *Press new shortcut key* box, and press the following key combination:

Alt+Ctrl+;

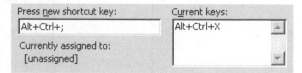

6) Click **Assign**. Word assigns the keyboard shortcut. The macro now has two keyboard shortcuts associated with it. In future, using either shortcut will run the macro.

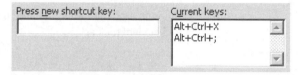

7) Click **Close** to close the *Customize Keyboard* dialog box, and click **Close** to close the *Customize* dialog box.

8) You have completed this exercise. You do not need to save any documents: the new keyboard assignment is already saved to your Normal template.

Working with macros and toolbar buttons

The procedure for assigning a macro to a toolbar button is very similar to that for assigning a macro to a keyboard shortcut. You can assign the macro when you record, as shown in Exercise 9.5, or at a later time, as in Exercise 9.6.

Exercise 9.5: Record a macro and assign it to a toolbar button

In this exercise, you will create a new macro and assign it to a button on a Word toolbar.

1) Is the Word toolbar to which you want to assign the macro displayed? If not, choose **View | Toolbars** to display it now.

2) Open the following document:

Chapter9_Exercise_9-5_Before.doc

3) Select the first paragraph of text in the document.

4) Choose **Tools | Macro | Record New Macro** to display the *Record Macro* dialog box.

5) In the *Macro name* box, type the following:

BlueCaps_Macro_Your_Name

6) Click the **Toolbars** button. Word now displays the *Customize* dialog box.

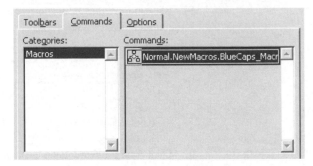

In the *Commands* list of the **Commands** tab, click on the macro that you have just named and drag it to the relevant toolbar.

In the example below, the button for the macro is positioned on the Standard toolbar.

When you have dragged the macro name to the toolbar, click **Close** to close the *Customize* dialog box.

7) You will now perform the sequence of actions for your macro to record:

- Choose **Format | Font**.

- Change the font colour to blue, and select the *All caps* checkbox.

- Click **OK**.

This completes the actions.

8) Click the **Stop Recording** button on the Stop Recording toolbar. Word removes the toolbar from the screen.

9) Your macro is now recorded. You can close the sample document without saving it. Your new macro is stored in the Normal template – not in the document.

10) Let's check that your macro is assigned correctly. Open the following document:

    Chapter9_Exercise_9-5_Before.doc

Select the second paragraph of text, and click the macro button on the toolbar. Your macro should have the effect shown.

Impressed·by·the·Internet's·rising·popularity,·many·businesses·have·established·an·online·
presence.·A·rich·variety·of·business·information·—·from·product·and·service·catalogues·to·
press

IMPRESSED·BY·THE·INTERNET'S·RISING·POPULARITY,·MANY·BUSINESSES·
HAVE·ESTABLISHED·AN·ONLINE·PRESENCE.·A·RICH·VARIETY·OF·BUSINESS·
INFORMATION·—·FROM·PRODUCT·AND·SERVICE·CATALOGUES·TO·PRESS·
RELEASES·TO·COMPANY·CONTACTS·—·IS·NOW·AVAILABLE·TO·INTERNET·
USERS.¶

11) Close and save your sample document with the following name:

   Chapter9_Exercise_9-5_After_Your_Name.doc

Exercise 9.6: Assign an existing macro to a toolbar button
In this exercise, you will assign a toolbar button to the macro that you previously created in Exercise 9.3.

1) Right-click any displayed Word toolbar, such as the Standard toolbar, choose **Customize** to display the *Customize* dialog box, and click the **Commands** tab.

2) In the *Categories* list, click *Macros*.

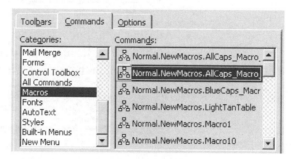

3) In the *Commands* list, click the macro that you created in Exercise 9.3 and drag it to the relevant toolbar.

   When finished, click **Close** to close the *Customize* dialog box.

4) Let's check that your macro is assigned correctly to the toolbar. Open the following document:

   Chapter9_Exercise_9-6_Before.doc

5) Select the third paragraph of body text, and click the macro button on the toolbar. Close and save your sample document with the following name:

   Chapter9_Exercise_9-6_After_*Your_Name*.doc

   Want to remove the macro button from your toolbar? Hold down the **Alt** key and drag the button down off the toolbar.

Working with macros and templates

A Word macro is not a separate file but is stored in a template or document.

- **Normal template**. If your current document is based on the Normal template (Normal.dot), Word gives you the choice of storing a new macro in the Normal template or in the current document.

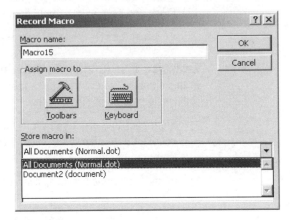

- **Another template**. If your current document is based on a template other than Normal.dot, you can store a new macro in Normal.dot, in the current template, or in the current document.

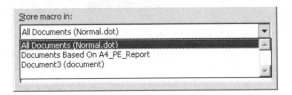

When you store a macro in the Normal template, it is available to all documents on *your* PC. When you store a macro in a document, it is available to any Word user who opens that document on *any* PC.

Macro projects and the Word 2000 Organizer

The area within a Word document or template in which macros are stored is called the *macro project*. A document or template may have more than one macro project. The first or default macro project in every Word document or template is called NewMacros.

Macro project

A group of one or more macros saved in an individual Word template or document. The first or default macro project in every document or template is called NewMacros.

Using the Word 2000 Organizer, you can copy a macro project (and all the macros it contains) between templates, between documents, and between documents and templates.

In the *Organizer* dialog box (available from the *Macros* dialog box), you can display two lists:

ECDL Advanced Word Processing

- **Macros in active document**. On the left, Word can display the macro projects stored in the active document, in Normal.dot and, if the current document is based on another template, in that other template.

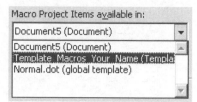

In the above example, you can select the macro project from any one of three locations: the current document (Document5), the current template (Template_Macros_ Your_Name) or Normal.dot.

- **Macros in Normal template**. On the right, Word shows the macro project in the Normal document template only.

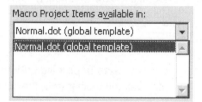

In Exercise 9.7, you will record a macro and store it in the current document rather than in a template. In Exercise 9.8, you use the Word 2000 Organizer to copy the macro project that contains your macro from the document to the Normal template.

Exercise 9.7: Record a macro and store it in a document

1) Open the following blank document:

   Chapter9_Exercise_9-7_Before.doc

2) Choose **Tools | Macro | Record New Macro** to display the *Record Macro* dialog box.

3) In the *Macro name* box, type the following name:

   Landscape_Macro_*Your_Name*

4) In the *Store macro in* list, select the current document option. Click **OK** to close the dialog box.

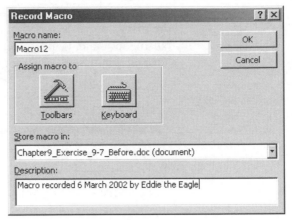

5) You will now perform the sequence of actions for your macro to record.

- Choose **File | Page Setup**.

- Click the **Paper Size** tab.

- Change the orientation to *Landscape*.

- Click **OK**.

This completes the actions.

6) Click the **Stop Recording** button on the Stop Recording toolbar. Word removes the toolbar from the screen. Your macro is now recorded.

7) Close and save the document with the following name:

Chapter9_Exercise_9-7_After_*Your_Name*.doc

In the next exercise, you will copy your macro, saved in the document, to the Normal template.

Exercise 9.8: Copy a macro using the Word 2000 Organizer

1) Open the document that you saved at the end of Exercise 9.7:

Chapter9_Exercise_9-7_After_*Your_Name*.doc

2) Choose **Tools | Macro | Macros** to display the *Macros* dialog box and click the **Organizer** button.

3) Select the **Macro Project Items** tab.

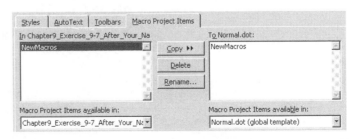

4) In the left-hand list, which shows the macro project for the current document, click *NewMacros* to select it, and then click **Copy**.

5) Word displays the following message box.

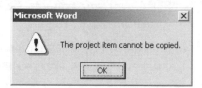

Why? Because you tried to copy a macro project named NewMacros to the Normal template, which already contains a macro project called NewMacros. You need to first rename the macro project before you can copy it.

6) With NewMacros still selected in the left list, click **Rename**, type the following new macro project name when prompted, and click **OK**:

MoreMacros

7) With MoreMacros still selected in the left list, click **Copy** to copy the macro project to the Normal template.

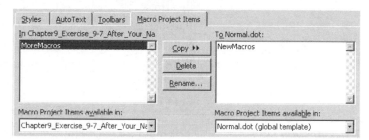

8) When finished, click **Close**.

9) Let's check that your landscape macro is actually stored in the Normal template, from where it is available to all documents based on that template.

Click the **New** button on the Standard toolbar to open a new document, choose **Tools | Macro | Macros**, and verify that your macro is present. When finished, you can close all open documents.

What a macro does and does not record

When you record a macro, which of your actions does the macro 'remember'? Macros record actions that affect the document, and ignore those that do not, such as switching display features on and off.

Macros and mouse actions

Macros do record mouse actions that choose menu commands (such as **File | Save**) and that click on toolbar buttons (such as the **Bold** button on the Formatting toolbar).

Macros do *not* record mouse actions that:

- **Change the location of the insertion point**. For example, to move a number of characters along a line, or to move forward or backward through a document

- **Select text**. For example, before copying a word or formatting a paragraph.

To record document-navigation and text-selection actions in a macro, you must use the relevant shortcut keys.

Navigation keys

The main shortcut keys for document navigation are:

Press	To move the insertion point
Left arrow	One character to the left.
Right arrow	One character to the right.
Ctrl+Left arrow	One word to the left.
Ctrl+ Right arrow	One word to the right.
Ctrl+Up arrow	One paragraph up.
Ctrl+Down arrow	One paragraph down.
Up arrow	Up one line.
Down arrow	Down one line.
End	To the end of a line.
Home	To the beginning of a line.
Ctrl+End	To the end of a document.
Ctrl+Home	To the beginning of a document.

Text-selection keys

The main text-selection shortcut keys are:

Press	To select text
Shift+ Right arrow	One character to the right.
Shift+Left arrow	One character to the left.
Ctrl+Shift+ Right arrow	To the end of a word.
Ctrl+Shift+Left arrow	To the beginning of a word.
Shift+End	To the end of a line.
Shift+Home	To the beginning of a line.
Shift+Down arrow	One line down.
Shift+Up arrow	One line up.
Ctrl+Shift+Down arrow	To the end of a paragraph.
Ctrl+Shift+Up arrow	To the beginning of a paragraph.
Ctrl+Shift+Home	To the beginning of a document.
Ctrl+Shift+End	To the end of a document.
Ctrl+A	The entire document.
F8+arrow keys	To a specific location in a document.

To display the document-navigation and text-selection keyboard shortcuts in Word's Online Help, choose **Help | Microsoft Word Help**, type 'shortcuts' in the search box, click **Search**, and then click *Keyboard Shortcuts* in the topics list. (Make sure you have hidden the Office Assistant before you do this.)

Before recording a macro

Here are some points to remember before recording any macro:

- **Templates**. Decide where you want to save the macro – in the current template or in the current document only.

- **Actions**. Plan the steps you want the macro to perform. It is possible to edit a macro, but you must be familiar with Visual Basic for Applications (VBA), the programming language in which macros are written. VBA is beyond the scope of this ECDL module and book.

- **Text selection**. If you are creating a macro that applies only to selected text in a document, consider whether you want the text-selection action recorded as part of the macro, or whether you want to select the text first before running the macro.

Chapter 9: quick reference

Macro properties

Property	Description
Name	This identifies the macro uniquely. Macro names can contain numbers, but they must begin with a letter and they cannot contain spaces.
	If you give a new macro the same name as an existing built-in Word macro, your new macro will replace the built-in Word macro – *without* warning!
Storage location	This can be the current template or document.
Description	Optionally, you can enter a description of your macro, up to 255 characters in length. This is your reference to help you remember what the macro does.
Keyboard shortcut	Optionally, you can assign a macro to a keyboard shortcut so that you can run it by pressing the appropriate keys.
Toolbar button	Optionally, you can assign a macro to a toolbar button so that you can run it by clicking the appropriate button.

Task	Procedure
Record a new macro.	Click the **REC** button on the Status Bar or choose **Tools | Macro | Record New Macro**. Type a name and click **OK**.
	Perform the actions you want the macro to record. When finished, click the **Stop Recording** button.
Assign a macro to a keyboard shortcut.	When recording the macro, click the **Keyboard** button in the *Record Macro* dialog box, press the relevant key combination, click **Assign** and click **Close**.
Assign a macro to a toolbar button.	When recording the macro, click the **Toolbar** button in the *Record Macro* dialog box. In the *Commands* list, click the macro and drag it to the relevant toolbar.
Copy a macro.	Choose **Tools | Macro | Record New Macro**, click **Organizer**, select the macro project, click **Copy** and then click **Close**.

Concepts summary

Word's macro feature enables you to *record* and, as often as needed, play back or *run* sequences of Word actions and menu commands. By recording frequently-performed and repetitive tasks in macros, you can speed up your work greatly. As the actions stored in a macro are performed in exactly the same way each time the macro is run, you can ensure that procedures are followed more reliably.

Macros are identified by a unique name and, optionally, can be assigned to a keyboard shortcut or toolbar button for fast access. You can make the keyboard or toolbar assignment when recording the macro or at a later time.

Word does *not* record the speed at which perform your actions. If you make a slight mistake, you can correct your error and keep going. If you make a serious error, stop the recording and begin again.

Macros *do* record *mouse actions* that choose menu commands and click on toolbar buttons, but they do not record mouse actions that change the location of the insertion point or select text. To record navigation and selection actions in a macro, you must use the relevant *shortcut keys*.

A Word macro is not a separate file but is stored in the current template or document. The area within a Word document or template in which macros are stored is called the *macro project*.

A document or template may have more than one macro project. The first or default macro project in every Word document or template is called *NewMacros*.

Using the *Word 2000 Organizer*, you can copy a macro project (and all the macros it contains) between templates, between documents, and between documents and templates.

Chapter 9: quick quiz

Circle the correct answer to each of the following multiple-choice questions about macros in Word.

Q1	A Word macro is …
A.	An AutoText entry that is inserted automatically when a new Word document opens.
B.	A built-in Word program that can copy text and graphics between templates.
C.	A series of recorded actions that, when run, performs those actions automatically.
D.	An AutoText entry that is inserted automatically when a Word document is saved and closed.

Q2	Which of the following statements about Word macros is untrue?
A.	Macros can be protected by passwords for security.
B.	Macros enable procedures to be followed consistently because the actions are performed in the same way each time the macro is run.
C.	Macros enable repetitive tasks to be recorded once and then run as often as needed.
D.	Macros can be stored in a document or a template.

Q3	Which button on Word's Status Bar can you click to begin recording a new macro?
A.	MACRO.
B.	RECORD.
C.	MAC REC.
D.	REC.

Q4	Which Word command can you choose to record a new macro?
A.	File | New | Macro.
B.	Tools | Macro | Record New Macro.
C.	Format | Automation | New Macros.
D.	Tools | Macro | New.

Q5	In Word, which of the following items must you specify for each new macro that you record?
A.	Macro description.
B.	Keyboard shortcut.
C.	Toolbar button.
D.	Macro name.

Q6	In Word, which of the following is the default storage location for a new macro that you record?
A.	The current document.
B.	The current template.
C.	The Normal template.
D.	AutoText Check.

Q7	In Word, which of the following keyboard shortcuts is a good choice for assigning a macro to?
A.	Ctrl+B.
B.	Ctrl+C.
C.	Ctrl+V.
D.	Alt+Ctrl+X.

Q8	In Word's *Record Macro* dialog box, which series of actions do you perform to assign a macro to a keyboard shortcut?
A.	Click the **Shortcut Key** button, press the relevant key combination, click the **Assign Now** button, and then click **OK**.
B.	Select an unassigned keyboard shortcut from the *Keyboard* list and click **Copy** to copy it to the *Assigned keys* list.
C.	Click the **Keyboard** button, press the relevant key combination, click the **Assign** button, and then click **Close**.
D.	Select an unassigned keyboard shortcut from the *Keyboard* list and click the **Assign** button.

Q9	In Word's *Record Macro* dialog box, which series of actions do you perform to assign a macro to a toolbar button?
A.	Click the **Toolbar** button. In the *Commands* list, click the macro to select it and drag it to the relevant toolbar.
B.	Click the **Toolbar** button. In the *Toolbars* list, click to select the relevant toolbar, click the **Assign** button and click **OK**.
C.	Click the **Assign Toolbar** button. In the *Macros* list, right-click the macro to select it and drag it to the relevant toolbar.
D.	Click the **Toolbar** button. In the *Available Toolbars* list, click to select the relevant toolbar, click the **Copy** button and click **OK**.

Q10	In Word, which series of actions do you perform to assign an already-recorded macro to a shortcut key?
A.	Right-click on the toolbar and choose **Customize**. On the *Commands* tab, click the **Keyboard** button, select *Macros* in the *Categories* list, select the macro in the *Macros* list, press the key combination, click **Assign**, click **Close,** and then click **Close** again.
B.	Choose **Tools | Macro | Macros**, click the **Shortcut Key** button, press the relevant key combination, click the **Assign Now** button, and then click **OK**.
C.	Right-click on the toolbar and choose **Customize**. On the **Commands** tab, click the **Keyboard** button, select the macro in the *Macros* list, press the key combination, click the **Assign** button, and click **OK**.
D.	Choose **Tools | Macro | Macros**, select an unassigned keyboard shortcut from the *Keyboard* list, click the **Assign** button, and click **OK**.

Q11	In Word, which series of actions do you perform to assign an already-recorded macro to a toolbar button?
A.	Choose **Tools | Macro | Macros**, click the **Shortcut Key** button, press the relevant key combination, click the **Assign Now** button, and then click **OK**.
B.	Right-click on the toolbar and choose **Customize**. On the **Commands** tab, select *Macros* in the *Categories* list, click the macro in the *Macros* list, drag it to the relevant toolbar, and click **Close**.
C.	Choose **Tools | Macro | Macros**, select a toolbar from the *Toolbars* list, select the macro from the *Macros* list, click the **Assign** button, and click **OK**.
D.	Right-click on the toolbar and choose **Customize**. On the **Commands** tab, right-click the macro in the *Available macros* list, drag it to the relevant toolbar, and click **OK**.

Q12	In Word, the area within a document or template in which macros are stored is called …
A.	A macro field.
B.	A macro subfolder.
C.	A macro AutoText entry.
D.	A macro project.

Q13	The first or default macro project in every Word document or template is called …
A.	DefaultMacros.
B.	NewMacros.
C.	Macros_Default.
D.	MacrosNew.

Q14	By default, the left-hand list in the *Word Organizer* dialog box shows …
A.	The macro projects stored in the Normal template.
B.	The macro projects stored in the Normal template and, if the current document is based on another template, in that other template.
C.	The macro projects stored in the current document.
D.	The macro projects stored in the active document, in Normal.dot and, if the current document is based on another template, in that other template.

Answers

1: C, **2:** A, **3:** D, **4:** B, **5:** D, **6:** C, **7:** D, **8:** C, **9:** A, **10:** A, **11:** B, **12:** D, **13:** B, **14:** D.

'Are you sure about this?': comments and document protection

- **AM3.3.4.1**. Add password protection to a document.

- **AM3.3.4.2**. Remove password protection from a document.

About comments

Any document you write will usually benefit from review by one or more of your colleagues. Word offers a *comments* feature to help document authors gather feedback from reviewers. Sometimes, authors insert comments for their own benefit – such as a reminder to add further text or to check particular facts. A few important points about comments in Word:

- Comments do not change the body of a document. Think of a comment as a kind of electronic Post-it™ note.

- The presence of a comment in a document is indicated by a comment mark. Double-click a comment mark to display the comment text in a separate *comment pane* at the bottom of the document window.

- Word numbers comments automatically, and labels each comment to identify the person making the comment.

- Comments can be edited and removed.

The Reviewing toolbar

Word offers a special toolbar for working with comments. To display it, choose **View | Toolbars | Reviewing**. Only four buttons are relevant to comments.

Insert new comment

Move insertion point forward or backward to the next comment in document

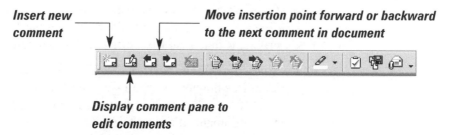

Display comment pane to edit comments

Comment
A short note or annotation applied to a particular location in a document. Comments do not affect a document's content.

Comments and printing

By default, Word does not print comments. To change this, choose **File | Print**, click **Options**, click the *Comments* checkbox and click **OK, OK**.

Word then prints the comments at the end of the document, beginning on a new page.

Comments and document protection

To ensure that your reviewers insert only comments and do not otherwise change your document, you can *password-protect* your document against modification.

Comments: the benefits for authors and reviewers

In the past, authors typically gathered feedback on a document by printing multiple copies, circulating the copies to reviewers, collecting the reviewed copies, and reading and implementing the reviewers' comments. Reviewers generally wrote their comments or annotations by hand on the printed review copies.

Word's comment feature streamlines the review process in three ways:

- **Electronic document distribution**. Documents can be circulated for review in electronic rather than printed form, eliminating the need for printing, photocopying and physical distribution.

- **Electronic comment capture**. Annotations are entered directly on the document file, removing the legibility problems that arise from difficult-to-read handwriting.

- **Single document version**. Because Word automatically identifies the person who inserts each comment, the same Word file can be reviewed successively by different people. This eliminates the version-management issues associated with multiple review copies of the same document.

Working with comments: the four tasks

Here are the four comment-related tasks you need to be able to perform:

- **Insert a comment in a document**. Exercise 10.1 takes you through the steps.

- **Display and hide comments**. You will learn about the various comment displays options in the text following Exercise 10.1.

- **Edit an existing comment**. You can edit comment text in the same way that you edit text in a document. See Exercise 10.2.

- **Remove a comment**. Typically, you will want to remove comments when preparing a final draft of a document. Exercise 10.3 shows you how.

Exercise 10.1: Insert a comment in a document

1) Start Word and open the following file:

    Chapter10_Exercise_10-1_Before.doc

2) Is the Reviewing toolbar displayed? If not, display it now by choosing **View | Toolbars | Reviewing**.

3) In the first line of the text under the document title, click just before the word 'committed'.

˙Elmsworth·Health·Trust:·Patients'·Charter¶
At·Elmsworth·Health·Trust,·we·are·committed·to·delivering·a·world-class·service.·Our·

Click here

Insert Comment button

4) Click the **Insert Comment** button on the Reviewing toolbar (or choose **Insert | Comment**). Word opens the comment pane at the bottom of the document window.

5) Type the comment 'totally' in the comment pane.

Comments From: All Reviewers

[EE1]totally¶

You can resize the comment pane by dragging the grey border between it and the document.

6) When finished, click **Close** on the comment pane.

Show/Hide button

7) Is the **Show/Hide** button on the Standard toolbar selected? If not, click it now.

Notice that Word displays a comment mark in the document to indicate that a comment is present at that location.

˙Elmsworth·Health·Trust:·Patients'·Charter¶
At·Elmsworth·Health·Trust,·we·are·committed·[EE1]to·delivering·a·world-class·service.·

Comment mark

8) Close and save your sample document with the following name:

    Chapter10_Exercise_10-1_After_*Your_Name*.doc

Comments are examples of Word's hidden text – text that can be hidden from display and shown only when you want to view it.

If you want to display hidden text at all times, and not just when the **Show/Hide** button on the Standard toolbar is selected:

- Choose **Tools | Options** and click the **View** tab.

- Select the *Hidden text* checkbox and click **OK**.

Another useful option on the **View** tab within the *Options* dialog box is the *ScreenTips* checkbox. When you select this, Word:

- Displays a yellow background behind comments, regardless of whether the **Show/Hide** button on the Standard toolbar is selected.

- Displays a yellow pop-up box when you position the cursor over a comment mark.

Elmsworth Health Trust  **Charter**

At Elmsworth Health Trust, we are committed [EE1]to delivering a world-class service. Our standards apply whether you are:

If your document contains comments from different reviewers, Word highlights each reviewer's comments with a different background colour.

If your document has been commented on by different reviewers, how can you tell which comments were made by individual reviewers?

Whenever a comment is inserted in a document, Word attaches the reviewer's details to that comment. Word takes the reviewer's details from the **User Information** tab of the dialog box accessed from **Tools | Options**. This information is entered during Word installation, but it may be amended at any stage.

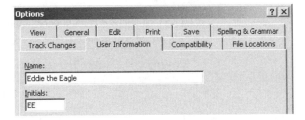

When using another person's PC to insert comments, you can use **Tools | Options** to change the user information details, and then change them back again when you have completed your comments.

In addition to user details, Word also attaches a sequentially increasing number to each comment, and displays the unique comment number in the comment mark. Word automatically updates the comment numbers as you add new comments and remove existing ones.

> ***Comment mark***
>
> *A mark that indicates the presence of a comment in a document. Comment marks identify the comment maker and show the comment's unique number.*

Exercise 10.2: Edit a comment

1) Open the following file:

    Chapter10_Exercise_10-2_Before.doc

2) Is the Reviewing toolbar displayed? If not, display it now by choosing **View | Toolbars | Reviewing**.

3) Double-click the comment mark after the word 'committed'.

Elmsworth Health Trust: Patients' Charter
At Elmsworth Health Trust, we are committed [EE1]to delivering a world-class service.

Double-click here

Word opens the comment pane at the bottom of the document window.

4) In the comment pane, change the text 'totally' to 'totally and absolutely'.

5) When finished, click **Close** on the comment pane.

6) Close and save your sample document with the following name:

    Chapter10_Exercise_10-2_After_*Your_Name*.doc

Exercise 10.3: Remove a comment

1) Open the following file:

    Chapter10_Exercise_10-3_Before.doc

2) Is the Reviewing toolbar displayed? If not, display it now by choosing **View | Toolbars | Reviewing**.

3) Right-click the comment mark after the word 'committed' to display a pop-up menu.

Elmsworth Health Trust: Patients' Charter

At Elmsworth Health Trust, we are committed ~~to delivering a world-class service.~~
Our standards apply whether you are:

- A patient
- A relative or friend of a patient
- Someone simply seeking advice.

This Patient Charter sets out what we can do for ~~led to.~~

Mission Statement

The purpose of the Elmsworth Health Trust is to:

- Promote good health

4) Choose **Delete Comment** to remove the comment and close the pop-up menu.

5) Close and save your sample document with the following name:

```
Chapter10_Exercise_10-3_After_Your_Name.doc
```

Document protection

To ensure that your reviewers insert only comments and do not alter the document itself, use Word's document-protection feature.

Word offers two kinds of password protection:

- **Document-open password protection**. You can protect a document so that it cannot be opened without the user entering the correct password.

- **Document-modify password protection**. You can protect a document so that it can be opened for reading by anyone, but only people who know the correct password can modify the document.

  This second option is suitable for documents that you want to circulate to reviewers, because reviewers can insert comments in a document-modify protected file without knowing the correct password.

  Note, however, that this option does not prevent someone saving your Word document under a new file name, and then making changes to it.

The procedures for applying the document-open and document-modify protections methods are very similar. You perform each from the same dialog box within the **File | Save As** command.

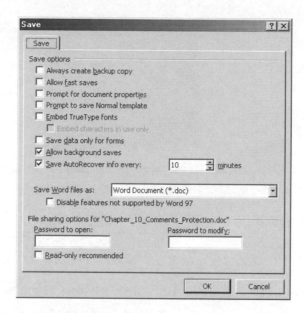

In Word, passwords are case sensitive and can contain up to 15 characters, including letters, numerals and symbols. You might want to write down your passwords and keep them in a secure place.

If you lose the password to a document-open protected Word file, you will not be able to open it. If you lose the password to a document-modify protected Word file, you will be able to open it only in read-only mode.

Working with document protection: the two tasks

Here are the two document protection tasks you need to be able to perform:

- **Add password protection to a document**. See Exercise 10.4.

- **Remove password protection from a document**. See Exercise 10.5.

Exercise 10.4: Add password protection to a document

1) Open the following file:

   Chapter10_Exercise_10-4_Before.doc

2) Choose **File | Save As**.

3) Click the **Tools** button in the dialog box, and from the pop-up menu select **General Options**.

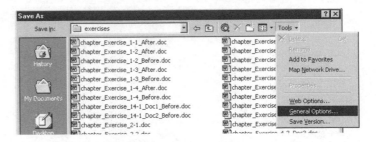

4) At the bottom of the dialog box, in the *Password to modify* box, type a password.

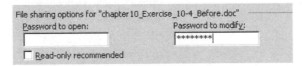

Word masks your password as you type it, displaying only asterisks.

5) Click **OK**. Word displays the *Confirm Password* dialog box.

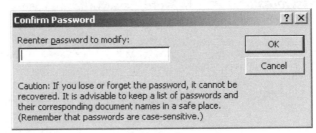

6) Retype your password and click **OK**.

7) You are returned to the *Save As* dialog box. In the *File name* box, type the following file name:

    Chapter10_Exercise_10-4_After_*Your_Name*.doc

8) Click **Save**.

You can now close your sample document.

Exercise 10.5: Remove password protection from a document

1) Open the following file:

    Chapter10_Exercise_10-5_Before.doc

2) Word prompts you to enter a password.

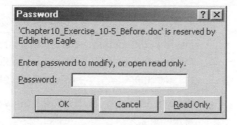

Password   ? X

'Chapter10_Exercise_10-5_Before.doc' is reserved by
Eddie the Eagle

Enter password to modify, or open read only.

Password: [   ]

    OK   Cancel   Read Only

3) Type the following password and click **OK**.

    blah

4) Word now opens your sample document. You now need to resave the document – but without the password protection.

    Choose **File | Save As**, click the **Tools** button and choose **General Options**.

5) Delete the password from the *Password to modify* box and click **OK**.

6) You are returned to the **Save As** dialog box. In the *File name* box, type the following file name:

    Chapter10_Exercise_10-5_After_*Your_Name*.doc

7) Click **Save**.

    You can now close your sample document.

    You can also use the procedure described in this exercise to change the password that protects a document.

Lesson 10: quick reference

Reviewing toolbar: comment buttons

Keys	Description
	Inserts a new comment at the insertion point in the current document.
	Displays the comment pane at the foot of the document window, enabling you to edit comments.
	Moves the insertion point forward to the location of the next comment in the document.
	Moves the insertion point back to the location of the previous comment in the document.

Task	Procedure
Insert a comment at the insertion point in the document.	Click the **Insert Comment** button on the Reviewing toolbar or choose **Insert	Comment**. Type the comment text and click **Close**.
Show/hide comments.	Click the **Show/Hide** button on the Standard toolbar.
Always show comments.	Choose **Tools	Options**, click the **View** tab, click the *Hidden text* checkbox, and click **OK**.
Show/hide coloured background behind comments.	Choose **Tools	Options**, click the **View** tab, select the *ScreenTips* checkbox, and click **OK**.
Edit a comment.	Double-click the comment mark to display the comment pane. Edit the text and click **Close**.
Delete a comment.	Right-click the comment mark and choose **Delete Comment** from the pop-up menu.

Task	Procedure
Apply password protection to a document.	Choose **File	Save As**, click the **Tools** button, choose **General Options**, enter open and/or modify password(s), click **OK**, retype password(s), click **OK** and click **Save**.
Remove password protection from a document.	Choose **File	Save As**, click the **Tools** button, choose **General Options**, delete and/or modify password(s), click **OK** and click **Save**.

Word's *comments* feature enables reviewers to insert annotations or short notes in a document.

The presence of a comment in a document is indicated by a *comment mark*, which shows a sequential comment number and the identity of the comment-maker. Double-clicking a comment mark displays the comment text in a separate *comment pane* at the bottom of the document window.

Once inserted, comments can be edited and removed as required.

By default, Word does not print comments. If comments are selected for printing, Word prints them on a separate page at the end of the document.

Comments do not change the content of a document. Think of a comment as a kind of electronic Post-it™ note.

Word allows you to *protect* a document so that it may not be opened without the entry of the correct password; alternatively, it may be opened but not modified without the entry of the correct password.

In Word, *passwords* are case sensitive and can contain up to 15 characters, including letters, numerals and symbols.

When a document is password-protected against modification, users who do not enter the correct password may open the document in *read-only* mode only. Users may insert comments in a read-only document, however. This makes this type of password protection suitable for documents circulated to reviewers.

Password-protecting a Word document against modification does not prevent anyone saving the document under a new file name and then making changes to it.

Chapter 10: quick quiz – comments

Circle the correct answer to each of the following multiple-choice questions about comments in Word.

Q1	In Word, a comment is …
A.	A text amendment in a Word document that is highlighted with a revision mark.
B.	A text item that is attached at a particular location in a Word document.
C.	One item in a list of amendments made to a document, and contained in a separate, automatically-created file.
D.	An annotation stored in the **File	Document Properties** dialog box.

Q2	Which of the following is not an advantage of using the comments feature in Word?
A.	Documents can be circulated for commenting in electronic rather than printed form.
B.	You are provided with a separate file containing all comments.
C.	Comments can be typed directly to the document file, rather than handwritten on a print-out.
D.	Each comment is labelled with the identity of the reviewer.

Q3	Which action do you take to insert a new comment in a Word document?
A.	Click the **New Comment** button on the Standard toolbar.
B.	Choose **Tools	Comment	New**.
C.	Choose **Insert	Comment**.
D.	Click the **New Comment** button on the Formatting toolbar.

Q4	In a Word document, which action do you take to ensure that comments are always displayed?
A.	Choose **Tools	Options**, click the **View** tab, select the *Show comments* checkbox, and click **OK**.
B.	Click the **Show Comments** button on the Reviewing toolbar.
C.	Choose **Tools	Options**, click the **View** tab, select the *Hidden text* checkbox, and click **OK**.
D.	Choose **Tools	Options**, click the **Comments** tab, select the *Show comments in document* checkbox, and click **OK**.

Q5	You want to edit a comment in a Word document. Which action do you *not* take?
A.	Right-click the comment mark and choose **Remove Comment** from the pop-up menu.
B.	Click the **Edit Comment** button on the Reviewing toolbar to display the comment text in the comment pane.
C.	Click anywhere in the comment mark and choose **Insert	Comments	Edit**.
D.	Double-click the comment mark to display the comment text in the comment pane.

Q6	You want to delete a comment from a Word document. Which action do you take?
A.	Right-click the comment mark and choose **Delete Comment** from the pop-up menu.
B.	Double-click the comment mark and choose **Delete Comment** from the pop-up menu.
C.	Choose **Insert	Comments	Remove**.
D.	Double-click the comment mark to display the comment pane, delete the comment and its label, and click **Close**.

Q7	To ensure Word always displays a coloured background behind comments you ...
A.	Choose **Tools	Options**, click the **View** tab, select the *ScreenTips* checkbox, and click **OK**.
B.	Click the **Show Comments** button on the Reviewing toolbar.
C.	Choose **Tools	Options**, click the **Comments** tab, select the *Show colored background* checkbox, and click **OK**.
D.	Choose **Tools	Options**, click the **View** tab, select the *Comment background* checkbox, and click **OK**.

Answers

1: B, **2:** B, **3:** C, **4:** C, *5:* A, **6:** A, **7:** A.

Chapter 10: quick quiz – password protection

Circle the correct answer to each of the following multiple-choice questions about password protection in Word.

Q1	Which of the following is a valid type of password protection in Word?
A.	Document-delete password protection.
B.	Document-format password protection.
C.	Document-modify password protection.
D.	Document-template password protection.

Q2	Which statement correctly describes document-modify password protection in Word?
A.	Without knowing the correct password, a user may not modify the document content but may insert comments in the document.
B.	Without knowing the correct password, a user may open the document but the document text is masked behind asterisks.
C.	Without knowing the correct password, a user may not modify the document content and may not insert comments in the document.
D.	Without knowing the correct password, a user may not open the document.

Q3	Which statement correctly describes document-open password protection in Word?
A.	Without knowing the correct password, a user may open the document but may not modify it in any way.
B.	Without knowing the correct password, a user may open the document but the document text is masked behind asterisks.
C.	Without knowing the correct password, a user may not modify the document content but may insert comments in the document.
D.	Without knowing the correct password, a user may not open the document.

Q4	Which of these statements about password protection of documents in Word is true?
A.	A user must specify the same password to protect a document against opening and against modification.
B.	The document-modify password protection feature prevents a user from resaving a Word document under a new file name and then making changes to it.
C.	A user may specify one password to protect a document against opening, and a different password to protect it against modification.
D.	Word stores on your PC a list of your document passwords that you can view in the event of you forgetting or losing a password.

Q5	Which of these statements about passwords in Word is untrue?
A.	Passwords can contain up to 15 characters.
B.	Passwords are case-sensitive.
C.	Passwords may include letters, numerals and symbols.
D.	Passwords, once entered, may not be amended.

Q6	Which command in Word do you choose to work with the password-protection options?
A.	**Tools	Security.**
B.	**File	Properties.**
C.	**Format	Password Protection.**
D.	**File	Save As.**

Answers

1: C, 2: A, 3: D, 4: C, 5: D, 6: D.

11

Displaying, accepting and rejecting revisions: change tracking

Objectives

In this chapter you will learn how to:

- Switch change tracking on and off
- Display and hide tracked changes
- Control how tracked changes are displayed
- Accept and reject tracked changes

New words

In this chapter you will meet the following terms:

- Change tracking
- Compare documents

Exercise files

In this chapter you will work with the following Word files:

- Chapter11_Exercise_11_4_Original_Before.doc
- Chapter11_Exercise_11_4_Edited_Before.doc

Syllabus reference

In this chapter you will cover the following items from the ECDL Advanced Word Processing Syllabus:

- **AM3.1.4.3**. Use highlighting options to track changes in a document.
- **AM3.1.4.4**. Accept or reject changes in a document.

About change tracking

Change tracking is a feature that records amendments made to a Word document by highlighting them with the following *revision marks*:

- **New text**. Word identifies text added to a document by formatting it in colour with underlining.
- **Deleted text**. Word identifies deleted text by formatting it in colour with strikethrough.

- **All amended text**. Word indicates all text additions and deletions by placing a vertical bar in the document's left margin.

Discharge·from·Hospital·¶

| ~~We·~~Staff·will·ensure·that·you·and·your·family·are·involved·in·the·planning·of·your· discharge·from·hospital, where·practical.¶

| A·discharge·plan·will·be·provided·for·your·continuing·health·and·social·care·needs.· This·will·be·communicated·to·your·General·Practitioner.·Your·GP·will·be·notified· ~~promptly~~·in·a·reasonable·period·of·time·regarding·~~of~~·your·discharge.¶

Change tracking helps authors locate the changes made by others to a Word document, identify who made the changes, and then accept or reject each change as required.

When different reviewers make changes to the same document, Word highlights each person's additions or deletions in a different colour.

The Reviewing toolbar

Word offers a special toolbar for working with tracked changes. To display it, choose **View | Toolbars | Reviewing**. Five buttons are relevant to change tracking.

Move insertion point forward/backward to next/previous change in document

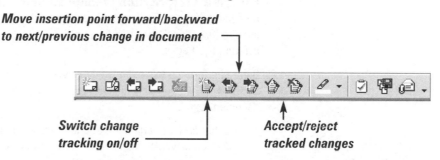

Switch change tracking on/off

Accept/reject tracked changes

Change tracking: the benefits to you

Change tracking offers two main benefits. It:

- **Highlights relevant areas**. The vertical bar in the left margin helps you locate reviewers' edits quickly. For long documents, this is a significant time-saver.

- **Saves retyping of reviewer feedback**. When you meet a change that you want to accept, a single mouse click is all that is needed to insert the change.

Change tracking

A feature that tracks additions or deletions made by reviewers to a Word document, highlights the changes with revision marks, and enables the author or editor to accept or reject such revisions.

Working with tracked changes: the four tasks

Here are the four tasks that you need to be able to perform with Word's tracked changes feature:

- **Switch change tracking on and off**. Change tracking is not appropriate for every document that you and your colleagues work on. Exercise 11.1 shows you how to switch this feature on and off.

- **Hide and display change tracking as you work**. Word gives you the option of displaying or hiding revisions marks as you work. See Exercise 11.2.

- **Control how tracked changes are displayed**. As Exercise 11.3 shows, Word allows you customize the display of tracked changes.

- **Accept or reject tracked changes**. Some changes from reviewers you will want to accept; others you will want to reject. Exercise 11.4 takes you through the steps of performing both tasks.

Exercise 11.1: Switch change tracking on and off

By default, change tracking is not activated in Word. To use it, you first need to turn it on. When you no longer want to track your changes, you can turn it off again.

Before performing this exercise, start Word and open a new, blank document. Change tracking is available only when you have at least one document open.

Track Changes button

1) Double-click the **TRK** button on the Status Bar at the foot of the main Word window. Alternatively, click the **Track Changes** button on the Reviewing toolbar. Repeat this step to switch change tracking off again.

Exercise 11.2: Hide and display change tracking on screen

With change tracking switched on, you may not always want to view your revisions recorded on screen as you work. This exercise shows you how to hide or display change tracking as you type.

Before performing this Exercise, first open a new, blank Word document. The **Tools | Track Changes** menu command is available only when you have at least one document open.

1) Choose **Tools | Track Changes | Highlight Changes**.

2) As required, deselect or select the *Highlight changes on screen* checkbox.

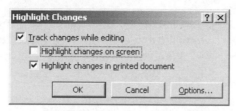

(Ensure that the *Track changes while editing* checkbox is selected.)

3) Click **OK**.

Exercise 11.3: Controlling how Word displays tracked changes

Revision marks indicate where a deletion, insertion or other editing change has been made in a document. This exercise shows how you can customize Word's display of revision marks.

Before performing this exercise, first open a new, blank Word document. The **Tools | Track Changes** menu command is available only when you have at least one document open.

1) Choose **Tools | Track Changes | Highlight Changes**, and click the **Options** button.

2) Word displays a dialog box that allows you to amend the mark and colour that you want applied to different kinds of revisions.

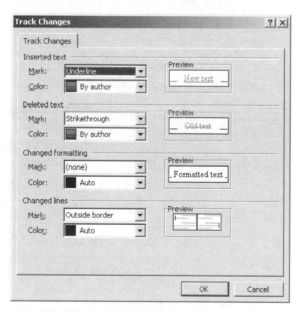

3) Make your amendments as required and click **OK, OK** to return to your document.

Accepting or rejecting tracked changes

You send a Word document to a reviewer. You ask the reviewer to make any edits directly in the document, with change tracking switched on. The reviewer then returns the document to you. What's next?

As the document author, you can use change tracking, in combination with another Word feature called compare documents, to:

- Identify the amendments made to a document.

- Accept or reject each amendment as appropriate, without having to retype amendments you accept.

> **Compare documents**
>
> *A feature that identifies differences between two open Word documents, typically the original document and a second, edited copy of the original.*

Exercise 11.4: Accept or reject tracked changes

In this exercise, you will open and work with two documents: an original document without tracked changes, and an edited document with tracked changes.

1) Open the following file, which represents the original, unedited document:

    Chapter11_Exercise_11_4_Original_Before.doc

2) Choose **Tools | Track Changes | Compare Documents**.

    Word opens the *Select File to Compare With Current Document* dialog box, prompting you to select the edited document against which you want to compare the original document. Select the following file and click **Open**:

    Chapter11_Exercise_11_4_Edited_Before.doc

    The first part of the original document should look like this:

    > **˙Elmsworth·Health·Trust:·Patients'·Charter**¶
    >
    > At·Elmsworth·Health·Trust↩·,·we·are·committed·to·delivering·a·world-class·service.· Our·standards·apply·whether·you·are:¶
    > • → A·patient¶
    > • → A·relative·or·friend·of·a·patient¶
    > • → Someone·simply·seeking·advice.¶
    > Our·This·Patient·Charter·sets·out·what·we·can·do·for·you·and·what·you·are·entitled·to.¶

    One way to accept or reject the reviewer's changes is to scroll through the document, locate each change, click anywhere in it, and then click the **Accept Change** or **Reject Change** button on the Reviewing toolbar.

Another method – one that gives you more information and options – is to choose **Tools | Track Changes | Accept or Reject Changes**. This displays the *Accept or Reject Changes* dialog box shown below.

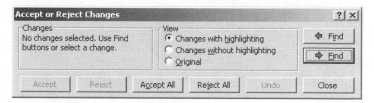

3) Click **-> Find** to tell Word to locate the first tracked change in the document.

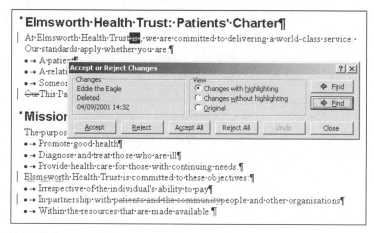

4) Click the **Accept** button to accept each change as Word leads you through the document.

5) When Word has presented you with all the tracked changes, it displays the following message box:

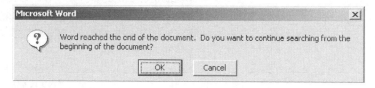

Click **Cancel**, and then click **Close** to close the *Accept or Reject Changes* dialog box.

6) Close and save your sample document under the following file name:

    Chapter11_Exercise_11_4_Final_Draft.doc

Chapter 11: quick reference

Button	Description
	Switches change tracking on or off.
	Moves the insertion point forward to the location of the next change in the document.
	Moves the insertion point back to the location of the previous change in the document.
	Accepts the selected change.
	Rejects the selected change.

Tasks summary

Task	Procedure
Turn change tracking on/off.	Double-click the **TRK** button on the Status Bar or click the **Track Changes** button on the Reviewing toolbar.
Show/hide revision marks on screen.	Choose **Tools	Track Changes	Highlight Changes**, select/deselect the *Highlight changes on screen* checkbox, and click **OK**.
Customize display of revision marks.	Choose **Tools	Track Changes	Highlight Changes**, click **Options**, customize the revision mark options, and click **OK**, **OK**.
Accept/reject tracked changes by comparing the original with the edited document.	Open the original document, choose **Tools	Track Changes	Compare Documents**, select the edited document and click **Open**.
	Choose **Tools	Track Changes	Accept or Reject Changes** and click **->Find**.
	Click **Accept** or **Reject** as Word leads you through the tracked changes in the document.
	When finished, click **Cancel** and **Close** when prompted.

Concepts summary

Change tracking is a feature that highlights amendments made to a Word with *revision marks*. New text is formatted in colour with underlining, and deleted text is formatted in colour with strikethrough. When different reviewers make changes to the same document, Word highlights each person's additions or deletions in a different colour.

Word flags all changes, whether additions or deletions, by positioning a *vertical bar* in the document's left margin. Word allows you to customize how you format the on-screen revision marks.

When you type and edit text with change tracking switched on, you may find the display of revision marks distracting. You can opt to hide the revision marks. Later, when you want to inspect your work, you can then switch them back on again.

An advantage of change tracking is that when used with the *compare documents* feature, it allows you to work with two documents – an original and an edited document – and selectively accept or reject changes made in the edited document.

Chapter 11: quick quiz

Circle the correct answer to each of the following multiple-choice questions about change tracking in Word.

Q1	Change tracking in Word is ...
A.	A feature that automatically corrects errors of spelling and grammar in a document.
B.	A feature that automatically generates a second copy of a document, and stores any changes separately in the second document.
C.	A feature that highlights changes with revision marks, and facilitates the acceptance or rejection of such changes.
D.	A feature that formats changes as hyperlinks, and offers the option to insert such changes by clicking on the hyperlinks.

Q2	By default, which revision mark does Word's change tracking feature use to indicate new text added to document?
A.	Colour with single-line underlining.
B.	Colour with double-line underlining.
C.	Colour with italics.
D.	Colour with strikethrough.

Q3	By default, which revision mark does Word's change tracking feature use to indicate text deleted from a document?
A.	Colour with single-line underlining.
B.	Colour with italics.
C.	Colour with bold.
D.	Colour with strikethrough.

Q4	By default, how does Word's change tracking feature indicate a change of any kind made to a document?
A.	Word places a grey background behind the amended text.
B.	Word places a vertical bar in the document's left margin.
C.	Word places a solid border around the amended text.
D.	Word places a vertical bar in the document's right margin.

Q5	Which action do you take to turn on change tracking in Word?
A.	Right-click the **TRK** button on the Status Bar at the foot of the main Word window.
B.	Choose **Tools	Change Tracking I On**.
C.	Double-click the **TRK** button on the Status Bar at the foot of the main Word window.
D.	Choose **Format	Track Changes**.

Q6	With change tracking switched on in Word, which action do you take to hide revision marks on the screen?
A.	Click the **Hide Revision Marks** button on the Reviewing toolbar.
B.	Choose **Tools	Track Changes	Highlight Changes**, deselect the *Highlight changes on screen* checkbox, and click **OK**.
C.	Double-click the **TRK** button on the Status Bar at the foot of the main Word window.
D.	Choose **Tools	Track Changes	Revision Marks**, deselect the *Highlight changes on screen* checkbox, and click **OK**.

Q7	In Word, which command do you choose to compare an original document with an edited copy of the same document?
A.	Open both documents, switch to the original document, and choose **Tools | Documents | Compare**.
B.	Open the edited document, choose **Tools | Track Changes | Compare Documents**, select the original document, and click **Open**.
C.	Open both documents, switch to the original document, and choose **Tools | Track Changes | Compare Documents**.
D.	Open the original document, choose **Tools | Track Changes | Compare Documents**, select the edited document, and click **Open**.

Q8	Which of the following is not an advantage of Word's change tracking feature?
A.	All amendments are highlighted, making them easier to locate.
B.	Errors in spelling and grammar are corrected automatically.
C.	The process of accepting or rejecting reviewers' amendments is simplified.
D.	All amendments are labelled with the identity of the reviewer, making document management easier.

Answers

1: C, **2:** A, **3:** D, **4:** B, **5:** C, **6:** B, **7:** D, **8:** B.

12

Many subdocuments, one document: master documents

What are master documents?

In Word, a *master document* is a file that can contain links to a series of individual Word documents called *subdocuments*. Master documents are used most commonly in networked environments because they enable different people on different PCs to work separately on different parts of a single large publication, such as a business plan, technical manual or annual report.

Master documents: the benefits to you

Imagine that you are a manager responsible for a publication project that consists of several, individual Word documents, some or all of which are written by different people. What benefits can you expect from using Word's master document feature?

- **Consistent style formatting**. Because all subdocuments are based on the template of the master document, it is easier for the manager to enforce common formatting standards throughout all the subdocuments in the publication.

- **Multi-document editing**. The manager can open and display all subdocuments in the master document at once, rearrange their order, and move text and graphics within and between subdocuments.

- **Automatic updating**. When any material is moved within or between subdocuments in the master document, Word automatically updates all numbered headings, footnotes, cross-references and page numbers to reflect their new location.

- **Multi-document navigation**.A single table of contents and index can be created and kept up to date for all the subdocuments in the master document.

- **Multi-document printing**. The manager can print all subdocuments in the master document in a single operation.

Different writers who work on individual subdocuments also gain from the use of the master document feature:

- **File size efficiency**. It is easier and faster to work on a small Word document than on a large one: the file opens and saves more quickly, and there is less need to navigate through large amounts of text.

- **Parallel production**. Individual writers can work on different subdocuments at the same time and focus only on their own contribution.

Master documents	Master documents are very similar to outlines: the publication
and outlines	manager works with master documents in Outline view, and the
	options needed are available as buttons on the Outlining toolbar.

You will learn the purpose of the toolbar buttons as you use them in the exercises. A list of buttons and their functions is included at the end of this chapter for easy reference.

> ### Master documents
>
> *A Word file that can act as a container for one or more individual Word documents, called subdocuments. Within a master document, subdocuments can be opened, formatted and edited as if they were single documents.*

Working with master documents: the four tasks

Here are the four master document tasks that you need to be able to perform:

- **Create a new master document and new subdocuments**. Exercise 12.1 shows you how to create a new master document, and then create subdocuments within it.

- **Create a new master document with inserted subdocuments**. In Exercise 12.2, you create a new master document by inserting existing Word documents as subdocuments within the master document.

- **Add a subdocument to a master document**. The procedure for adding subdocuments to a master document is similar to that for creating a master document by the insertion of subdocuments. See Exercise 12.3.

- **Remove a subdocument from a master document**. No longer need a subdocument within a master document? Exercise 12.4 shows you how to remove a subdocument.

Working with new master documents

In effect, a master document is a Word document that contains one or more subdocuments. Word allows you to create subdocuments, and as a result, transform your currently open document into a master document, in either of two ways. You can convert outline headings to new subdocuments or insert existing documents as subdocuments. Let's examine each approach in more detail.

Converting outline headings to new subdocuments

Here are the main steps in this approach:

- You begin by creating a new document or opening an existing one. This document will become your master document.

- You switch to Outline view. If this is a new document, you create your outline headings. If it is an existing document, you ensure that your headings are formatted with heading styles.

Create Subdocument button

- Finally, you designate some or all of your outline headings as subdocuments by selecting them and clicking the **Create Subdocument** button on the Outlining toolbar.

Because your current document now contains subdocuments, it is a master document.

Exercise 12.1 provides an example of this approach.

Inserting existing documents as subdocuments

Here are the main steps in this approach:

- You create a new document or open an existing one.

- You switch to Outline view.

Insert Subdocument button

- You insert one or more existing Word documents as subdocuments in your open document. You do this using the **Insert Subdocument** button on the Outlining toolbar.

This is the approach that you follow in Exercise 12.2.

Which is the better way to create master documents?

Creating an outline and then converting the outline headings to subdocuments gives you more control over the document management process. In practice, however, a publication manager is often asked to build a master document from a number of already-written documents.

On many occasions, a hybrid approach may be necessary: you may begin with a new outline, convert some outline headings to subdocuments, and then insert some already-written documents into your master document.

Saving a master document

You save a master document as you would any Word document – by pressing **CTRL+S**, clicking the **Save** button on the Standard toolbar, or choosing **File | Save** – but the effect is very different.

When you save a master document containing outline headings that you have selected for conversion to subdocuments, Word:

- Creates a new, separate file for each subdocument.

- Assigns subdocument file names based on the text of the outline headings.

- Stores the subdocuments in the same folder as the master document.

If you are managing a multi-author document on a PC network, it's a good idea to create a special folder for holding the master document and the subdocuments, and inform your colleagues of its location.

Exercise 12.1: Convert outline headings to subdocuments

In this exercise you, will open a Word document, display it in Outline view, designate all the level-1 headings as subdocuments, and then save it as a master document with subdocuments.

1) Open Word and open the following Word file:

    Chapter12_Exercise_12-1_Before.doc

2) Choose **View | Outline**. As you can see, the document has been formatted using Word styles that display as outline headings in Outline view.

    You want to split your open document into a series of smaller subdocuments, with each level-1 heading indicating the start of a new subdocument.

3) Click the **Show Heading 1** button on the Outlining toolbar so that Word displays only level-1 headings.

Create Subdocument button

4) Select the four level-1 headings by dragging across them with the mouse.

5) Click the **Create Subdocument** button on the Outlining toolbar.

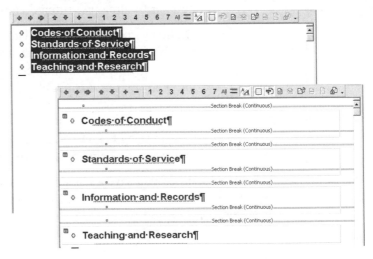

Word converts your selected outline headings to subdocuments.

Notice that it separates the subdocuments with continuous section breaks, surrounds each subdocument with a thin, grey border, and displays a subdocument icon at the top-left corner of each subdocument.

6) Click the **Show Heading 3** button on the Outlining toolbar to see how Word displays the subdocuments in this view.

The section breaks are not shown, but a grey border still surrounds each subdocument.

7) Click the **Show All Headings** button on the Outlining toolbar to see how Word displays the subdocuments.

Both the sections breaks and the grey borders are shown in this view.

8) Save your new master document with the following file name, and close it:

```
Chapter12_Exercise_12-1_After_Your_Name.doc
```

In the final stage of this exercise, you will open your saved master document and verify that Word created the subdocuments as separate files.

9) Open the master document that you saved and named in step 8. It should look like this.

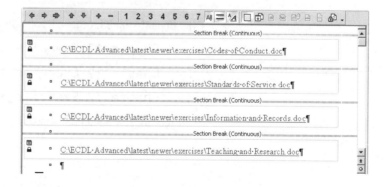

(The file path names may be different on your PC.)

10) Close your master document. Using Windows Explorer or My Computer, verify that the subdocument files, shown in your master document, actually exist on your PC.

In Exercise 12.1, you converted all level-1 headings in the outline to subdocuments. Word allows you to convert one or a selection of heading levels to a subdocument or subdocuments:

- **Single outline heading**. You can select and then convert any individual outline heading to a subdocument.

- **Selection of outline headings**. You can select and then convert a group of outline headings to subdocuments. Ensure that the *first* heading in your selection is in the heading level you want to use for splitting your document.

  For example, if you select a number of headings, the first one of which is at heading level 2, Word creates a new subdocument for every heading level 2 in your selection, even if the selection contains text formatted with heading level 1.

Exercise 12.2: Insert existing documents as subdocuments

In this exercise, you insert existing Word documents as subdocuments within a new, blank document, and then save the document as a master document.

1) Open a new, blank document and choose **View | Outline**.

Insert Subdocument button

2) On the Outlining toolbar, click the **Insert Subdocument** button to display the *Insert Subdocument* dialog box.

3) Select the following document and click the **Open** button:

   `Chapter12_Exercise_12-2_SubDoc1`

   Word inserts the selected file and moves the insertion point to the next line.

4) Repeat step 3 for the following documents:

   `Chapter12_Exercise_12-2_SubDoc2`

   `Chapter12_Exercise_12-2_SubDoc2`

   `Chapter12_Exercise_12-2_SubDoc4`

   Your master document should now look like this.

Codes·of·Conduct¶

——————————————————Section Break (Continuous)——————————————————

——————————————————Section Break (Continuous)——————————————————

Standards·of·Service¶

——————————————————Section Break (Continuous)——————————————————

——————————————————Section Break (Continuous)——————————————————

Information·and·Records¶

——————————————————Section Break (Continuous)——————————————————

——————————————————Section Break (Continuous)——————————————————

Teaching·and·Research¶

¶

5) Save your document with the following name and close it:

    Chapter12_Exercise_12-2_After_*Your_Name*.doc

6) Open your saved master document. You should see the subdocuments as hyperlinked path and file names. As a test, click once on any subdocument to open it.

7) Close your master document and close the open subdocument.

Working with existing master documents

Here are some important points about working with master documents and subdocuments:

- **Displaying subdocuments within the master document**. When you open a master document in Outline view, the subdocuments are hidden – that is, they are collapsed into the master document and displayed only as hyperlinks.

Expand Subdocuments button

Collapse Subdocuments button

  When the subdocuments are hidden, click the **Expand Subdocuments** button to view them. You can then switch to Normal or Print Layout view, as required.

  To hide the subdocuments, click the **Collapse Subdocuments** button. The subdocuments appear as hyperlinked file names. Click on a hyperlink for Word to display a subdocument in a separate document window.

- **Working with a subdocument in the master document**. As a publication manager, you will typically work with subdocuments from within the master document.

  If the subdocuments are collapsed, just click on a subdocument name to display it. If they are expanded, switch to Normal or Print Layout view.

- **Working with subdocuments as separate files**. Individual writers open and work with subdocuments as separate Word files rather than from within the master document.

Locking subdocuments

Whenever you open a master document in Outline view, Word displays a small padlock icon to the left of each subdocument.

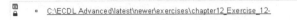
C:\ECDL Advanced\latest\newer\exercises\chapter12_Exercise_12-

This indicates that Word has *locked* the subdocuments so that they can be displayed but not modified.

Click the **Expand Subdocuments** button on the Outlining toolbar to unlock the subdocuments. If any subdocument remains locked, it is because another person is working on it, or the author has password-protected it, or it is in a folder to which you have read-only access.

Unlock/Lock Document button

You can attempt to unlock a locked document by clicking the **Unlock/Lock Document** button on the Outlining toolbar.

Subdocument locations and filenames

It is important that individual authors do not save subdocuments to a different location or rename them. If they do, the links to the subdocuments within the master document are no longer valid, and the subdocuments disappear from the master document.

Exercise 12.3: Adding and removing subdocuments

You can add further subdocuments to a master document at any stage. The procedure is similar to the one you followed in Exercise 12.2 for building a master document by inserting subdocuments.

1) Open the master document that you created and saved in Exercise 12.2. Word opens the document in Outline view.

Expand Subdocuments button

2) Click the **Expand Subdocuments** button on the Outlining toolbar.

3) In this example, you want to add a Word document as the new third subdocument in the master document. It will be located after the 'Standards of Service' subdocument and before the 'Information and Records' subdocument.

Click on the section break before the location where you want to insert the additional subdocument.

4) Press the **Enter** key to insert a new paragraph mark.

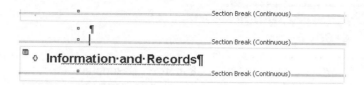

5) With the insertion point positioned at the new paragraph mark, click the **Insert Subdocument** button on the Outlining toolbar.

Insert Subdocument button

In the *Insert Subdocument* dialog box, select the following document and click **Open**:

```
Chapter12_Exercise_12-3_SubDocNew.doc
```

Word inserts your selected document as a subdocument within the master document.

6) Close and save your document with the following name:

```
Chapter12_Exercise_12-3_After_Your_Name.doc
```

Exercise 12.4: Removing a subdocument from a master document

1) Open the master document that you saved in Exercise 12.3. Word opens the document in Outline view.

2) Click the **Expand Subdocuments** button on the Outlining toolbar.

Expand Subdocuments button

3) Click the icon for the subdocument that you want to remove. In this example, click the icon to the left of the third subdocument, as shown.

Remove Subdocument button

4) Click the **Remove Subdocument** button on the Outlining toolbar.

5) Close and save your document with the following name.

```
Chapter12_Exercise_12-4_After_Your_Name.doc
```

Word breaks the connection between the removed subdocument and the master document, but the subdocument's content remains in the master document. You can delete some or all of this content from the master document, as required. If you no longer need a subdocument file, use My Computer or Windows Explorer to delete it.

Chapter 12: quick reference

Outlining toolbar: master document and subdocument buttons

Button	Description
	Creates subdocument(s) from the selected outline heading(s).
	Displays a dialog box that allows you to insert a Word document as a subdocument of the currently open document.
	Expands the subdocuments of the current master document so you can view and work with their content in Outline, Normal or Print Layout view.
	Collapses the subdocuments of the currently open master document. Word displays only the path and file names of the subdocuments as hyperlinks.

Tasks summary

Task	Procedure
Designate an outline heading as a subdocument.	Select the outline heading and click the **Create Subdocument** button on the Outlining toolbar.
Insert a subdocument in an outline.	Position the insertion point at the location where you want to insert the subdocument, click the **Insert Subdocument** button on the Outlining toolbar, select the Word document, and click **Open**.
Expand/collapse subdocuments.	In Outline view, click the **Expand Subdocuments** or **Collapse Subdocuments** button on the Outlining toolbar.
Add a subdocument to a master document.	In Outline view, click on the section break before the location where you want to insert the subdocument, press **Enter**, click the **Insert Subdocument** button on the Outlining toolbar, select the Word document, and click **Open**.
Remove a subdocument from a master document.	In Outline view, click the icon for the subdocument that you want to remove, and click the **Remove Subdocument** button on the Outlining toolbar.

Word's *master document* feature enables a publication manager to open, display, format and create a table of contents and index for several individual Word documents as if they were a single document.

The individual Word documents are called *subdocuments*. The containing document that integrates the subdocuments is called the *master document*.

You work with a master document in *Outline view*, and use the relevant buttons on the *Outlining toolbar*. You can create a master document in two ways: by *converting outline headings* to subdocuments, or *inserting existing Word documents* as subdocuments.

When you save a master document containing outline headings that have been converted to subdocuments, Word creates a new, separate file for each subdocument, assigns subdocument file names based on the text of the outline headings, and stores the subdocuments in the same folder as the master document.

Different contributors to a publication can open and work on different subdocuments simultaneously. The publication manager, however, typically works on subdocuments from within the master document.

When a master document is opened, Word displays only a hyperlinked path and file name for each subdocument. Click a hyperlink to open the subdocument in its own window. To work on the master document as a whole, click the **Expand Subdocuments** button on the Outlining toolbar and switch to Normal or Print Layout view.

Chapter 12: quick quiz

Circle the correct answer to each of the following multiple-choice questions about master documents and subdocuments in Word.

Q1	In Word, a master document is ...
A.	A Word file that contains style definitions and standard text that can be used in multiple Word documents.
B.	A Word document that has been checked for errors in spelling and grammar and that is formatted with styles.
C.	A Word file that contains one or more individual Word documents, called subdocuments.
D.	A Word document that has been saved with the **File	Save As Master Document**.

Q2	In Word, which of the following is not an advantage of using the master document feature?
A.	Word automatically generates and displays version numbers in the headers of all subdocuments in the master document.
B.	A single table of contents and index can be generated for all subdocuments in the master document.
C.	Consistent style formatting because all subdocuments are based on the template of the master document.
D.	All the subdocuments can be edited as a single file.

Q3	In Word, which document view do you use when working with master documents and subdocuments?
A.	Print Layout view.
B.	Outline view.
C.	Master view.
D.	Master Document view.

Q4	In Word, which of the following statements about subdocuments is untrue?
A.	The document manager typically views and works with subdocuments from within the master document.
B.	Individual writers can open and work with subdocuments just as they would regular Word documents.
C.	Different writers can work on different subdocuments of the same master document simultaneously.
D.	Subdocuments can be opened as individual Word documents; but they can be edited and formatted only from within the master document.

Q5	In Word Outline view, which action do you take to designate a selected outline heading as a subdocument?
A.	Click the **Create Subdocument** button on the Outlining toolbar.
B.	Press **Shift+Tab**.
C.	Click the **Convert to Subdocument** button on the Master Document toolbar.
D.	Click the **New Subdocument** button on the Master Document toolbar.

Q6	In Word, what happens when you save a new master document containing outline headings that you have designated as new subdocuments?
A.	Word saves the master document and all the designated subdocuments within a new file.
B.	Word saves the master document and creates a new, separate file for each subdocument.
C.	Word saves the master document in one file and all the designated subdocuments in a second file.
D.	Word saves only the master document.

Q7	In Word Outline view, which action do you take to insert a Word document as a subdocument in a master document?
A.	Click the **New Subdocument** button on the Master Document toolbar, select the document, and click **Insert**.
B.	Click **Insert+Tab**.
C.	Choose **File	Insert	Subdocument**, select the Word document, and click **OK**.
D.	Click the **Create Subdocument** button on the Outlining toolbar, select the document, and click **Open**.

Q.8	What type of break does Word insert between subdocuments in a master document?
A.	A continuous section break.
B.	An odd page break.
C.	An odd page section break.
D.	An even page break.

Q.9	By default, how does Word display a master document when it is opened?
A.	Word displays the first heading level only for each subdocument.
B.	Subdocuments are show only as hyperlinked file names.
C.	Word displays the first three heading levels only for each subdocument.
D.	Subdocuments are shown only as hyperlinked file and path names.

Q.10	On Word's Outlining toolbar, which button do you click to designate an outline heading as a new subdocument?
A.	
B.	
C.	
D.	

Q11	On Word's Outlining toolbar, which button do you click to insert a Word document as a subdocument in a master document?
A.	
B.	
C.	
D.	

Q12	On Word's Outlining toolbar, which button do you click to view the subdocuments within a master document?
A.	
B.	
C.	
D.	

Answers

1: C, **2:** A, **3:** B, **4:** D, **5:** A, **6:** B, **7:** D, **8:** A, **9:** D, **10:** A, **11:** B, **12:** C.

13 'Please complete and return': Word forms

Syllabus reference	In this chapter you will cover the following items from the ECDL Advanced Word Processing Syllabus:

- **AM3.4.2.1**. Create and edit a form.

- **AM3.4.2.2**. Use available form field options: text field, checkbox, drop-down menu, and so on.

- **AM3.4.2.3**. Delete fields in a form.

- **AM3.4.2.4**. Protect a form.

So many forms, so little time

How many forms have you completed in your life? The answer is probably 'a lot' (or perhaps 'too many'). Typically, forms are of two main types:

- **Paper-based forms**. Examples include applications (for organization membership, for bank loans and mortgages), compliance documents (for employers and regulators), and satisfaction questionnaires (for customers).

- **Web-based forms**. Some websites ask you to complete an online form in which you reveal details of your personal or business interests. If you purchase a product over the web, you are typically requested to type your credit card details into an online form.

Now meet a third type of form: a Word form.

Word forms: how they are different

What makes a Word form different from a regular Word file? A Word form has identifying features:

- **Form fields**. It contains *interactive* areas called form fields in which users can type information.

- **Protection**. A Word form is a *protected* document. The result is that users can only input text and select options – they cannot amend the form content or layout.

- **Templates**. A Word form is made available as a template. When users open the template, Word opens a *copy of the form* on their screens, ready for them to complete.

In summary, if a Word file is a template, is protected, and contains form fields, it's a form.

Form fields

Word offers three types of form fields – text, drop-down list and checkboxes.

- **Text form fields**. These are blank boxes in which users type details such as their name, address, age, etc. In this context, the term 'text' also includes numbers and dates.

- **Drop-down form fields**. These display a list of preset choices from which a user may select only one.

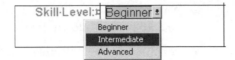

- **Checkbox form fields**. These enable you to offer users the ability to select more than one option from a given list.

Drop-down and checkbox form fields offer advantages for both the form creator and the form users:

- **For the form creator**. As you specify the options from which users may choose, you eliminate the risk of typos or other 'bad data' in your form.

- **For form users**. They help users to complete the form quickly and with a minimum of typing. Also, users need not remember the names of your products or services.

You will learn more about each type of form field later in this chapter.

Form field

An interactive area in a Word form where users type information in response to a question or indicate an appropriate response by choosing from drop-down lists or a series of checkboxes.

The Forms toolbar

As a form creator, you work with form fields using Word's Forms toolbar. To display this Toolbar, choose **View | Toolbars | Forms**.

You will learn the purpose of each Forms toolbar button as you use it in the exercises.

You work with the parts of a form that are not form fields – the identifying text, instructions and questions – in the same way as you would work with text in a non-form Word document. You can also insert pictures and other graphics (such as a company logo) in a form.

Typically, tables are used when creating Word forms as they help the form creator to position questions and form fields left to right across the page.

> **Word form**
>
> *A Word file that contains form fields, is protected, and is made available as a template. Form fields and descriptive text are typically arranged using one or more Word tables.*

Word forms: the lifecycle

Consider the stages in the life of a Word form:

- **Form creation**. Someone creates a Word form using the Form toolbar for the form fields and Word's text editing, formatting, tables and graphics features for the remainder of the form.

- **Form distribution**. Two options here: *physical* (passing the form around on a diskette) or *network-based* (making the form available for downloading from a server or attaching it to an e-mail.)

- **Form completion**. Users open a copy of the form based on the form template, and 'fill in' and 'tick' the form fields, as appropriate.

- **Form collection**. Users return the completed form document, typically by the same means as they received it.

- **Data collation**. Someone extracts the users' responses from the returned Word forms. The collated responses are typically inserted into a database for reporting and analysis.

This chapter is essentially about learning two skills:

- The ability to choose the correct type of form field for a particular information-gathering task.

- The ability to use the options available on the Forms toolbar and the form field dialog boxes.

Working with forms: the six tasks

Here are the six tasks that you need to be able to perform with forms in Word:

- **Create a new form**. Exercise 13.1 takes you through the steps of inserting form fields in a Word document.

- **Protect a form**. In Exercises 13.2 and 13.3, you discover how to protect a form, without and with a password.

- **Work with text fields**. Learn how to manipulate form fields of this type in Exercises 13.4 and 13.5.

- **Work with drop-down list fields**. See Exercise 13.6.

- **Work with checkbox fields**. See Exercise 13.7.

- **Delete form fields**. See Exercise 13.8.

Working with new forms

In the first exercise, you will open a Word document and insert text, drop-down and checkbox form fields into it. The document already contains labels – text that identifies the purpose of each form field. A table is used to position both the field labels and the form fields.

Exercise 13.1: Creating a New Form

1) Start Word and open the following file:

    Chapter13_Exercise_13-1_Before.doc

2) Choose **View | Toolbars | Forms**.

3) Click in the second cell of the first row.

4) Click the **Text Form Field** button on the Forms toolbar.

    Word displays your inserted text form field as a grey rectangle containing a number of hollow dots.

5) Click in the fourth cell of the first row.

6) Click the **Text Form Field** button on the Forms toolbar. The first row of your table should now look like this:

---

ab|

Text Form Field button

7) Click in the second cell of the third row.

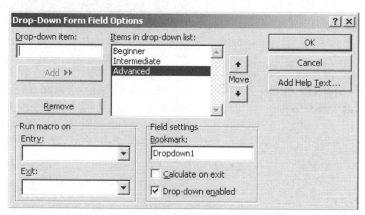

Click here

***Drop Down Form
Field button***

8) Click the **Drop-Down Form Field** button on the Forms toolbar.

Word displays your inserted drop-down form field as a solid grey rectangle.

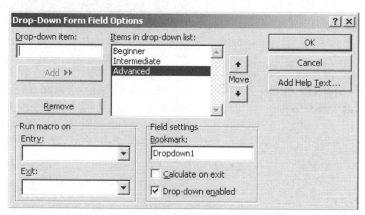

***Form Field
Options button***

9) Click anywhere in your drop-down list and click the **Form Field Options** button on the Forms toolbar. Alternatively, right-click on the field and choose **Properties** from the pop-up menu displayed.

In the *Drop-down item* box, type the three options, 'Beginner', 'Intermediate' and 'Advanced', clicking the **Add** button after each one.

When finished, click **OK** to close the dialog box.

10) On the third row, click in the cell to the right of the word 'Amex'.

Click here ───────

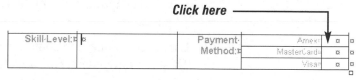

11) Click the **Check Box Form Field** button on the Forms toolbar.

Word displays your inserted checkbox form field as a grey square block containing a smaller, hollow black square.

***Check Box
Form Field
button***

12) Repeat step 11 in the cells to the right of the words 'MasterCard' and 'Visa'. Your document should look like this:

TRAINING·BOOKING·FORM¶

First·Name:¤	¤¤¤¤¤¤ ¤		Surname:¤	¤¤¤¤¤¤ ¤		¤
¤	¤		¤	¤		¤
Skill·Level:¤	¤		Payment· Method:¤	Amex¤	☐ ¤	¤
				MasterCard¤	☐ ¤	¤
				Visa¤	☐ ¤	¤

13) Close and save your sample document with the following name:

Chapter13_Exercise_13-1_After_*Your_Name*.doc

Checkboxes and exclusive options

In Exercise 13.1, you used checkboxes for the credit card options. These are *exclusive* choices: you want your form users to select only *one* credit card. A drop-down list is a safer choice for such a purpose, as it prevents users from incorrectly selecting more than one option.

For form users, however, checkboxes are more convenient, because they need to click just once to indicate a choice. A drop-down list demands that users click twice – once to open the list, and a second time to select the required option.

Working with form protection

The form that you created and saved in Exercise 13.1 is not yet interactive. That is, information cannot be typed into its text fields, nor can options be selected from its drop-down or checkbox fields. A form becomes interactive only after it has been *protected*.

Word offers you two ways of protecting a form:

- **Without a password**. A form that is protected without a password can be unprotected by anyone.

- **With a password**. A form that is protected with a password can be unprotected only by someone who knows the correct password.

Users cannot alter the content or layout of a protected form. They can only interact with its form fields.

Which type of protection is better? Typically, the form creator first protects the form without a password and then tests the form's fields. When the creator is satisfied that the fields work correctly, he or she then applies password protection to the form, saves it as a template, and makes it available for use.

In the next two exercises, you apply protection to a form without and with a password.

Exercise 13.2: Protecting a form without a password

1) Open the following Word file:

    Chapter13_Exercise_13-2_Before.doc

    Is the Forms toolbar displayed? If not, choose **View | Toolbars | Forms**.

Protect Form button

2) Click the **Protect Form** button on the Forms toolbar.

    Alternatively, choose **Tools | Protect Document** to display the *Protect Document* dialog box. In the *Protect document for* area, select *Forms* and click **OK**.

    Your form is now protected. Let's check that its fields work correctly.

3) Click in the *First Name* field and type 'Charles'. Press **Tab** to move the insertion to the *Surname* field and type 'Kennedy'.

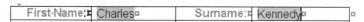

4) Click anywhere in the *Skill Level* field. Notice that Word displays a drop-down list. Select the *Advanced* option.

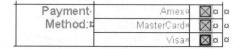

5) In the *Payment Method* area of your form, click in each of the three credit card fields. Notice that Word displays an 'X' in each field that you click on.

Payment· Method:¤	Amex¤	☒ ¤	¤
	MasterCard¤	☒ ¤	¤
	Visa¤	☒ ¤	¤

6) Your form appears to work correctly. Before continuing further, you need to remove the test information.

    Click again in each credit card field to deselect it. Click in the *Skill Level* drop-down list and select the *Beginner option*. Click in the *First Name* and *Surname* fields and use the **Backspace** or **Delete** keys to remove the text.

7) Close and save your sample protected form with the following name:

    Chapter13_Exercise_13-2_After_*Your_Name*.doc

Exercise 13.3: Protecting a form with a password

1) Open the following Word file:

    Chapter13_Exercise_13-3_Before.doc

    Is the Forms toolbar displayed? If not, choose **View | Toolbars | Forms**.

Protect Form button

2) The form is currently protected *without* a password. Your first task is to unprotect it.

Click the **Protect Form** button on the Forms toolbar. Alternatively, choose **Tools | Unprotect Document**. You have removed the protection from the form.

3) Choose **Tools | Protect Document** to display the *Protect Document* dialog box.

4) In the *Protect document for* area, select *Forms*. Type the password 'hello', and click **OK**.

5) Word prompts you to re-enter your password.

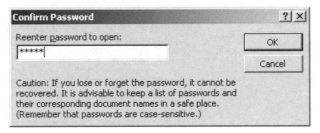

Type 'hello' again and click **OK**.

6) Close and save your password-protected form with the following name:

`Chapter13_Exercise_13-3_After_`*`Your_Name`*`.doc`

You can unprotect the form at any time by choosing **Tools | Unprotect Document** and entering the correct password when prompted.

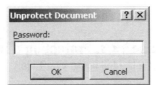

You cannot apply or remove password protection by using the **Protect Form** button on the Forms toolbar. You must use the **Tools | Protect Document** or **Tools | Unprotect Document** command on the Tools menu. The **Protect Form** button applies or removes only non-password protection.

Form fields and default values

To speed up users' completion of a form, you can provide preset responses – *default values* – in your form fields.

Text fields may contain default text, numbers or dates. In a drop-down list, the first item is selected by default; a checkbox may be defined as selected.

Default value

In a Word form, a choice made by the form creator when the user does not type information, or select an alternative answer or option.

Working with text form fields

Text form fields offer a range of attributes. For example, you can specify the type of text that users may enter (options include regular text, a date, a number or a calculation), the maximum number of characters, and the text case. The full list of options for text form fields is shown at the end of this chapter.

Text form field

In a Word form, an area in which users can type a text response to a question or instruction. Depending on the format specified, the field can contain alphanumeric characters, numbers only, dates, times or calculations.

Exercise 13.4: Working with text form fields

In this exercise, you will amend the properties of text form fields in a Word form.

1) Open the following Word file:

    Chapter13_Exercise_13-4_Before.doc

    Is the Forms toolbar displayed? If not, choose **View | Toolbars | Forms**.

2) A text form field is located to the right of the words 'Invoice Number:'. Right-click on it and choose the **Properties** command from the pop-up menu.

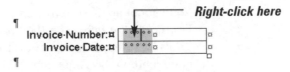

Right-click here

Word displays the *Text Form Field Options* dialog box.

In the *Type* box, select the *Number* option and click **OK**.

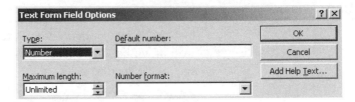

3) Right-click in the text form field to the right of 'Invoice Date:' and choose the **Properties** command.

    In the *Type* box, select the *Current date* option. In the *Date format* box, select *dd/MM/yyyy* and click **OK**.

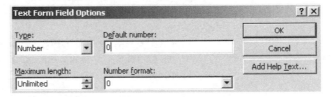

4) Right-click in the text form field beneath the 'Qty' heading and choose the **Properties** command.

    In the *Type* box, select the *Number* option. In the *Default number* box, type 0; in the *Number format* box, select 0. Click **OK**.

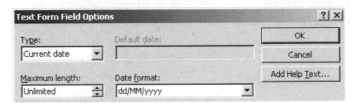

5) Select the text form field that you amended in step 4 by dragging across it.

    Press **Ctrl+C** and use **Ctrl+V** to paste it successively in each of the other five cells in the 'Qty' column. Your fields should look like this:

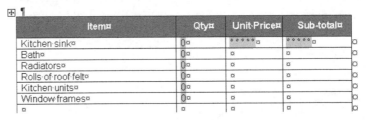

Item¤	Qty¤	Unit·Price¤	Sub-total¤	
Kitchen·sink¤	0¤	° ° ° ° °¤	° ° ° ° °¤	¤
Bath¤	0¤	¤	¤	¤
Radiators¤	0¤	¤	¤	¤
Rolls·of·roof·felt¤	0¤	¤	¤	¤
Kitchen·units¤	0¤	¤	¤	¤
Window·frames¤	0¤	¤	¤	¤
¤	¤	¤	¤	¤

ECDL Advanced Word Processing

6) Right-click in the text form field beneath the 'Unit Price' heading and choose the **Properties** command.

In the *Type* box, select the *Number* option. In the *Default number* box, type 0. In the *Number format* box, select the currency option – it's displayed as £#,##0.00;(£#,##0.00). Click **OK**.

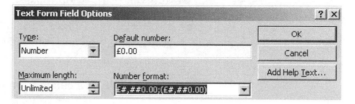

7) Select the text form field that you amended in step 6 by dragging across it.

Press **Ctrl+C** and use **Ctrl+V** to paste it successively in each of the other five cells in the 'Unit Price' column.

8) Right-click in the text form field beneath the 'Sub-total' heading and choose the **Properties** command.

9) In the *Type* box, select the *Number* option. In the *Default number* box, type 0. In the *Number format* box, select the currency option. Click **OK**.

10) Select the text form field that you amended in step 9 by dragging across it.

Press **Ctrl+C**, and use **Ctrl+V** to paste it successively in each of the other five cells in the 'Sub-total' column. Also, paste it in the *Total* field at the bottom right of the form. Your fields should look like this:

Item¤	Qty¤	Unit·Price¤	Sub-total¤	
Kitchen·sink¤	0¤	£0.00¤	£0.00¤	¤
Bath¤	0¤	£0.00¤	£0.00¤	¤
Radiators¤	0¤	£0.00¤	£0.00¤	¤
Rolls·of·roof·felt¤	0¤	£0.00¤	£0.00¤	¤
Kitchen·units¤	0¤	£0.00¤	£0.00¤	¤
Window·frames¤	0¤	£0.00¤	£0.00¤	¤
¤	¤	¤	¤	¤
¤	¤	¤	¤	¤
¤	¤	¤	¤	¤
¤	¤	¤	¤	¤
Total¤	¤	¤	£0.00¤	¤

11) Click the **Protect Form** button on the Forms toolbar to protect your form.

12) Close and save your sample form with the following name:

Chapter13_Exercise_13-4_After_*Your_Name*.doc

Calculations in text form fields

The form that you created in Exercise 13.4 does not take advantage of a very useful type of text form field – the *calculation* type. This field type can generate a result based on values entered by the form user in other fields of the form.

By inserting text form fields of the calculation type, your Word form can act like an Excel worksheet. As with formulas and functions in Excel, calculation fields in Word always being within an equals (=) sign. How do you identify which fields in your form contain the values needed to generate the result? Word gives you two options:

- **Table cell references**. If your form fields are located in a Word table, you can reference the cells in the table in the same way as you would the cells in an Excel worksheet.

    An example of a calculation using table cell references is:

    =SUM(C1:C4)

    In this instance, C1 is the cell in the third column of the first row, and C4 is the cell in the third column of the fourth row.

- **Form field bookmarks**. Word automatically assigns a bookmark name to each form field that you insert. You can view a form field's bookmark by selecting it and clicking the **Form Field Options** button on the Forms toolbar.

An example of a calculation using bookmarks is:

    =SUM(Text5:Text8)

To use a form field as the basis for a calculation, you must select the *Calculate on exit* checkbox for that field. You do not select this checkbox for the field that performs the actual calculation. Exercise 13.5 provides an example of calculation-type text form fields in action.

Exercise 13.5: Working with calculations in text form fields

1) Open the following Word file:

    Chapter13_Exercise_13-5_Before.doc

    Is the Forms toolbar displayed? If not, choose **View | Toolbars | Forms**.

2) In turn, click on each of the six fields in the 'Qty' column of the form, click the **Form Field Options** button on the Forms toolbar, select the *Calculate on exit* checkbox, and click **OK**.

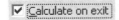

3) Repeat step 2 for each of the six fields in the 'Unit Price' column.

4) Click on the first field in the 'Sub-total' column beneath the column heading, click the **Form Field Options** button on the Forms toolbar, change the *Type* from *Number* to *Calculation*, and type the following in the *Expression* box:

    =b2*c2

Cell references b2 and c2 represent the cells in the 'Qty' and 'Unit Price' columns of the same row of the table. Do not select the *Calculate on exit* option. Notice that the *Fill-in enabled* option is deselected.

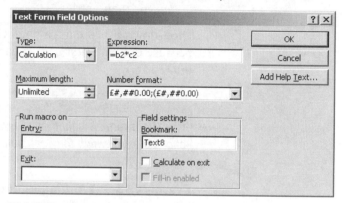

Click **OK** to close the dialog box.

5) Repeat step 4 for the other five cells in the 'Sub-total' column, but type different cell references in the *Expression* box for each cell, as follows:

    =b3*c3
    =b4*c4
    =b5*c5
    =b6*c6
    =b7*c7

6) Click in the *Total* cell at the bottom right of your form, change the *Type* from *Number* to *Calculation*, and type the following in the *Expression* box:

    =sum(d2:d7)

Click **OK** to close the dialog box.

7) Click the **Protect Form** button on the Forms toolbar to protect your document without a password.

8) Close and save your sample document with the following name:

    Chapter13_Exercise_13-5_After_*Your_Name*.doc

9) Open your form and type some sample numbers and amounts in the 'Qty' and 'Unit Price' columns. Press the **Tab** key to move from one cell to the next.

Notice that Word generates new results in the 'Sub-total' column each time you enter or amend values in the 'Qty' or 'Unit Price' columns. You can close your form without saving it.

Working with drop-down form fields

A drop-down form field lets users select *one option* from a list of mutually exclusive alternatives. Drop-down form fields help to:

■ Ensure accuracy, because users do not need to remember product or service names.

■ Eliminate the risk of typos, because form users do not need to type their entries

Drop-down lists are not a good choice for printed forms because only the first item in each list will appear on the printed form.

Drop-down form field

In a Word form, a field that allows users to display a list of choices from which they can select a single response.

Exercise 13.6: Working with drop-down form fields
In this exercise, you will insert one drop-down form field, change the order of items in a second field, and remove and add items in a third field.

1) Open the following file:

    Chapter13_Exercise_13-6_Before.doc

    Is the Forms toolbar displayed? If not, display it now.

2) Click in the cell beneath the 'Flying To:' heading.

Click here

**Drop-Down Form
Field button**

**Form Field
Options button**

3) Click the **Drop-Down Form Field** button on the Forms toolbar. Word displays your inserted drop-down form field as a solid grey rectangle.

4) With the insertion point in the cell containing the field that you inserted in step 2, click the **Form Field Options** button on the Forms toolbar. Word displays the *Drop-Down Form Field Options* dialog box.

5) In the *Drop-down item* box, type the following locations, clicking the **Add** button after each one:

```
Berlin
Cork
Frankfurt
Glasgow
```

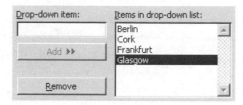

When finished, click **OK** to close the dialog box.

6) Right-click on the field in the field beneath the 'Departure Month' heading and choose **Properties** from the pop-up menu displayed. Word displays the *Drop-Down Form Field Options* dialog box.

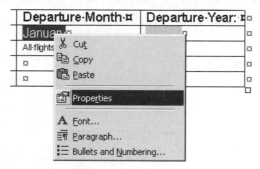

7) In the *Items in drop-down list* box, click March, and then click the **Move Up** button.

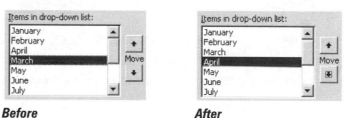

Before   **After**

The months are now in the correct order. When finished, click **OK**.

8) Right-click in the field beneath the 'Departure Year' heading and choose **Properties**. Word displays the *Drop-Down Form Field Options* dialog box.

9) In the *Items in drop-down list* box, click 2000 and then click **Remove**.

10) In the *Drop-down item* box, type '2003'. Click **Add** and then **OK**.

11) Close and save your sample document with the following name:

    Chapter13_Exercise_13-6_After_*Your_Name*.doc

Working with checkbox form fields

Checkbox fields help users complete a Word form quickly because they don't need to type their responses. Unlike the drop-down form fields, where users can select only one option, checkboxes allow form users to make multiple choices.

Checkbox form field
In a Word form, a field that allows users to select from among multiple options by clicking a checkbox.

Exercise 13.7: Working with checkbox form fields

1) Open the following file:

   ```
   Chapter13_Exercise_13-7_Before.doc
   ```

   Is the Forms toolbar displayed? If not, display it now.

2) Click in the cell to the right of the cell containing the word 'Mozzarella'.

Click here

Check Box Form Field button

3) Click the **Check Box Form Field** button on the Forms toolbar. Word displays your inserted checkbox form field as a grey square block containing a smaller, hollow, black square.

   □

4) Select the checkbox form field that you inserted in step 3 by dragging across it.

5) Press **Ctrl+C** and use **Ctrl+V** to paste it successively in each of the other seven cells that represent pizza toppings. Your fields should look like this:

Form Field Options button

6) Click in the table cell containing the checkbox field for the mozzarella topping, and click the **Form Field Options** button. Word displays the *Check Box Form Field Options* dialog box.

7) In the *Default value* area, select the *Checked* option. Click **OK** to close the dialog box.

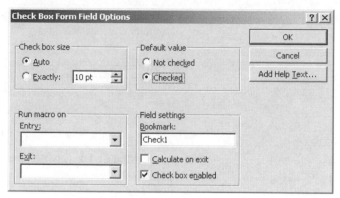

The mozzarella topping checkbox now looks like this:

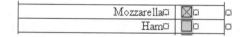

Protect Form button

8) Click the **Protect Form** button on the Form toolbar. Your form is now protected.

9) Close and save your sample document with the following name:

Chapter13_Exercise_13-7_After_*Your_Name*.doc

In the final exercise of this chapter, you will learn how to delete fields from a form.

Exercise 13.8: Deleting a form field

1) Open the following file:

Chapter13_Exercise_13-8_Before.doc

Is the Forms toolbar displayed? If not, display it now.

2) Click in the second cell of the first row to select the text form field. Word displays the selected field as a solid black rectangle.

Press the **Delete** key to remove the field from the form.

3) Click in the fourth cell of the first row to select the text form field, and press **Delete** to remove the field.

4) Click in the second cell of the third row to position the insertion point in the cell. Press **Delete** once to select the field and a second time to remove it.

5) In the third row, click in the cell to the right of the word 'Amex'.

Press **Delete**. Word selects the checkbox field. Press **Delete** a second time to remove the field.

6) Repeat step 5 to remove the other two credit card fields. Your table should now look like this:

First·Name:¤	¤		Surname:¤	¤		¤
¤	¤		¤	¤		¤
Skill·Level:¤	¤		Payment· Method:¤	Amex¤	¤	¤
				MasterCard¤	¤	¤
				Visa¤	¤	¤

7) Close and save your sample document with the following name:

Chapter13_Exercise_13-8_After_*Your_Name*.doc

Chapter 13: quick reference

Forms toolbar

Button	Description
ab|	Inserts a text box field in a document.
☑	Inserts a checkbox field in a document.
	Inserts a drop-down field in a document.
	Displays the *Form Field Options* dialog box for the selected field.
🔒	Protects the form to enable users to interact with its fields.

Form fields

Field type	When used
Text	The user's response consists of text, a number or a date.
Checkbox	The user may select *multiple* choices from a series.
Drop-down list	The user must select one choice from a list.

Text form field types

Text field type	Permitted content
Regular text	Any characters, including letters, numbers and symbols.
Number	Numeric entries only. If you specify a number format, Word converts the user's entries accordingly.
Date	Calendar date entries only. If you specify a date format, Word converts the user's entries accordingly.
Current date	A display-only field that shows the date on which the user opened the form.
Current time	A display-only field that shows the time on which the user opened the form.
Calculation	Arithmetic expressions. For example, the total of a column of numbers, or the order quantity multiplied by the unit price.

Tasks summary

Task	Procedure
Insert a form field.	Click the appropriate form field button on the Forms toolbar.
Amend the properties of a form field.	Select the field and click the **Form Field Options** button on the Forms toolbar. Alternatively, right-click on the field and choose **Properties** from the drop-down menu.
Delete a form field.	Select the field and press **Delete**.
Protect a form without a password.	Click the **Protect Form** button on the Forms toolbar.
	Alternatively, select the field, choose **Tools | Protect Document**, select *Forms* in the *Protect document for* area, and click **OK**.
Protect a form with a password.	Choose **Tools | Protect Document**, select *Forms* in the *Protect document for* area, type your password, click **OK**, retype your password and click **OK**.
Unprotect a form.	If not password-protected, click the **Protect Form** button on the Forms toolbar.
	If password-protected, choose **Tools | Unprotect Document**, type the password, and click **OK**.

Concepts summary

A form is a Word *template* file that contains interactive areas called *form fields* in which users can type information and select options. When users open the template, Word opens a copy of the form on their screens, ready for them to complete. A Word form is a protected document. Users can input text and select options but cannot amend the form content or layout.

Word offers three kinds of form fields: *text* (blank boxes in which users can enter text, numbers, date and calculations), *drop-down* (which offer a list of preset choices from which a user may select only one), and *checkbox* (which allow users to select more than one option from a given range). You can specify default values for each field type to speed up form completion.

Chapter13: quick quiz

Circle the correct answer to each of the following multiple-choice questions about forms in Word.

Q1	Which of the following is not an essential feature of a Word form?
A.	A Word form is a protected document.
B.	A Word form is distributed as a template.
C.	A Word form is formatted using heading styles.
D.	A Word form must contain at least one form field.

Q2	Why are Word forms made available as templates?
A.	It enables users to create and complete a new Word document that is based on the selected form template, without affecting the template itself.
B.	Templates are easier to share among multiple users on a PC network.
C.	Form fields can be inserted in Word templates only and not in Word documents.
D.	Word templates can be password-protected against unwanted modification. Word documents cannot.

Q3	In Word, which of the following is not a type of form field?
A.	Drop-down list.
B.	Form ID.
C.	Text.
D.	Checkbox.

Q4	On the Forms toolbar in Word, which button do you click to insert a text form field?
A.	
B.	
C.	
D.	ab|

Q5	In a Word form, which form field type would you use to accept the entry of a person's date of birth?
A.	Text form field.
B.	Date form field.
C.	Calendar form field.
D.	Checkbox form field.

Q6	In a Word form, which form field type would you use to accept the entry of a financial amount?
A.	Floating-point form field.
B.	Currency form field.
C.	Text form field.
D.	Checkbox form field.

Chapter 13: 'Please complete and return': Word forms

Q7	In a Word form, which type of user entry is permitted in a text form field?
A.	Text.
B.	Calculation.
C.	Number.
D.	All of the above.

Q8	In a Word form, which of the following would not be accepted as a valid calculation in a text form field?
A.	=B2*B4/52
B.	=SUM(E2:E6)
C.	=Text1+Text3
D.	SUM(D2:E6)

Q9	When defining a text form field in a Word form, what is the effect of selecting the *Calculate on exit* checkbox?
A.	The field's user-entered value can be the input to a calculation that is defined in another field on the form.
B.	Word automatically updates all the form's text fields whenever the user saves the form.
C.	The field can calculate a result that is based on values entered in other fields by the form user.
D.	Word automatically updates all the form's text fields whenever the user closes the form, regardless of whether the user saves the form.

Q10	On the Forms toolbar in Word, which button do you click to insert a drop-down form field?
A.	
B.	
C.	
D.	ab|

Q11	When creating a Word form, you would insert a drop-down list field when you want ...
A.	The form user to enter a calendar date.
B.	To allow the form user to select more than one response from a series of options.
C.	The form user to enter a number.
D.	To prevent the form user from selecting more than one response from a series of options.

Q12	In Word, which of the following statements about drop-down list form fields is untrue?
A.	The first option in the list is the default choice.
B.	The form creator can edit the drop-down list to rearrange the order of the options in the list.
C.	The form user can select more than one option from the drop-down list.
D.	The form creator can remove an option from a drop-down list.

Q13	On the Forms toolbar in Word, which button do you click to insert a checkbox form field?
A.	
B.	
C.	
D.	ab|

Q14	When creating a Word form, you would insert a checkbox field when you want ...
A.	The form user to enter a calendar date.
B.	To allow the form user to select more than one response from a series of options.
C.	The form user to enter the input to a calculation.
D.	To prevent the form user from selecting more than one response from a series of options.

Q15	In Word, which of the following statements about checkbox form fields is untrue?
A.	The form creator can specify that a checkbox is selected by default.
B.	Form users can interact with a checkbox field in either of three ways: they leave it deselected, they can click to select it, or they can double-click to double-select it.
C.	Word automatically applies a bookmark name to each checkbox inserted by the form creator.
D.	The form creator can remove a checkbox from a form.

Q16	On the Forms toolbar in Word, which button do you click to apply or remove form protection?
A.	
B.	
C.	
D.	

Q17	In Word, which of the following statements about form protection is true?
A.	The form creator does not need to protect a form to enable the form users to interact with the fields on the form.
B.	Form protection without a password prevents form users from changing the form content or layout.
C.	Form protection without a password does not enable the form users to interact with the form fields.
D.	Form protection with a password enables the form users to interact with the form's fields but prevents them from changing the form content or layout.

Q18	In Word, which of the following statements about form protection is true?
A.	The form creator can apply or remove password-protection using the relevant buttons on the Forms toolbar.
B.	The form creator can apply or remove password-protection using the **Protect Document** or **Unprotect Document** commands on the **Tools** menu.
C.	The form creator cannot apply or remove non-password protection using the relevant buttons on the Forms toolbar.
D.	Password protection, once applied to a form, cannot be removed at a later stage.

Answers

1: C, **2:** A, **3:** B, **4:** D, **5:** A, **6:** C, **7:** D, **8:** D, **9:** A, **10:** A, **11:** D, **12:** C, **13:** B, **14:** B, **15:** B, **16:** D, **17:** D, **18:** B.

14

Tables: merging, splitting, sorting and totalling

Objectives	In this chapter you will learn how to:
	■ Convert tabbed text to a table
	■ Merge and split cells in a table
	■ Sort cells in a table
	■ Total columns of numbers in a table

New words

In this chapter you will meet the following terms:

■ Table

■ Sorting

■ Separator character

■ Sort order

Exercise files

In this chapter you will work with the following Word files:

■ Chapter14_Exercise_14-1_Before.doc

■ Chapter14_Exercise_14-2_Before.doc

■ Chapter14_Exercise_14-4_Before.doc

■ Chapter14_Exercise_14-5_Before.doc

■ Chapter14_Exercise_14-6_Before.doc

Syllabus reference

In this chapter you will cover the following items from the ECDL Advanced Word Processing Syllabus:

■ **AM3.4.1.1**. Use merge and split cell options in a table.

■ **AM3.4.1.2**. Convert tabbed text into a table.

■ **AM3.4.1.3**. Sort data (alphabetic or numeric) in a table (ascending or descending order).

- **AM3.4.1.4**. Perform addition calculations on a numeric list in a table.

About tables

Tables provide a way of arranging content – text, numbers, images or fields – in vertical *columns* and horizontal *rows*. The rectangular boxes in a table are called *cells*.

Column

UK Premiership Top Scorers 2000-01

Player	Team	From Play	Penalties	Total Goals
Phillips	Sunderland	24	6	30
Shearer	Newcastle	18	5	23
Yorke	Manchester United	20	0	20
Bridges	Leeds United	19	0	19
Cole	Manchester United	19	0	19
Henry	Arsenal	15	2	17
Di Canio	West Ham	14	2	16
Iversen	Tottenham Hotspur	14	0	14
Quinn	Sunderland	14	0	14

Row →

Cell

Tables: when you need to use them

In Word, you will most commonly use tables to:

- **Present numerical information**. Material that includes numbers (such as a sales report) or conveys some kind of ranking (such as a list of best-selling products) is generally shown in tables.

- **Create multicolumn layout**. For brochures and other highly formatted documents, tables offer a quick, precise way of arranging content in multiple columns. (See Chapter 25 for more about Word's newspaper-style columns, which allow text to flow between columns.)

- **Design Word forms**. Tables offer the best way of positioning fields and labels in Word electronic forms (see Chapter 13).

When table cells contain numbers, you can perform arithmetical and statistical calculations on those numbers. In effect, you can use such a table as a spreadsheet.

> **Table**
>
> *An arrangement of material (text, numbers, images or fields) in rows and columns. The individual elements of a table are called cells.*

Working with tables: the four tasks

Here are the four tasks that you need to be able to perform with tables in Word:

- **Convert tabbed text to a table**. Exercise 14.1 takes you through the steps of creating a table from paragraphs of text that contain tabs.

- **Merge and split cells**. Sometimes, you may want to merge two or more cells into a single cell. At other times, you may want to split a single cell into a number of smaller cells. Exercises 14.2 and 14.3 show you how.

- **Sort cells in a table**. As Exercises 14.4 and 14.5 show, you can change the order of rows in a table.

- **Perform calculations in a table**. Tables are not just for layout. You can also perform calculations in tables. See Exercise 14.6.

Converting tabbed text to tables

Word provides an option for quickly converting text to a table when that material contains two *separator characters*:

- **A column separator character**. Word can use this character – typically a tab – to identify the beginning of a new column.

- **A row separator character**. Word can use this character – typically a paragraph mark or line break – to identify the beginning of a new row.

Generally, there are two situations when you want to converted tabbed text to tables:

- **The information was entered in tabbed format**. Tabs are an alternative to tables for creating multiple column layouts.

- **The information was imported in tab-delimited format**. You may find yourself working with text that has been imported, in tab-delimited format, from a non-Word file.

  As its name suggests, a tab-delimited file is one where text on the same row but in different columns is separated by tab characters.

Separator character

A character such as a tab or paragraph break that represents a logical division in the structure of a set of information.

When converting tabbed text to a table, ensure that each paragraph of text that you select for conversion contains the same number of tabs.

Extra tabs within any paragraph result in Word creating a row with empty, unwanted cells.

Exercise 14.1: Converting tabbed text to a table

In this exercise, you create a table by selecting and converting a number of paragraphs that contain tabs. The material is taken from *Designing Tomorrow's Education: Promoting Innovation with New Technologies*, EU Commission, March 2000.

1) Start Word and open the following file:

    Chapter14_Exercise_14-1_Before.doc

2) Select all the paragraphs of text that contain tabs.

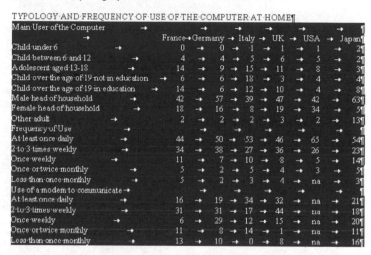

3) Choose **Table | Convert Text to Table** to display the *Convert Text to Table* dialog box.

4) Word examines all your selected lines, finds the line containing the greatest number of tabs, and displays this number as the suggested value in the *Number of columns* box.

   In this example, accept the suggested value of seven columns.

   You cannot change the value in the *Number of rows* box. This is fixed by the number of paragraph marks or line breaks in the selected text.

Of the three available AutoFit options, select *AutoFit to contents*. This tells Word to adapt the width of each column to accommodate the text within it.

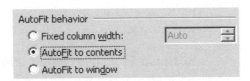

5) Word gives you the option of applying an AutoFormat layout to format your table by. Leave this field at its default value of *None*.

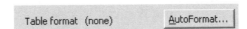

6) As your selected text contains tabs, Word correctly guesses that tabs are the separator character for the table conversion operation.

Separate text at
- ○ Paragraphs   ○ Commas
- ● Tabs   ○ Other: `-`

Click **OK**, and then click anywhere outside your table to deselect it. Your converted table should look like this:

⊞ TYPOLOGY·AND·FREQUENCY·OF·USE·OF·THE·COMPUTER·AT·HOME¶

Main·User·of·the·Computer¤	¤	¤	¤	¤	¤	¤	¤
¤	France¤	Germany¤	Italy¤	UK¤	USA¤	Japan¤	¤
Child·under·6¤	0¤	0¤	·1¤	1¤	1¤	2¤	¤
Child·between·6·and·12¤	4¤	4¤	5¤	6¤	5¤	2¤	¤
Adolescent·aged·13-18¤	14¤	9¤	15¤	11¤	8¤	3¤	¤
Child·over·the·age·of·19·not·in·education¤	6¤	6¤	18¤	3¤	4¤	4¤	¤
Child·over·the·age·of·19·in·education¤	14¤	6¤	12¤	10¤	4¤	8¤	¤
Male·head·of·household¤	42¤	57¤	39¤	47¤	42¤	63¤	¤
Female·head·of·household¤	18¤	16¤	8¤	19¤	34¤	5¤	¤
Other·adult¤	2¤	2¤	2¤	3¤	2¤	13¤	¤
Frequency·of·Use¤	¤	¤	¤	¤	¤	¤	¤
At·least·once·daily¤	44¤	50¤	·53¤	46¤	65¤	54¤	¤
2·to·3·times·weekly¤	34¤	38¤	27¤	36¤	26¤	23¤	¤
Once·weekly¤	11¤	7¤	10¤	·8¤	5¤	14¤	¤
Once·or·twice·monthly¤	5¤	2¤	5¤	4¤	3¤	5¤	¤
Less·than·once·monthly¤	5¤	2¤	3¤	4¤	na¤	3¤	¤
Use·of·a·modem·to·communicate¤	¤	¤	¤	¤	¤	¤	¤
At·least·once·daily¤	16¤	19¤	34¤	32¤	na¤	21¤	¤
2·to·3·times·weekly¤	31¤	31¤	17¤	44¤	na¤	18¤	¤
Once·weekly¤	6¤	29¤	12¤	15¤	na¤	20¤	¤
Once·or·twice·monthly¤	11¤	8¤	14¤	1¤	na¤	11¤	¤
Less·than·once·monthly¤	13¤	10¤	0¤	8¤	na¤	16¤	¤

7) Save your sample document with the following name, and close it:

Chapter14_Exercise_14-1_After_*Your_Name*.doc

Merging and splitting cells in tables

When you create a table, you must specify the number of columns that you want it to contain. As you work with a table, however, you may want to reduce or increase the number of cells in a particular row or rows. Word allows you to manipulate

ECDL Advanced Word Processing

the number of cells in selected rows by merging or splitting their cells.

Exercise 14.2: Merging cells in a table

In this exercise, you will open an existing table and merge cells within some of its rows.

1) Open the following file:

```
Chapter14_Exercise_14-2_Before.doc
```

2) Select the first row of the table by clicking just to the left of it.

TYPOLOGY·AND·FREQUENCY·OF·USE·OF·THE·COMPUTER·AT·HOME¶							
Main·User·of·the·Computer¤	¤	¤	¤	¤	¤	¤	¤
¤	France¤	Germany¤	Italy¤	UK¤	USA¤	Japan¤	¤
Child·under·6¤	0¤	·0¤	·1¤	1¤	1¤	2¤	¤

3) Choose **Table | Merge Cells**.

Word merges the seven cells so that the row now contains just a single cell. Click anywhere outside the row to deselect it. It should look like this:

TYPOLOGY·AND·FREQUENCY·OF·USE·OF·THE·COMPUTER·AT·HOME¶							
Main·User·of·the·Computer¤							¤
¤	France¤	Germany¤	Italy¤	UK¤	USA¤	Japan¤	¤
Child·under·6¤	0¤	·0¤	·1¤	1¤	1¤	2¤	¤

4) Select the row that contains the words 'Frequency of Use' and repeat step 3.

Other·adult¤	2¤	2¤	2¤	3¤	2¤	13¤	¤
Frequency·of·Use¤	¤	¤	¤	¤	¤	¤	¤
At·least·once·daily¤	44¤	50¤	·53¤	46¤	65¤	54¤	¤

5) Select the row that contains the words 'Use of a Modem to Communicate' and repeat step 3.

Less·than·once·monthly¤	5¤	2¤	3¤	4¤	na¤	3¤	¤
Use·of·a·Modem·to·Communicate¤	¤	¤	¤	¤	¤	¤	¤
At·least·once·daily¤	16¤	19¤	34¤	32¤	na¤	21¤	¤

6) Save your sample document with the following name, and close it:

```
Chapter13_Exercise_14-2_After_Your_Name.doc
```

What happens when the cells you select for merging contain text? The answer is that Word inserts paragraph marks to separate the text that was originally in different cells.

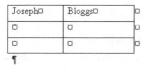

Before   ***After***

Exercise 14.3: Splitting cells in a table

In this exercise, you will create a table and then split a selected cell within it.

1) Click the **New** button on the Standard toolbar to create a new, blank document.

2) Choose **Table | Insert Table**, accept the dialog box default options as shown below, and click **OK**.

Word creates a new table as shown:

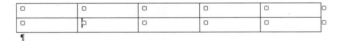

3) Click in the last cell of the second row and choose **Table | Split Cells**.

4) Accept the default dialog box options as shown, and click **OK**.

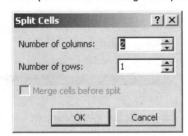

5) Click anywhere outside the table to deselect it. Your table should now look like this:

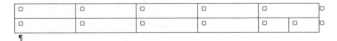

You can close the sample document without saving it.

What happens when the cell you select for splitting contains text? Word positions the text that was in the original cell in the *first* of the new cells.

If the text in the original, single cell contained paragraph marks, Word positions the text after the first paragraph mark in the second split cell, the text after the second paragraph mark in the third split cell, and so on.

Sorting rows in tables

Word allows you to rearrange the rows of a table, so that the rows are displayed in an order different to that in which they are currently displayed.

- **Alphabetically**. You may want to sort the rows alphabetically, in ascending (A–Z) or descending (Z–A) order.

  For example, when working with a table containing various customer details, it is generally easier to find a particular customer when the rows are sorted alphabetically by customer name.

Table sorted in ascending alphabetical order based on Name column →

Name¤	Area¤	First·Sale¤	Sales·Value¤	¤
Andrews※	Region·4※	21/05/99※	234,987※	¤
Byrne※	Region·2※	12/09/00※	340,344※	¤
Carlton※	Region·6※	03/07/01※	125,000※	¤
Dunlop※	Region·1※	01/01/01※	456,234※	¤
Engert※	Region·2※	12/09/01※	520,988※	¤
Friars※	Region·5※	30/10/00※	198,643※	¤
Greyfield※	Region·4※	17/10/99※	231,040※	¤

- **Numerically**. You can also sort table rows according to the values of the numbers that they contain. Again, you can select an ascending (0–9) or descending (9–0) sort order.

  In the example of a table containing customer details, you might want to show customers in the order of their sales value.

Name¤	Area¤	First·Sale¤	Sales·Value¤	¤
Engert※	Region·2※	12/09/01※	520,988※	¤
Dunlop※	Region·1※	01/01/01※	456,234※	¤
Byrne※	Region·2※	12/09/00※	340,344※	¤
Andrews※	Region·4※	21/05/99※	234,987※	¤
Greyfield※	Region·4※	17/10/99※	231,040※	¤
Friars※	Region·5※	30/10/00※	198,643※	¤
Carlton※	Region·6※	03/07/01※	125,000※	¤

Table sorted in descending numeric order based on Sales Value column

Sorting does not change the content of a table, only the order in which the table rows are displayed.

> **Sorting**
>
> *Rearranging rows in a table based on the values in one or more columns.*

Exercise 14.4: Sorting rows in a table

In this exercise, you will sort a table that displays the top goal scorers in the English Football Premiership for the 2000–2001 season. This is an example of a one-level or 'simple' sort.

1) Open the following file:

    `Chapter14_Exercise_14-4_Before.doc`

The rows are currently sorted in order of total goals scored, with the top scorers listed first.

UK·Premiership·Top·Scorers·2000-01¶

Name¤	Team¤	From·Play¤	Penalties¤	Total·Goals¤
Phillips¤	Sunderland¤	24¤	6¤	30¤
Shearer¤	Newcastle¤	18¤	5¤	23¤
Yorke¤	Manchester·United¤	20¤	0¤	20¤
Bridges¤	Leeds·United¤	19¤	0¤	19¤
Cole¤	Manchester·United¤	19¤	0¤	19¤
Henry¤	Arsenal¤	15¤	2¤	17¤
Di·Canio¤	West·Ham¤	14¤	2¤	16¤
Iversen¤	Tottenham·Hotspur¤	14¤	0¤	14¤
Quinn¤	Sunderland¤	14¤	0¤	14¤

¶

2) Click in any cell of the *Name* column, and choose **Table | Sort** to display the *Sort* dialog box.

3) Notice that Word detects the column (in this case the *Name* column) in which you placed the insertion point.

For text items, the sort order always defaults to ascending (A–Z). Also selected by default is the *Header row* option. Typically, your tables contain header rows that you do not want included in the sort operation.

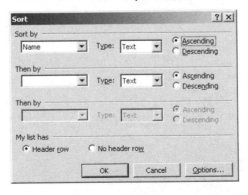

Accept the default dialog box values as shown above and click **OK**.

4) Word reorders the table rows in ascending order of player name, so that Bridges is listed first, Cole second and Yorke last.

UK·Premiership·Top·Scorers·2000–01¶

Name¤	Team¤	From·Play¤	Penalties¤	Total·Goals¤	¤
Bridges¤	Leeds·United¤	19¤	0¤	19¤	¤
Cole¤	Manchester·United¤	19¤	0¤	19¤	¤
Di·Canio¤	West·Ham¤	14¤	2¤	16¤	¤
Henry¤	Arsenal¤	15¤	2¤	17¤	¤
Iversen¤	Tottenham·Hotspur¤	14¤	0¤	14¤	¤
Phillips¤	Sunderland¤	24¤	6¤	30¤	¤
Quinn¤	Sunderland¤	14¤	0¤	14¤	¤
Shearer¤	Newcastle¤	18¤	5¤	23¤	¤
Yorke¤	Manchester·United¤	20¤	0¤	20¤	¤

Save your sample document with the following name, and close it:

Chapter14_Exercise_14-4_After_*Your_Name*.doc

Sorting by more than one column

Word enables you to specify up to three levels of sorting:

- **Single-level sort**. Rows are sorted according to the values in one column only (see Exercise 14.4).

- **Two-level sort**. Rows are sorted according to values in one column, *and*, where multiple rows contain the same value, the second sort order determines how these rows are ranked.

  Imagine that you have a customer table containing several customers who share the name Smith. If you sort the table by descending sales value within customer name, the Smiths with the higher sales values are listed first.

- **Three-level sort**. An example would be a customer table sorted by sales region within sales value within customer name. The third sort order takes effect only when multiple customers share the same name *and* the same sales value. In such rows, the values in the sales region column determine how the customers are listed.

Sort order

A way of sorting a table. Sort orders can be alphabetical or numeric, and can be in ascending (0–9, A–Z) or descending (Z–A, 9–0) sequence.

Exercise 14.5: Performing a two-level sort

In this exercise, you will perform a two-level sort: by player name within total goals scored. That is, you will list the table rows in order of goals scored. Where two players have scored the same number of goals, they will be sorted by name.

1) Open the following file:

    Chapter14_Exercise_14-5_Before.doc

2) Click anywhere in the table and choose **Table | Sort** to display the *Sort* dialog box.

3) In the *Sort by* area, select *Total Goals*, *Number* and *Descending*.

4) In the *Then by* area, select *Name*, *Text* and *Ascending*.

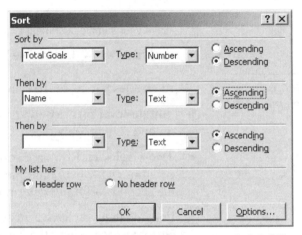

Accept the default setting of *Header row* and click **OK**.

5) Word sorts the table rows as shown below:

UK·Premiership·Top·Scorers·2000-01¶

Name¤	Team¤	From·Play¤	Penalties¤	Total·Goals¤	¤
Phillips¤	Sunderland¤	24¤	6¤	30¤	¤
Shearer¤	Newcastle¤	18¤	5¤	23¤	¤
Yorke¤	Manchester·United¤	20¤	0¤	20¤	¤
Bridges¤	Leeds·United¤	19¤	0¤	19¤	¤
Cole¤	Manchester·United¤	19¤	0¤	19¤	¤
Henry¤	Arsenal¤	15¤	2¤	17¤	¤
Di·Canio¤	West·Ham¤	14¤	2¤	16¤	¤
Iversen¤	Tottenham·Hotspur¤	14¤	0¤	14¤	¤
Quinn¤	Sunderland¤	14¤	0¤	14¤	¤

¶

Notice that rows 4 and 5 under the header row contain the same value in the *Total Goals* column (19), but that Bridges is listed before Cole. And in rows 7 and 8 (*Total Goals*, 14) Iversen appears before Quinn.

6) Save your sample document with the following name, and close it:

   Chapter13_Exercise_14-5_After_*Your_Name*.doc

Performing calculations in tables

A table in Word also offers the ability to arrange content in multiple columns, and, where the cells contain numbers, to perform spreadsheet-like calculations.

Exercise 14.6: Totalling numbers in a table

In this exercise, you add numbers that are arranged in vertical and horizontal lists within a table.

1) Open the following file:

   Chapter14_Exercise_14-6_Before.doc

2) Click in the second cell on the bottom row of the table.

Customer¤	Jan¤	Feb¤	Mar¤	Total¤
Andrews¤	23¤	45¤	12¤	¤
Brittan¤	34¤	50¤	45¤	¤
Cranshaw¤	12¤	29¤	41¤	¤
Dunlop¤	45¤	63¤	71¤	¤
Edgars¤	12¤	18¤	31¤	¤
¤	¤	¤	¤	¤
¤	¤	¤	¤	¤

Click here

3) Choose **Table | Formula** to display the *Formula* dialog box.

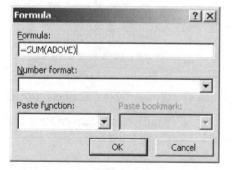

Word guesses correctly that you want to add numbers in the cells directly above the selected cell. Click **OK** to close the dialog box.

Word displays the sum of the cells in the second column (126) in the selected cell.

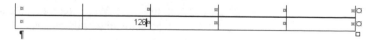

4) Click in the third cell on the bottom row of the table, and choose **Table | Formula** to display the *Formula* dialog box.

In this case, Word guesses – incorrectly – that you want to add the cells to the left of the selected cell.

Formula:
=SUM(LEFT)

Amend the value in the *Formula* box to the following:

=SUM(ABOVE)

Click **OK**.

5) Word displays the sum of the cells in the third column (205) in the selected cell.

Click in the fourth cell of the bottom row and repeat step 4. Word should display the number 200 in this cell.

6) In the above steps, you have added numbers *vertically* in the table. In the remaining steps, you will add numbers *horizontally* across the table rows.

Click in the last cell of the first row under the table header.

Click here

Customer¤	Jan¤	Feb¤	Mar¤	Total¤	
Andrews¤	23¤	45¤	12¤		¤
Brittan¤	34¤	50¤	45¤		¤
Cranshaw¤	12¤	29¤	41¤		¤
Dunlop¤	45¤	63¤	71¤		¤
Edgars¤	12¤	18¤	31¤		¤
¤		¤	¤		¤
¤	126¤	205¤	200¤		¤

¶

7) Choose **Table | Formula** to display the *Formula* dialog box.

Word guesses correctly that you want to add the cells to the left of the selected cell.

Formula:
=SUM(LEFT)

Click **OK** to close the dialog box.

8) Click in the last cell of the second row under the header row and choose **Table | Formula** to display the *Formula* dialog box.

In this case, Word guesses – incorrectly – that you want to add the cells above the selected cell.

Amend the value in the *Formula* box to the following:

```
=SUM(LEFT)
```

Click **OK**.

9) Click in the last cell of the third, fourth, fifth and seventh rows under the header row, and repeat step 9 in each case.

Your table should now look like this:

Customer¤	Jan¤	Feb¤	Mar¤	Total¤
Andrews¤	23¤	45¤	12¤	80¤
Brittan¤	34¤	50¤	45¤	129¤
Cranshaw¤	12¤	29¤	41¤	82¤
Dunlop¤	45¤	63¤	71¤	179¤
Edgars¤	12¤	18¤	31¤	61¤
¤	¤	¤	¤	¤
¤	126¤	205¤	200¤	531¤

Save your sample document with the following name, and close it:

```
Chapter14_Exercise_14-6_After_Your_Name.doc
```

Chapter 14: quick reference

Tasks summary

Task	Procedure
Convert tabbed text to a table.	Select the text, choose **Table | Convert Text to Table**, select the number of columns, the column width, and the tab separator character, and click **OK**.
Merge multiple cells.	Select the cells and choose **Table | Merge Cells**.
Split a single cell.	Select the cell, choose **Table | Split Cells**, specify the number of columns and the rows that you want to split the selected cell into, and click **OK**.
Sort table rows.	Click in any cell, choose **Table | Sort**, select the column(s) to sort by and their sort order(s), specify whether the table contains a header row, and click **OK**.
Total numbers in a row or column.	Click in any cell, choose Table | Formula, accept or amend the suggested formula, and click **OK**. Typical formulas are as follows: `=SUM(ABOVE)` and `=SUM(LEFT)`

Typically, you will use tables in Word to present *numerical information*, to create *multicolumn* layouts for brochures and newsletters, and to position fields and labels in Word *forms*.

You can *merge* multiple cells into a single cell, or *split* a single cell in multiple cells.

Tabbed text, including text imported in tab-delimited format, can be converted quickly to a table. The conversion process is based on Word identifying the tab character as the beginning of a new column and the paragraph mark or line break character as the beginning of a new row. Each tabbed paragraph should contain the same number of tabs. Extra tabs within any paragraph result in Word creating a row with empty, unwanted cells.

You can *sort* the rows of a table on the basis of the values in one, two or three columns. The *sort orders* available are alphabetical or numeric, and ascending (0–9, A–Z) or descending (Z–A, 9–0).

When table cells contain numbers, you can perform spreadsheet-like *calculations* on them.

Chapter 14: quick quiz

Circle the correct answer to each of the following multiple-choice questions about tables in Word.

Q1	Which of the following items cannot be stored in a Word table?
A.	A field.
B.	An image.
C.	A macro.
D.	Text.

Q2	In Word, which action do you take to begin converting selected tabbed text to a table?
A.	Click the **Convert Tabbed Text** button on the Tables and Borders toolbar.
B.	Right-click on the selected tabbed text and choose the **Convert Now** command from the pop-up menu.
C.	Choose the **Table	Convert Text to Table** command.
D.	Choose the **Tools	Conversion Options	Tabbed Text to Table** command.

Q3	Which of the statements about tabbed-text-to-table conversion in Word is not true?
A.	Word uses the tab character to identify where a new column should begin.
B.	Word uses the tab character to identify where a new row should begin.
C.	Word uses the line break character to identify where a new row should begin.
D.	For best results, all lines in the selected text should have the same number of tabs.

Q4	In a Word table, you merge four cells, each of which contains text, into a single new cell. Which statement describes the result?
A.	Word deletes the text that was in the original, pre-merged cells.
B.	Word displays the text that was in the first of the four cells in the new, merged cell. The text that was in the other cells is deleted.
C.	Word displays the text of the original cells in the single cell, with paragraph marks indicating the pre-merged cell boundaries.
D.	None of the above – you cannot merge a cell that contains text.

Q5	In a Word table, you split a cell that contains text into four new cells. Which statement describes the result?
A.	Word displays the text in the first of the four split cells.
B.	Word deletes the text that was in the original, unsplit cell.
C.	Word displays the text in all four of the new cells.
D.	None of the above – you cannot split a cell that contains text.

Q6	A single-column Word table lists numbers in the following order: 3, 8, 12, 45. How is the table sorted?
A.	Alphabetical, ascending.
B.	Numeric, ascending.
C.	Numeric, descending.
D.	Alphabetical, descending.

Q7	A single-column Word table lists names in the following order: Adams, Bergkamp, Dixon, Henry. How is the table sorted?
A.	Alphabetical, ascending.
B.	Numeric, descending.
C.	Numeric, ascending.
D.	Alphabetical, descending.

Q8	A Word table is sorted by customer name within sales value. What does this mean?
A.	Rows are listed in order of customer name. When two or more customers share the same name, the relevant rows are listed in order of sales value.
B.	The customer with the highest sales value is shown first, and the customer whose name begins with Z is shown last.
C.	Rows are listed in order of sales value. When two or more customers share the sales value, the relevant rows are listed in order of customer name.
D.	The customer with the highest sales value is shown last, and the customer whose name begins with Z is shown last.

Q9	Which of the following is a valid formula for adding numeric cells in a Word table?
A.	=ADD(LEFT)
B.	=TOTAL(ABOVE)
C.	=SUM(BENEATH)
D.	=SUM(LEFT)

Answers   **1:** C, **2:** C, **3:** B, **4:** C, **5:** A, **6:** B, **7:** A, **8:** A, **9:** D.

15 *Spreadsheets in Word*

Objectives

In this chapter you will learn how to:

- Embed worksheet cells in a Word document
- Modify embedded spreadsheet cells in Word

New words

In this chapter you will meet the following term:

- Embedded object

Exercise files

In this chapter you will work with the following files:

- `Chapter15_Exercise_15-1_Before.doc`
- `Chapter15_Exercise_15-1_Before.xls`
- `Chapter15_Exercise_15-2_Before.doc`

Syllabus reference

In this chapter you will cover the following item from the ECDL Advanced Word Processing Syllabus:

- **AM3.4.4.1:** Modify an embedded worksheet in a document.

About embedded objects

When working with files created in different MS Office 2000 applications, such as Word, Excel and PowerPoint, you can:

- Copy or cut an item from one type of file to the Clipboard.
- Use the **Edit | Paste Special** command to *embed* that item in the second type of file.

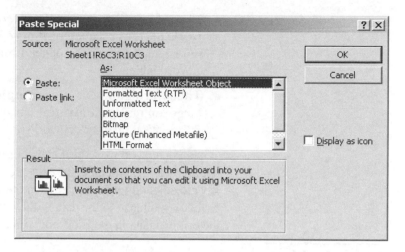

In this chapter, you will work with cells copied from Excel worksheets and embedded into Word documents. The cells are examples of *embedded objects*.

<table>
<tr><td>

Pasting versus embedding

</td><td>

How does embedding differ from pasting?

- **Pasting.** When you paste Excel cells into a Word document, Word treats the worksheet cells as a Word table. You can edit and format the cells in the same way as you would the cells of a table.

  In effect, the pasted data become part of the Word document.

- **Embedding**. When you embed Excel cells into a Word document, the embedded cells bring with them the functionality of the worksheet from which they came. When you double-click the embedded cells, Word's menus and toolbars disappear from the screen and are replaced by Excel's.

  Although they are positioned within the Word document, the embedded data or 'objects' remain, in effect, part of Excel.

</td></tr>
</table>

Embedded object

Data created in one MS Office application that are positioned in another application but that retain all the functionality of the original application.

Embedded objects: the benefits to you

Generally, there is a combination of two reasons why you will want to embed selected Excel cells, or an entire Excel worksheet, into a Word document:

- **The information is already entered in an Excel worksheet**. Consequently, it makes no sense to retype the information and any associated formulas and functions into a Word table.

- **The information contains complex calculations and/or large amounts of data**. It is easier to work with such information in an Excel worksheet than in a Word table.

When you embed worksheet cells in a Word document, you can use all of Excel's menu commands, toolbar buttons and shortcut keys to edit and format the cells in the embedded worksheet. Any changes you make to the data in the embedded object do not affect the original data in the file from which the object was copied.

Working with spreadsheets in Word: the two tasks

Here are the two tasks that you need to be able to perform with embedded spreadsheet cells in Word:

- **Embed worksheet cells in a Word document**. Exercise 15.1 takes you through the steps of embedding selected worksheet cells in a Word document.

- **Modify embedded spreadsheet cells in Word**. In Exercise 15.2 you discover how to manipulate worksheet cells that have been embedded in Word documents.

Embedding spreadsheet cells in Word

Exercise 15.1: Embed Excel worksheet cells in a Word document

In this exercise, you will select and copy a cell range from an Excel worksheet and then embed the cells in a Word document.

1) Start Word and open the following document:

   `Chapter15_Exercise_15-1_Before.doc`

2) Start Excel and open the following Excel workbook:

   `Chapter15_Exercise_15-1_Before.xls`

3) From Sheet1 in the Excel workbook, select the cell range B1:G39 and copy it to the Clipboard. You may now close the Excel workbook.

4) In the Word document, click at the second paragraph mark beneath the heading 'Balance Sheet for XYZ Enterprises'. This is the place at which you will embed the worksheet cells.

5) Choose **Edit | Paste Special** to display the *Paste Special* dialog box. In the *As* section of the dialog box, select *Paste* and select *Microsoft Excel Worksheet Object*.

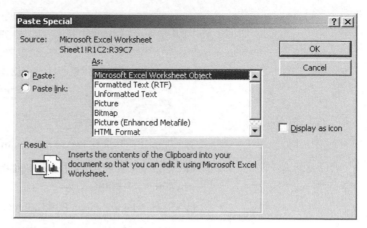

Click **OK**.

Word pastes the worksheets cells in your document as an embedded object.

6) Save your sample document with the following name, and close it:

Chapter15_Exercise_15-1_After_*Your_Name*.doc

Working with worksheet cells embedded in Word

When you create a table, you must specify the number of columns that you want it to contain. As you work with a table, however, you may want to reduce or increase the number of cells in a particular row or rows. Word allows you to manipulate the number of cells in selected rows by merging or splitting their cells.

Exercise 15.2: Amend embedded worksheet cells

In this exercise, you will amend a Word document that contains embedded worksheet cells and then edit and format those cells using Excel's functionality.

1) Open the following file:

Chapter15_Exercise_15-2_Before.doc

2) Double-click on the embedded worksheet cells, and click in the cell containing the words 'BALANCE SHEET'.

Notice that Word's menus and toolbars are replaced by the corresponding Excel ones.

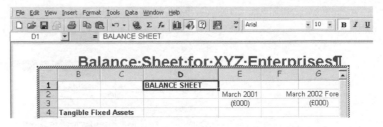

3) Press the **Delete** key to remove the words 'BALANCE SHEET'.

4) Click in cell E22 to select it, edit the cell content from '560' to '650', and press **Enter**.

5) Select the cell range B39:G39 and choose **Format | Cells**.

6) Click the **Borders** tab, select the *Outline* border, and click **OK**. Word places a border around the selected cells.

7) Scroll back up to the top of the embedded cells.

8) Double-click anywhere outside the embedded cells to deselect them. Notice that Excel's menus and toolbars disappear and are replaced by the corresponding Word ones.

9) Save your sample document with the following name, and close it:

   Chapter15_Exercise_15-2_After_*Your_Name*.doc

Chapter 15: quick reference

Tasks summary

Keys	Description
Embed Excel worksheet cells in a Word document.	In Excel, select the cells and copy or cut them to the Clipboard.
	In Word, position the insertion point where you want to locate the cells and choose **Edit	Paste Special**.
	In the *As* section of the dialog box, select *Paste* and *Microsoft Excel Worksheet Object*, and click **OK**.
Modify worksheet cells that have been embedded in a Word document.	Double-click anywhere in the embedded cells to replace Word's menus and toolbars with the corresponding Excel ones.
	Perform the required actions. When finished, double-click anywhere outside the embedded cells to redisplay Word's menus and toolbars.

When Excel cells are *embedded* into a Word document, they bring with them the functionality of the worksheet from which they came. When you double-click the embedded cells, Word's menus and toolbars disappear from the screen and are replaced by Excel's.

Chapter 15: quick quiz

Circle the correct answer to each of the following multiple-choice questions about embedded objects in Word.

Q1	Which one of the following commands do you choose to embed worksheet cells in a Word document?
A.	Edit | Paste.
B.	Insert | Embedded Objects.
C.	Edit | Paste Special.
D.	Insert | New Objects.

Q2	In Word, which of the following statements about embedded objects is untrue?
A.	Embedded objects bring with them the functionality of the application from which they came.
B.	You can embed data only from Excel in Word documents, and not data from PowerPoint or other MS Office applications.
C.	If you double-click on an embedded object, Word's menus and toolbars are replaced with those of the application in which the object was created.
D.	It is easier to work with complex calculations and/or large amounts of data in an embedded Excel worksheet than in a Word table.

Q3	In Word's *Paste Special* dialog box, which option do you select to embed cells from an Excel worksheet?
A.	Microsoft Excel Worksheet Object.
B.	Microsoft Workbook Object.
C.	Excel Worksheet Cells.
D.	Microsoft Excel Worksheet Cell Range.

Answers

1: C, **2:** B, **3:** A.

16   *Charts in Word*

Objectives

In this chapter you will learn how to:

- Create a chart with Microsoft Graph
- Modify chart formatting
- Reposition a chart in a Word document

New words

In this chapter you will meet the following terms:

- Microsoft Graph
- Data series
- Data label
- Plot area
- Datasheet
- Data point
- Chart area

Exercise files

In this chapter you will work with the following Word files:

- Chapter16_Exercise_16-1_Before.doc
- Chapter16_Exercise_16-2_Before.doc
- Chapter16_Exercise_16-3_Before.doc
- Chapter16_Exercise_16-4_Before.doc
- Chapter16_Exercise_16-5_Before.doc
- Chapter16_Exercise_16-6_Before.doc
- Chapter16_Exercise_16-7_Before.doc
- Chapter16_Exercise_16-8_Before.doc

- `Chapter16_Exercise_16-9_Before.doc`

- `Chapter16_Exercise_16-10_Before.doc`

- `Chapter16_Exercise_16-11_Before.doc`

- `Chapter16_Exercise_16-12_Before.doc`

- `Chapter16_Exercise_16-13_Before.doc`

Syllabus reference

In this chapter you will cover the following items from the ECDL Advanced Word Processing Syllabus:

- **AM3.4.4.2**: Create a chart from a table or pasted worksheet data in a document.

- **AM3.4.4.3**: Modify the formatting of a chart created from a table or pasted worksheet data.

- **AM3.4.4.4**: Position a chart in a document.

About Microsoft Graph

Word is supplied with a small application call *Microsoft Graph* that enables you to create and amend a variety of bar, column, pie and other charts based on information contained in tables. To present data in a Word table as a chart, you:

- Select the table, or cells within the table, in the Word document.

- Choose **Insert | Picture | Chart** to activate the Microsoft Graph application.

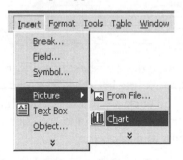

Microsoft Graph then creates a chart of the default type – a 3D bar chart – as an *embedded object* within your Word document.

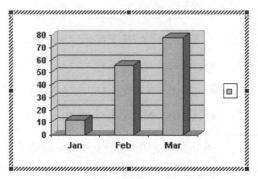

Want to change your chart format in any way? Just right-click on it to access a wide range of options that allow you to change the chart type and amend selected chart elements, such as font, background, axes and data labels. When finished, you can click outside the chart to return to Word.

Microsoft graph

A small application supplied with Word that enables you to create charts based on data in a table.

Charts and datasheets

Whenever you double-click a chart, you are shown another element called the *datasheet* – a small window that you use to modify the chart content. You do this by typing in your own numbers and text, over-writing those already present.

Document2 - Datasheet		A	B	C	D	E
		Jan	Feb	Mar		
1	3-D Colum	12	56	78		
2						
3						
4						

To relocate the datasheet to a different part of your screen, click and drag its title bar. The datasheet is removed from the screen when you click anywhere outside the embedded chart. When you change an item in the datasheet, Microsoft Graph updates the chart immediately.

Datasheet

A table displayed by Microsoft Graph with every chart. You use the datasheet to modify the chart content.

Chart menu commands

When your embedded chart is active – that is, when you double-click on it – Word's menus disappear from the screen and are replaced by Microsoft Graph menus of charting commands.

Working with charts in Word: the three tasks

Here are the three charting tasks that you need to be able to perform in Word:

■ **Create a chart from a table**. Exercise 16.1 takes you through the steps of creating a chart from data in a Word table.

■ **Modify chart formatting**. In Exercises 16.2 to 16.12, you discover the various options for amending the format of an embedded chart.

■ **Reposition a chart in a document**. In Exercise 16.13, you learn how to relocate an embedded chart within a Word document.

Working with new charts

The starting point for the creation of a new chart is a table containing numbers and, usually, some text to identify the numbers. The table:

■ may have been created directly in the Word document itself; or

■ may have been created as a result of pasting Excel worksheet cells into the Word document.

Exercise 16.1: Create a chart from a word table

1) Start Word and open the following document:

```
Chapter16_Exercise_16-1_Before.doc
```

2) Select all the columns except *Totals* on the right.

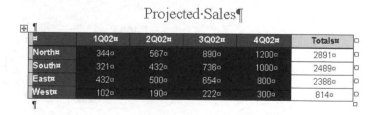

3) Choose **Insert | Picture | Chart**.

4) Word activates Microsoft Graph, which inserts an embedded chart and an associated datasheet in your Word document.

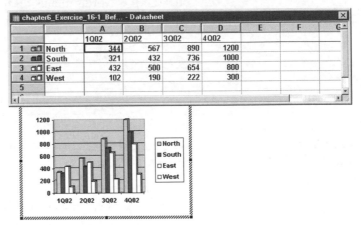

You can move the datasheet to a different part of your screen by dragging its title bar.

Click anywhere outside the embedded chart to close Microsoft Graph and return to Word.

5) Click once on your chart and drag its bottom right sizing handle until your chart is about the same width as the Word table above it. Click anywhere outside the chart to deselect it. Your document should look like this:

Projected·Sales¶

¤	1Q02¤	2Q02¤	3Q02¤	4Q02¤	Totals¤	
North¤	344¤	567¤	890¤	1200¤	2891¤	
South¤	321¤	432¤	736¤	1000¤	2489¤	
East¤	432¤	500¤	654¤	800¤	2386¤	
West¤	102¤	190¤	222¤	300¤	814¤	

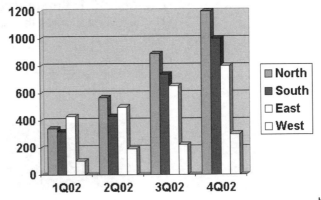

6) Save your sample document with the following name, and close it:

Chapter16_Exercise_16-1_After_*Your_Name*.doc

Working with chart elements

Data points, data series and data labels

Before working with chart formatting, it is important to understand a number of key terms relating to charting operations.

All charts are made up of *data points*. Each data point contains an item and its numerical value. Consider the four examples below:

Item	Value		Item	Value
Apples	4		January	£ 1,965.34
Pears	3		February	£ 2,451.50
Bananas	6		March	£ 8,301.49

Item	Value		Item	Value
Mary	15.00%		Sales	£4,954,032.00
Catherine	50.00%		Costs	£394,823.00
Margaret	35.00%		Overheads	£25,068.00

Each example consists of individual items (fruit, months, people and financial categories) and their associated numerical values. In the first example, the three data points are apples and 4, pears and 3, and bananas and 6. Other data points from the above examples are February and £2,451.50, Catherine and 50%, and overheads and £25,068.00

Data point
An item being measured and its measured value.

A collection of data points is called a *data series*. For instance, you may want to create a chart that shows the company's sales figures for different months, or a chart that compares one month's sales figures for different departments.

Data series
A group of related data points. A data series may compare different items measured at the same time, for example, or single items measured at different times.

By default, Microsoft Graph does not display labels. You can add two types of data labels to a chart:

- **Value labels**. These indicate the numerical values of the individual data points. See Exercise 16.2.

- **Text labels**. These display the names of the data points. By default, Microsoft Graph already displays these names on an axis. See Exercise 16.3.

Chart area and plot area

The region within an embedded chart consists of two distinct areas: the chart area and the plot area.

Chart area: the margin area surrounding the actual chart

Plot area: the area of the plotted chart

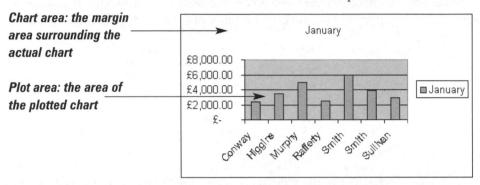

Exercise 16.2: Add value labels to a chart

1) Open the following document:

   Chapter16_Exercise_16-2_Before.doc

2) Double-click anywhere on the chart to activate Microsoft Graph.

3) Right-click on the chart area (the margin area surrounding the actual chart), choose **Chart Options** from the pop-up menu, and select the **Data Labels** tab of the dialog box.

4) Select the *Show Value* option and click **OK**.

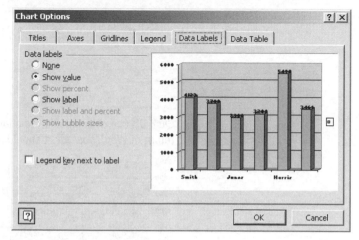

5) Right-click on the chart area, choose **Chart Type** from the pop-up menu, and select the 1D clustered column chart subtype.

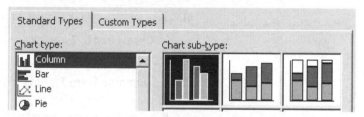

6) Click OK and click outside the chart to close Microsoft Graph and return to Word. Your chart should look like this.

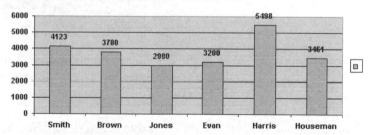

7) Save your sample document with the following name, and close it:

    Chapter16_Exercise_16-2_After_*Your_Name*.doc

Exercise 16.3: Add text labels to a chart

1) Open the following document:

    Chapter16_Exercise_16-3_Before.doc

2) Double-click anywhere on the chart to activate Microsoft Graph.

3) Right-click on the chart area (the margin area surrounding the actual chart), choose **Chart Options** from the pop-up menu, and select the **Data Labels** tab of the dialog box.

4) Select the *Show label* option.

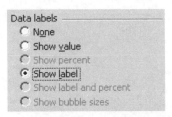

5) Click **OK** and click outside the chart to close Microsoft Graph and return to Word. Your chart should look like this:

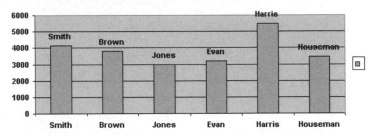

6) Save your sample document with the following name, and close it:

    `Chapter16_Exercise_16-3_After_Your_Name`.doc

To format text and value labels, right-click on a label and choose **Format Data Labels** from the pop-up menu.

Select your required options from the following four dialog box tabs – **Patterns, Font**, **Number** and **Alignment** – and click **OK**.

Chart titles and legends

A chart title is text describing the chart. By default, Microsoft Graph centres the chart title in the chart area above the plot area.

A legend is a box that identifies the colours or patterns that are assigned to the data series or categories in a chart. Microsoft Graph offers the following placement options for a chart legend: bottom, corner, top, right and left. By default, the legend is located on the right. If you select a different placement, Microsoft Graph resizes the plot area automatically to accommodate it.

Exercise 16.4: Add a chart title

1) Open the following document:

    `Chapter16_Exercise_16-4_Before.doc`

2) Double-click anywhere on the chart to activate Microsoft Graph.

3) Right-click on the chart area (the margin area surrounding the actual chart), choose **Chart Options** from the pop-up menu, and select the **Titles** tab of the dialog box.

4) In the *Chart title* box, type the following text and click **OK**:

    Unit Sales in Third Quarter

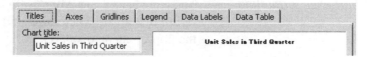

Click outside the chart to close Microsoft Graph and return to Word.

5) Save your sample document with the following name, and close it:

    Chapter16_Exercise_16-4_After_*Your_Name*.doc

To edit the chart title, double-click the chart to activate Microsoft Graph, and then click anywhere within the title text. You can now edit the text. To remove the chart title, click on it once and press **Delete**.

To reformat the chart title, right-click anywhere on it and choose **Format Chart Title** from the pop-up menu displayed.

Select the options you require from the three tabs of the dialog box – **Patterns**, **Font** and **Alignment** – and click **OK** when finished.

Exercise 16.5: Move and delete a chart legend

1) Open the following document:

    Chapter16_Exercise_16-5_Before.doc

2) Double-click anywhere on the chart to activate Microsoft Graph.

3) Right-click on the chart area (the margin area surrounding the actual chart), choose **Chart Options** from the pop-up menu, and select the **Legend** tab of the dialog box.

4) Click on the various *Placement* options and notice the effect of relocating the legend in the preview area on the right of the dialog box.

5) Click the show *legend* option to deselect it and click **OK**.

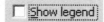

6) Click outside the chart to close Microsoft Graph and return to Word. You can see that the legend is no longer displayed.

7) Save your sample document with the following name, and close it:

Chapter16_Exercise_16-5_After_*Your_Name*.doc

Chart axes formatting

You can change how Microsoft Graph displays a chart axis by right-clicking anywhere on it and choosing **Format Axis** from the pop-up menu displayed.

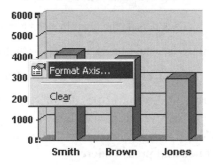

Select the options you require from the five tabs of the dialog box – **Patterns**, **Scale**, **Font**, **Number** and **Alignment** – and click **OK** when finished.

Exercise 16.6: Amend chart axis format

1) Open the following document:

Chapter16_Exercise_16-6_Before.doc

2) Double-click anywhere on the chart to activate Microsoft Graph.

3) Right-click on the horizontal category axis and choose the **Format Axis** command from the pop-up menu displayed.

4) In the dialog box displayed, click the **Font** tab and change the colour to red.

5) Click the **Patterns** tab and change the colour to red.

6) Click **OK** to close the dialog box.

7) Repeat steps 3 to 6 for the horizontal category value axis.

8) Click outside the chart to close Microsoft Graph and return to Word. You can see that the axis text is in the colour you chose.

9) Save your sample document with the following name, and close it:

Chapter16_Exercise_16-6_After_*Your_Name*.doc

Chart axes values

On the **Scale** tab of the *Format Axis* dialog box, Microsoft Graph allows you to change the minimum, maximum and increment values displayed for each axis, the units in which the chart values are shown, and the point at which the two axes cross. The three more commonly used options that can help you make a chart axis more readable are:

- **Minimum value**. Typically, you will want your chart to highlight the *relative differences* between the various data series rather than the absolute value of each series. See Exercise 16.7.

- **Units**. Does your chart consist of large numbers? If, for example, the chart values range from 1,000,000 to 50,000,000, you can display the numbers on the axis as 1 to 50 and show a label that indicates that the units express millions. See Exercise 16.8.

- **Increment value**. If the axis values are too crowded, you can increase the increment between each display value, say, from 1000 to 2000. See Exercise 16.9.

Exercise 16.7: Change the minimum axis value

1) Open the following Word document:

    Chapter16_Exercise_16-7_Before.doc

2) You can see that none of the data series have a value of less than 3000.

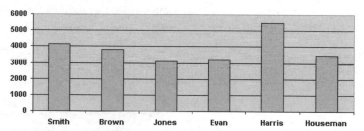

By changing the minimum value to 3000, you will be able to see more clearly how the various data series differ from each other.

Double-click anywhere on the chart to activate Microsoft Graph.

3) Right-click on the vertical value axis and choose the **Format Axis** command from the pop-up menu displayed.

4) In the dialog box displayed, click the **Scale** tab, and change the *Minimum* value to 3000. The *Category (X) Axis Crosses* at value automatically changes to 3000.

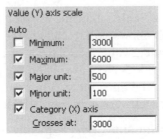

Value (Y) axis scale	
Auto	
☐ Minimum:	3000
☑ Maximum:	6000
☑ Major unit:	500
☑ Minor unit:	100
☑ Category (X) axis	
Crosses at:	3000

5) Click **OK** to close the dialog box. Click outside the chart to close Microsoft Graph and return to Word. Your chart should now look like this:

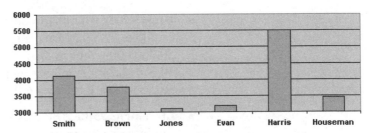

6) Save your sample document with the following name, and close it:

Chapter16_Exercise_16-7_After_*Your_Name*.doc

Exercise 16.8: Change the axis units

1) Open the following Word document:

Chapter16_Exercise_16-8_Before.doc

2) You can see that the data series values range from 300,000 to 600,000.

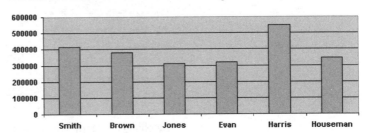

By changing the chart units to thousands, you can make your *y* axis easier to read.

Double-click anywhere on the chart to activate Microsoft Graph.

3) Right-click on the vertical value axis and choose the **Format Axis** command from the pop-up menu displayed.

4) In the dialog box displayed, click the **Scale** tab, and select the *Thousands* option from the *Display units* drop-down list.

Ensure that the *Show display units label on chart* checkbox is selected.

5) Click **OK** to close the dialog box. Click outside the chart to close Microsoft Graph and return to Word. Your chart should now look like this:

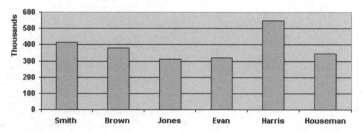

6) Save your sample document with the following name, and close it:

Chapter16_Exercise_16-8_After_*Your_Name*.doc

Exercise 16.9: Change the axis unit increments

1) Open the following Word document:

Chapter16_Exercise_16-9_Before.doc

You can see that the *y* axis is divided into increments of 1000.

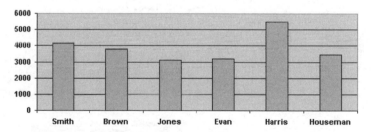

2) Double-click anywhere on the chart to activate Microsoft Graph.

3) Right-click on the vertical value axis and choose the **Format Axis** command from the pop-up menu displayed.

4) In the dialog box displayed, click the **Scale** tab, and change the value in the *Major unit* box from 1000 to 2000.

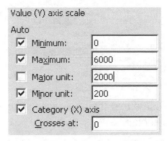

Value (Y) axis scale
Auto
☑ Mi̱nimum: 0
☑ Ma̱ximum: 6000
☐ Ma̱jor unit: 2000|
☑ Mi̱nor unit: 200
☑ Category (X) axis
  C̱rosses at: 0

5) Click **OK** to close the dialog box. Click outside the chart to close Microsoft Graph and return to Word. Your chart should now look like this:

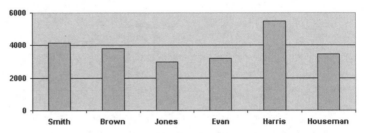

6) Save your sample document with the following name, and close it:

Chapter16_Exercise_16-9_After_*Your_Name*.doc

Chart gridlines

Gridlines are lines that extend across the plot area from the increment values on one or both axes. They make it easier for the reader to evaluate the chart's data values.

- On column charts, gridlines typically extend only from the *y* axis.

- On bar charts, gridlines typically extend only from the *x* axis.

Microsoft Graph offers two kinds of gridlines: *major gridlines*, which are displayed by default, and *minor gridlines* for more precise data evaluation. Pie charts have no gridlines.

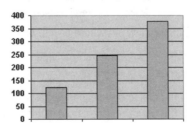

Column chart with gridlines from y axis

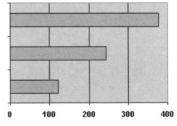

Bar chart with gridlines from x axis

Exercise 16.10: Amend chart gridlines

1) Open the following Word document:

    Chapter16_Exercise_16-10_Before.doc

    You can see major gridlines extending horizontally from the *y* axis.

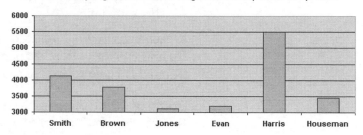

2) Double-click anywhere on the chart to activate Microsoft Graph.

3) Right-click on the chart area (the margin area surrounding the actual chart), choose **Chart Options** from the pop-up menu, and select the **Gridlines** tab.

4) In the dialog box displayed, click the *Minor gridlines* checkbox in the *Value (y) axis* section. The *Major gridlines* checkbox is selected by default.

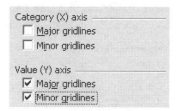

5) Click **OK** to close the dialog box. Click outside the chart to close Microsoft Graph and return to Word. You chart now looks as shown.

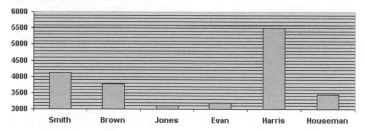

6) Save your sample document with the following name, and close it:

    Chapter16_Exercise_16-10_After_*Your_Name*.doc

Working with chart colours

Microsoft Graph enables you to change the colours of three parts of a chart:

- **Chart area**. This is the margin area surrounding the chart.

- **Plot area**. This is the area of the actual chart.

- **Data series**. This is the data plotted by the chart. Depending on the chart type, this can consist of columns, bars or 'slices' of a pie.

In each case, you right-click on the relevant element, choose the **Format** command from the pop-up menu, and select your required fill colour. See Exercise 16.11.

Exercise 16.11: Amend chart colours

1) Open the following Word document:

    Chapter16_Exercise_16-11_Before.doc

    As you can see, the chart area is currently coloured white, the plot area is grey, and the data series is blue.

2) Double-click anywhere on the chart to activate Microsoft Graph.

3) Right-click on the chart area, choose **Format Chart Area** from the pop-up menu, select a light yellow colour, and click **OK**.

4) Right-click on the plot area, choose **Format Plot Area** from the pop-up menu, select a red colour, and click **OK**.

5) Right-click on any column, choose **Format Data Series** from the pop-up menu, select white, and click **OK**.

    Click **OK** to close the dialog box. Click outside the chart to close Microsoft Graph and return to Word.

6) Save your sample document with the following name, and close it:

    Chapter16_Exercise_16-11_After_*Your_Name*.doc

Working with chart types

Microsoft Graph offers more than a dozen chart types. Here are the three main ones:

- **Column chart**. The default type, in which items are shown horizontally and values vertically.

- **Bar chart**. A sideways column chart that shows items horizontally and values vertically.

- **Pie chart**. Shows the proportion of each item that makes up the total.

Changing the chart type

To change the current type of a chart, double-click the chart to activate Microsoft Graph, right-click anywhere within the chart, choose the **Chart Type** command from the pop-up menu, and select a different type (or subtype) from the *Chart Type* dialog box.

In Exercise 16.12 you will convert an existing column chart, the default type, to a bar chart.

Exercise 16.12: Changing a column chart to a bar chart

1) Open the following Word document:

Chapter16_Exercise_16-12_Before.doc

2) Double-click anywhere on the column chart to activate Microsoft Graph.

3) Right-click on the chart area, and choose **Chart Type** from the pop-up menu.

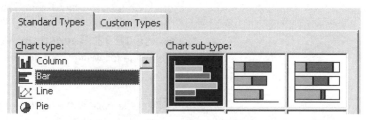

4) In the *Chart type* area, select *Bar* and click **OK** to close the dialog box.

5) Click outside the chart to close Microsoft Graph and return to Word. Your chart should now look like this:

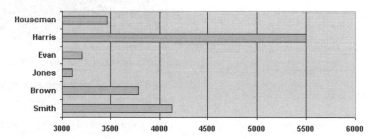

6) Save your sample document with the following name, and close it:

Chapter16_Exercise_16-12_After_*Your_Name*.doc

Repositioning and resizing a chart

When you double-click on an embedded chart, you activate Microsoft Graph and can use all its charting functions. When you have finished working with the chart, you can then click anywhere outside the chart area to return to Word.

When you click *once* on an embedded chart, you remain within Word and you can work with the chart as if it were an inserted picture.

- **Repositioning a chart**. By default, Word treats an embedded chart as a paragraph, just as it does an inserted picture. You can reposition such a chart with the **Format | Paragraph** command.

  Alternatively, you can right-click the embedded chart, choose **Format Object**, click the **Layout** tab, select the *Behind text* or *In front of text* option, and click **OK**.

  Your embedded chart is no longer a paragraph but a free-floating object that you can click on and drag to a new position with the mouse.

- **Resizing a chart**. Click once anywhere in the chart to select it, click on a sizing handle, and then drag it to the required size.

Exercise 16.13: Reposition a chart

1) Open the following Word document:

   Chapter16_Exercise_16-13_Before.doc

2) Select the table at the bottom of the page.

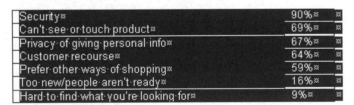

3) Choose **Insert | Picture | Chart**.

4) Word activates Microsoft Graph, which inserts an embedded chart and an associated datasheet in your Word document.

   Click anywhere outside the chart to return to Word.

5) Select the table that supplied the data for the chart, and choose **Edit | Cut** to remove it from the Word document.

6) Click the chart once, choose **Format | Paragraph**, change the left indentation from 5 to 0 cm, and click **OK**.

7) Click once on your chart, and drag its bottom-right sizing handle to the right margin of the page.

8) Double-click anywhere on the column chart to activate Microsoft Graph.

9) Right-click on the chart legend, choose **Format Legend** from the pop-up menu, click the **Font** tab, change the font to 10 point, and click **OK**.

10) Right-click on the *y* axis, choose **Format Axis** from the pop-up menu, click the **Font** tab, change the font to 10 point, and click **OK**. Your sample document should now look like this:

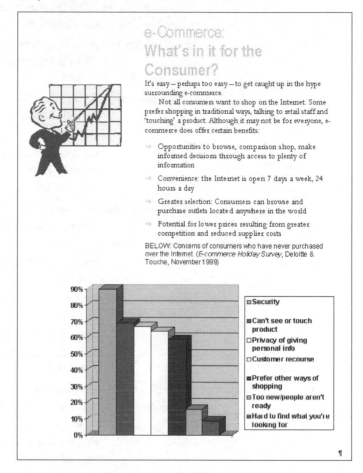

11) Save your sample document with the following name, and close it:

Chapter16_Exercise_16-13_After_*Your_Name*.doc

Tasks summary

Task	Procedure
Create a chart based on data in a table.	Select the table, or cells within the table, in the Word document, and choose **Insert	Picture	Chart**.
Add value labels to a chart.	Right-click on the chart area, choose **Chart Options**, click the **Data Labels** tab, select the Show Value option, and click **OK**.
Add text labels to a chart.	Right-click on the chart area, choose **Chart Options**, click the **Data Labels** tab, select the *Show label* option, and click **OK**.
Add a chart title.	Right-click on the chart area, choose **Chart Options**, click the **Titles** tab, enter the title in the *Chart title* box, and click **OK**.
Reposition or delete a legend.	Right-click on the chart area, choose **Chart Options**, click the **Legend** tab, select your required options, and click **OK**.
Amend axis format.	Right-click on an axis, choose **Format Axis**, select your required options on the **Font** and **Patterns** tabs, and click **OK**.
Change axis minimum value.	Right-click on an axis, choose **Format Axis**, click the **Scale** tab, change the minimum value, and click **OK**.
Change axis units.	Right-click on an axis, choose **Format Axis**, click the **Scale** tab, select from the *Display units* drop-down list, and click **OK**.
Change the chart axis unit increments.	Right-click on an axis, choose **Format Axis**, click the **Scale** tab, change the major unit, and click **OK**.
Amend gridlines display.	Right-click on the chart area, choose **Chart Options**, click the **Gridlines** tab, select your required options, and click **OK**.
Amend chart colours.	Right-click on the chart area, plot area or a data series, choose **Format**, select your required fill colour, and click **OK**.
Change chart type.	Right-click on the chart area, choose **Chart Type**, select a different type (or subtype), and click **OK**.
Reposition a chart.	In Word, click the chart, choose **Format	Paragraph**, enter your new value(s), and click **OK**.
	Alternatively, right-click the chart, choose **Format Object**, click the **Layout** tab, select the *Behind text* or *In front of text* option, and click **OK**. You can then drag the chart with the mouse.

Concepts summary

Word is supplied with a small application named *Microsoft Graph* that enables you to create and amend a variety of bar, column, pie and other charts based on information contained in tables.

To present data in a Word table as a chart, select all or part of the table and choose **Insert | Picture | Chart**. Microsoft Graph then creates a chart of the default type – a 3D bar chart – as an *embedded object* within your Word document. You can return to Word by clicking anywhere outside the chart.

Associated with every chart is a *datasheet* – a small window that you use to modify the chart content. You do this by typing in your own numbers and text, over-writing those already present.

A chart contains three main areas: the *chart area* (the margin area surrounding the chart), the *plot area* (the area of the actual chart), and the *data series* (the data plotted by the chart). Depending on the *chart type*, the data series can consist of columns, bars or slices of a pie.

In any chart, a *data point* is an item being measured and its measured value. You can add *value labels* to indicate the numerical values of the individual data points, and *text labels* to display the names of the data points. You can also add a *chart title* to describe the chart, and you can amend, move or delete the chart legend – the box that identifies the colours or patterns of the data series.

Options for working with the *chart axes* include the ability to change the *minimum value* to highlight the relative rather than absolute value of the data series, the units in which the values are expressed (for example, hundreds or thousands), and, if the axis values are too crowded, the increment value.

Gridlines are lines that extend across the plot area from the increment values on one or both axes. They make it easier for the reader to evaluate the chart's data values. Microsoft Graph offers major gridlines (displayed by default) and optional minor gridlines for more precise data evaluation. Pie charts have no gridlines.

You can change the colour of any element by right-clicking on it, choosing the **Format** command from the pop-up menu, and selecting your required fill colour.

By default, Word treats an embedded chart as a paragraph, just as it does an inserted picture. You can reposition such a chart with the **Format | Paragraph** command. Alternatively, you can right-click the embedded chart, choose **Format Object**, click the **Layout** tab, select the *Behind text* or *In front of text* option, and click **OK**. You can then drag the chart with the mouse.

Chapter 16: quick quiz

Circle the correct answer to each of the following multiple-choice questions about charts in Word.

Q1	What is the name of the application supplied with Word that enables users to create and work with charts?
A.	Microsoft Chart Maker.
B.	Microsoft Graph Builder.
C.	Microsoft Chart.
D.	Microsoft Graph.

Q2	In Word, which command do you choose to create a chart based on data contained in table cells?
A.	**Insert | Picture | Chart.**
B.	**Format | Chart | New.**
C.	**Tools | Insert | Chart.**
D.	**Format | Chart | Insert.**

Q3	By default, which item(s) does Microsoft Graph display within the area of an embedded chart?
A.	The chart only.
B.	The datasheet only.
C.	The chart and its associated datasheet.
D.	The chart and its associated worksheet.

Q4	In Word, which action do you take to return from Microsoft Graph to the Word document that contains the chart?
A.	Click anywhere outside the chart.
B.	Choose **Chart	Exit**.
C.	Choose **File	Close Chart and Return to Word**.
D.	Choose **File	Close**.

Q5	In a Word document, which action do you take to work with an embedded chart?
A.	Right-click anywhere on the chart.
B.	Double-click anywhere on the chart.
C.	Right-click on the plot area.
D.	Right-click on the plot area and choose **Format	Object**.

Q6	In Microsoft Graph, which action do you take to access the options for changing the format of a chart axis?
A.	Right-click on the axis, choose **Axis Pattern**, and select your required options from the **Font** and **Shading** tabs.
B.	Click to select the axis and select your required options on the **Format** tab.
C.	Right-click on the axis, choose **Format Axis**, and select your required options on the **Font** and **Pattern** tabs.
D.	Click to select the axis and select your required options on the **Format** and **Color** tabs.

Q7	In Microsoft Graph, which of the following chart axis actions can you not perform?
A.	Change the minimum value displayed by the chart axis.
B.	Set the chart axis width to zero.
C.	Amend the units in which the chart axis values are displayed.
D.	Change the increment between the displayed chart axis units.

Q8	In Microsoft Graph, which of the following statements about gridlines is untrue?		
A.	On column charts, gridlines extend by default only from the *y* axis.
B.	Pie charts do not display gridlines by default.
C.	On bar charts, gridlines extend by default only from the *x* axis.
D.	Column charts do not display gridlines by default.

Q9	In Microsoft Graph, which of the following statements is untrue?		
A.	The chart area is the plot area and the data series it contains.
B.	A data point indicates a particular value within a data series.
C.	The plot area is the area of the actual chart. It is bounded by the two chart axes and is enclosed within the chart area
D.	A data series is a collection of data points. Depending on the chart type, the data series can consist of columns, bars or slices of a pie.

Answers

1: D, **2:** A, **3:** C, **4:** A, **5:** B, **6:** C, **7:** B, **8:** D, **9:** A.

17 *Footnotes and endnotes*

Objectives

In this chapter you will learn how to:

- Create footnotes and endnotes
- Amend the content, format and placement of footnotes and endnotes
- Remove footnotes and endnotes

New words

In this chapter you will meet the following terms:

- Footnote
- Endnote

Exercise files

In this chapter you will work with the following Word files:

- `Chapter17_Exercise_17-1_Before.doc`
- `Chapter17_Exercise_17-2_Before.doc`
- `Chapter17_Exercise_17-3_Before.doc`
- `Chapter17_Exercise_17-4_Before.doc`
- `Chapter17_Exercise_17-5_Before.doc`
- `Chapter17_Exercise_17-6_Before.doc`
- `Chapter17_Exercise_17-7_Before.doc`

Syllabus reference

In this chapter you will cover the following items from the ECDL Advanced Word Processing Syllabus:

- **AM3.3.3.1:** Create or delete footnotes and endnotes.
- **AM3.3.3.2:** Modify existing footnotes or endnotes.
- **AM3.3.3.3:** Modify format and positioning of footnotes or endnotes.

About footnotes and endnotes

You can use footnotes and endnotes to supply additional information about text in a document, or to cite references or sources. The main difference between footnotes and endnotes is their location. Here are some important points about footnotes and endnotes:

- **Positioning**. Footnotes typically appear at the bottom of individual pages. Endnotes typically appear at the end of the document.

- **Footnotes and endnotes together**. You can include both footnotes and endnotes in the same document.

- **Reference marks**. Every footnote or endnote consists of text and an indicator called a reference mark – this is a superscripted symbol or number that appears in the body of the document to indicate that a footnote or endnote is present.

purchased·over·the·Internet·revealed·that·the·three·main·barriers·to·
online·shopping·were·concerns·over·payment·security·(90%),·
inability·to·physically·inspect·the·products·offered·(69%)·and·fears·
of·loss·of·privacy·(67%).

Reference mark

E-commerce·Holiday·Survey, Deloitte·&·Touche, November·1999¶

- **Symbol reference marks**. Symbols are a good choice as reference marks when you have only one or two footnotes or endnotes in a document. For example, *Subject to status or availability* or *Certain conditions may apply.*

- **Sequential numbering**. By default, Word inserts sequential numbers as references marks. When you move, delete or relocate a numbered footnote or endnote, Word automatically updates all other footnotes or endnotes in the document.

- **Editing and formatting**. In Print Layout view, you edit and format footnote and endnote text in the same way that you edit and format text in the body of a document.

The Footnote and Endnote dialog box

You insert footnotes and endnotes with the **Insert | Footnote** command.

Footnotes, endnotes and document views

In Print Layout view, you edit and format individual footnotes and endnotes simply by positioning the insertion point over them and clicking and selecting the note text, as required.

In Normal view, Word does not display notes by default. To view them, choose **View | Footnotes**. Word opens a separate window at the bottom of your screen in which you can access and work with all footnotes and endnotes in your document.

Working with footnotes: the four tasks

Here are the four tasks that you need to be able to perform with footnotes and endnotes in Word:

- **Create footnotes and endnotes**. Exercises 17.1 and 17.2 take you through the steps of creating footnotes with sequential numbers and with custom symbols. In Exercise 17.6, you learn how to create numbered endnotes.

- **Edit note text**. Exercise 17.3 shows you how to amend footnote text. You edit endnote text in a similar way.

- **Amend note format**. In Exercise 17.4, you discover the various options for modifying footnote format. You reformat endnotes in a similar way.

- **Delete notes**. You delete a footnote in Exercise 17.5 and delete an endnote in Exercise 17.7.

Working with new footnotes

In the first two exercises, you will create new footnotes in two documents.

Exercise 17.1: Create numbered footnotes

1) Start Word and open the following document:

    Chapter17_Exercise_17-1_Before.doc

2) Are you in Print Layout view? If not, choose **View | Print Layout**.

3) Click in the location where you want the footnote reference mark to appear.

In this example, click at the end of the first paragraph of body text, after the '2005' but before the full stop.

INTRODUCTION¶

Internet·usage·continues·to·grow·dramatically·throughout·the·world.·
From·a·base·of·40·million·users·in·1996,·the·number·of·online·users·
is·predicted·to·reach·1·billion·in·2005▮¶

4) Choose **Insert | Footnote** to display the *Footnote and Endnote* dialog box.

5) In the *Insert* area, select *Footnote*. In the *Numbering* area, select *AutoNumber*. The default numbering system for footnotes is 1,2,3, …

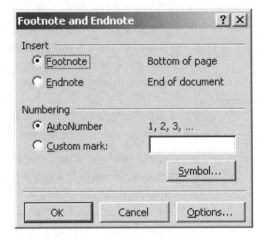

Click **OK**.

6) Word moves the insertion point to the bottom of the page. You can see a line and the number 1. This is where the footnote will appear.

Type the following footnote text:

```
Angus Reid Group
```

ECDL Advanced Word Processing

7) Move to the second page of the sample document, and locate the paragraph of body text that begins with 'By 2003'.

8) Click in the end of the paragraph, after the word 'models' but before the full stop.

> only·2.7%·of·new·car·sales·currently·take·place·over·the·Net,·but·as·
> many·as·40%·of·purchases·involve·the·Net·at·some·point,·with·
> consumers·using·it·to·compare·prices·or·look·at·the·latest·models.¶

9) Choose **Insert | Footnote**, select *Footnote*, select *AutoNumber*, and click **OK**.

Word moves the insertion point to the bottom of the page. Type the following footnote text:

    The Economist, Feb. 2000

10) Drag over the words 'The Economist', and click the **Italics** button on the Formatting toolbar. Your footnote should now look like this:

> ² *The·Economist*,·Feb.·2000¶

11) Move to the next paragraph, which begins with the words 'Not all consumers'. Click at the end of the paragraph, after the '(67%)' but before the full stop.

> online·shopping·were·concerns·over·payment·security·(90%),·
> inability·to·physically·inspect·the·products·offered·(69%)·and·fears·
> of·loss·of·privacy·(67%).¶

12) Choose **Insert | Footnote**, select *Footnote*, select *AutoNumber*, and click **OK**.

13) Word moves the insertion point to the bottom of the page. Type the following footnote text:

    E-commerce Holiday Survey, Deloitte &
    Touche, November 1999

14) Drag over the words 'E-commerce Holiday Survey', and click the **Italics** button on the Formatting toolbar. Your footnote should now look like this:

> ² *The·Economist*,·Feb.·2000¶
>
> ³ *E-commerce·Holiday·Survey*,·Deloitte·&·Touche,·November·1999¶

15) Click anywhere in the body text of your sample document. Save your document with the following name, and close:

Chapter17_Exercise_17-1_After_*Your_Name*.doc

Exercise 17.2: Create footnotes with custom symbols

1) Open the following Word document:

Chapter17_Exercise_17-2_Before.doc

Are you in Print Layout view? If not, choose **View | Print Layout**.

Click in the end of the first paragraph of body text, after the '2005' but before the full stop.

INTRODUCTION¶
Internet·usage·continues·to·grow·dramatically·throughout·the·world.·
From·a·base·of·40·million·users·in·1996,·the·number·of·online·users·
is·predicted·to·reach·1·billion·in·2005.¶

2) Choose **Insert | Footnote** to display the *Footnote and Endnote* dialog box.

3) In the *Insert* area, select *Footnote*. In the *Numbering* area, click the **Symbol** button.

4) Word displays the *Symbol* dialog box. Click the asterisk symbol (*) to select it and click **OK**.

5) You are returned to the *Footnote and Endnote* dialog box. Notice that the *Custom mark* checkbox is selected and the asterisk is shown in the box to its right.

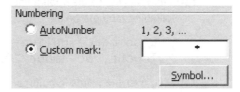

6) Click **OK**.

7) Word moves the insertion point to the bottom of the page. You can see a line and the asterisk symbol. This is where the footnote will appear.

8) Type the following footnote text:

    Angus Reid Group

9) Move to the second page of the sample document, and locate the paragraph of body text that begins with 'By 2003'.

    Click in the end of the paragraph, after the word 'models' but before the full stop.

    only·2.7%·of·new·car·sales·currently·take·place·over·the·Net,·but·as·many·as·40%·of·purchases·involve·the·Net·at·some·point,·with·consumers·using·it·to·compare·prices·or·look·at·the·latest·models¶

10) Choose **Insert | Footnote**. In the *Insert* area, select *Footnote*. In the *Numbering* area, click the **Symbol** button.

11) In the *Symbol* dialog box, click the diamond symbol (♦) to select it and click **OK**.

12) Word moves the insertion point to the bottom of the page. Type the following footnote text:

    The Economist, Feb. 2000

13) Drag over the words 'The Economist', and click the **Italics** button on the Formatting toolbar. Your footnote should now look like this:

    ♦·*The·Economist,·*Feb.·2000¶

14) Move to the paragraph, that begins with the words 'Not all consumers'. Click in the end of the paragraph, after the '(67%)' but before the full stop.

    online·shopping·were·concerns·over·payment·security·(90%),·inability·to·physically·inspect·the·products·offered·(69%)·and·fears·of·loss·of·privacy·(67%)¶

15) Choose **Insert | Footnote**. In the *Insert* area, select *Footnote*. In the *Numbering* area, click the **Symbol** button.

16) In the *Symbol* dialog box, click the degree symbol (°) to select it and click **OK**.

17) Word moves the insertion point to the bottom of the page. Type the following footnote text:

    E-commerce Holiday Survey, Deloitte & Touche, November 1999

18) Drag over the words 'E-commerce Holiday Survey', and click the **Italics** button on the Formatting toolbar. Your footnote should now look like this:

*·*The Economist,·*Feb.·2000¶

*·*E-commerce·Holiday·Survey,·Deloitte·&·Touche,·November·1999¶

19) Click anywhere in the body text of your sample document. Save your document with the following name, and close:

Chapter17_Exercise_17-2_After_*Your_Name*.doc

Working with footnote content

In Exercise 17.3, you will edit the content of an existing footnote.

Exercise 17.3: Amend the content of footnotes

1) Open the following Word document:

Chapter17_Exercise_17-3_Before.doc

Are you in Print Layout view? If not, choose **View | Print Layout**.

2) Move to the footnote at the bottom of the first page, and edit the text from 'Angus Reid Group' to 'XYZ Consultants'.

Your footnote should now look like this:

¹·XYZ·Consultants¶

3) Click anywhere in the body text of your sample document. Save your document with the following name, and close:

Chapter17_Exercise_17-3_After_*Your_Name*.doc

Working with footnote format

Word allows you to amend the format of a footnote in a number of ways:

- **Font**. You can select all or part of a footnote and amend aspects of its appearance – such as the font or font colour – with the **Format | Font** command.

  Alternatively, as in Exercises 17.1 and 17.2, you can amend the format of selected footnote text by clicking the relevant buttons on the Formatting toolbar.

- **Paragraph**. You can select a footnote and amend its left and right indents, and the spacing above and below it, with the **Format | Paragraph** command.

- **Style**. You can change the font and paragraph attributes of *all* footnotes in a document, or in all documents based on a particular template, by changing the built-in Footnote Text style with the **Format | Style** command.

- **Separator line**. You can delete the horizontal line that Word inserts above footnotes and, optionally, insert an alternative. To do so, switch to Normal view and use the options within the **View | Footnotes** command.

- **Numbering format**. When your footnotes follow an automatic sequence, you use the **Options** button within the **Insert | Footnote** command to change from the default pattern (1,2,3, …) to another of your choice (such as a,b,c, ...).

- **Placement**. You can change the placement of all footnotes in a document from the default location at the bottom of the page to beneath the last line of text on each page.

Exercise 17.4: Amend the format of a footnote

1) Open the following Word document:

    Chapter17_Exercise_17-4_Before.doc

    Are you in Print Layout view? If not, choose **View | Print Layout**.

2) Click anywhere in the footnote at the bottom of the first page, and choose **Format | Style**. Word displays the *Style* dialog box with Footnote Text style selected automatically. Click the **Modify** button.

3) In the *Modify Style* dialog box, click **Format** and then **Font**.

4) Change the font to Arial, 10 point, and change the font colour to blue. Click **OK**, **OK** and **Apply**.

5) Move to the second page of your sample document and verify that the other footnotes have also changed appearance.

6) Choose **View | Normal** to switch to Normal view, and then choose **View | Footnotes**. Word opens a separate footnote pane at the bottom of your screen.

7) Click *Footnote Separator* in the drop-down list that appears just above the footnotes.

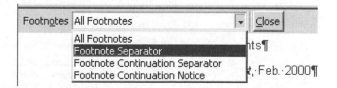

8) Click to the left of the separator line to select it.

9) Press **Delete** to remove it.

10) Click at the paragraph mark where the separator line used to be.

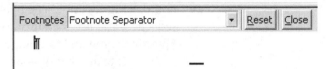

Choose **Format | Borders and Shading**. On the **Borders** tab, click *Box*, change the style to a double line, and deselect all borders except the bottom one.

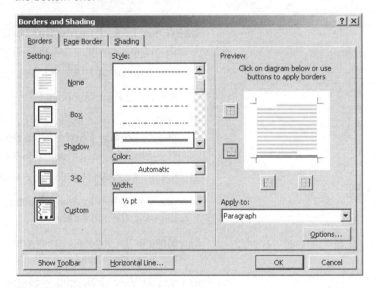

Click **OK**.

11) Choose **View | Print Layout** and verify that your footnote separator has changed.

12) Click anywhere in the footnote at the bottom of the sample document's first page and choose **Insert | Footnote**.

13) Click the **Options** button. In the *Place at* list, select *Beneath text*. In the *Number format* list, select *A, B, C, ...*

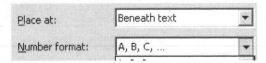

When finished, click **OK** and **OK**.

Notice that Word has inserted a new footnote symbol. This is as a result of using the **Insert | Footnote** command.

¶
_____

🔲XYZ·Consultants¶

Click to the left of this and press **Backspace**. Your footnote should now look like this:

¶
_____

🔲XYZ·Consultants¶

14) Move to the second page of your sample document to verify that the footnote numbering sequence and placement has changed.

15) Click anywhere in the body text of your sample document. Save your document with the following name, and close:

Chapter17_Exercise_17-4_After_*Your_Name*.doc.

Want to remove a footnote? Just select the reference marker in the body text and press **Backspace** or **Delete**. Word removes the footnote and, if you are using the AutoNumber option, automatically renumbers all remaining footnotes. See Exercise 17.5.

Exercise 17.5: Deleting a footnote

1) Open the following Word document:

Chapter17_Exercise_17-5_Before.doc

Are you in Print Layout view? If not, choose **View | Print Layout**.

2) Select the first footnote marker in your document by dragging across it.

Internet·usage·continues·to·grow·dramatically·throughout·the·world. From·a·base·of·40·million·users·in·1996,·the·number·of·online·users· is·predicted·to·reach·1·billion·in·2005▮¶

3) Press **Delete** or **Backspace**. Word removes the footnote.

4) Move to the second page of your sample document to verify that the footnote numbering sequence has changed.

5) Click anywhere in the body text of your sample document. Save your document with the following name, and close:

Chapter17_Exercise_17-5_After_*Your_Name*.doc

In Exercise 17.6, you will create new endnotes in a sample document.

Exercise 17.6: Create numbered endnotes

1) Start Word and open the following document:

   `Chapter17_Exercise_17-6_Before.doc`

2) Are you in Print Layout view? If not, choose **View | Print Layout**.

3) Click in the location where you want the endnote reference mark to appear.

   In this example, click at the end of the first paragraph of body text, after the '2005' but before the full stop.

   INTRODUCTION¶

   Internet·usage·continues·to·grow·dramatically·throughout·the·world.· From·a·base·of·40·million·users·in·1996,·the·number·of·online·users· is·predicted·to·reach·1·billion·in·2005.¶

4) Choose **Insert | Footnote** to display the *Footnote and Endnote* dialog box.

5) In the *Insert* area, select *Endnote*. In the *Numbering* area, select *AutoNumber*. The default numbering system for endnotes is 1,2,3, …

6) Click **OK**.

7) Word moves the insertion point to the end of your document. You can see a line and the number 1. This is where the endnote will appear.

Type the following endnote text:

```
Angus Reid Group
```

‖ Angus Reid Group¶

8) Move to the second page of the sample document, and locate the paragraph of body text that begins with 'By 2003'.

Click in the end of the paragraph, after the word 'models' but before the full stop.

only·2.7%·of·new·car·sales·currently·take·place·over·the·Net,·but·as·many·as·40%·of·purchases·involve·the·Net·at·some·point,·with·consumers·using·it·to·compare·prices·or·look·at·the·latest·models¦¶

9) Choose **Insert | Footnote**, select *Endnote*, select *AutoNumber*, and click **OK**.

10) Word moves the insertion point to the end of your document. Type the following endnote text:

```
The Economist, Feb. 2000
```

11) Drag over the words 'The Economist', and click the **Italics** button on the Formatting toolbar. Your endnote should now look like this:

¾ *The Economist,* Feb. 2000¶

12) Move to the next paragraph, which begins with the words 'Not all consumers'. Click at the end of the paragraph, after the '(67%)' but before the full stop.

online·shopping·were·concerns·over·payment·security·(90%),·inability·to·physically·inspect·the·products·offered·(69%)·and·fears·of·loss·of·privacy·(67%)¦¶

13) Choose **Insert | Endnote**, select *Endnote*, select *AutoNumber*, and click **OK**.

14) Word moves the insertion point to the end of the document. Type the following endnote text:

```
E-commerce Holiday Survey, Deloitte &
Touche, November 1999
```

15) Drag over the words 'E-commerce Holiday Survey', and click the **Italics** button on the Formatting toolbar. Your endnotes should now look like this:

---

[i] Angus·Reid·Group¶

[ii] *The·Economist*,·Feb.·2000¶

[iii] *E-commerce·Holiday·Survey*,·Deloitte·&·Touche,·November·1999¶

16) Click anywhere in the body text of your sample document. Save your document with the following name, and close:

    `Chapter17_Exercise_17-6_After_`*`Your_Name`*`.doc`

Working with endnote content and format

The procedures for modifying existing endnotes are similar to those for working with footnotes:

- **Content**. To change the text of any endnote in Print Layout view, click in the endnote and make the text changes.

- **Font**. You can select all or part of an endnote and amend aspects of its appearance – such as the font or font colour – with the **Format | Font** command.

  Alternatively, as in Exercise 17.4, you can amend the format of selected endnote text by clicking the relevant buttons on the Formatting toolbar.

- **Paragraph**. You can select an endnote and amend its left and right indents, and the spacing above and below it, with the **Format | Paragraph** command.

- **Style**. You can change the font and paragraph attributes of *all* endnotes in a document, or in all documents based on a particular template, by changing the built-in Endnote Text style with the **Format | Style** command.

- **Separator line**. You can delete the horizontal line that Word inserts above endnotes and insert an alternative. To do so, switch to Normal view and use the options within the **View | Footnotes** command.

- **Numbering Format**. When your endnotes follow an automatic sequence, you use the **Options** button within the **Insert | Footnote** command to change from the default pattern (1,2,3, …) to another of your choice (such as a,b,c, ...).

Exercise 17.7: Deleting a endnote

1) Open the following Word document:

    `Chapter17_Exercise_17-7_Before.doc`

Are you in Print Layout view? If not, choose **View | Print Layout**.

2) Select the first endnote marker in your document by dragging across it.

Internet·usage·continues·to·grow·dramatically·throughout·the·world.·
From·a·base·of·40·million·users·in·1996,·the·number·of·online·users·is·
predicted·to·reach·1·billion·in·2005.¶

3) Press **Delete** or **Backspace**. Word removes the endnote.

4) Move to the end of your sample document to verify that the endnote numbering sequence has changed.

⌐*The·Economist*,·Feb.·2000¶

⌐*E-commerce·Holiday·Survey*,·Deloitte·&·Touche,·November·1999¶

5) Click anywhere in the body text of your sample document. Save your document with the following name, and close:

Chapter17_Exercise_17-7_After_*Your_Name*.doc

Chapter 17: quick reference

Tasks summary

Task	Procedure
Insert a footnote or endnote.	Position the insertion point where you want to reference mark to appear, choose **Insert | Footnote**, select the required options, and click **OK**.
Edit a footnote or endnote.	In Print Layout view, you can edit notes in the same way that you edit and format text in the body of a document.
Reformat a footnote or endnote.	In Print Layout view, select the note text and click the buttons on the Formatting toolbar, or use the options within the **Font**, **Paragraph** and **Style** commands on the **Format** menu.
Modifying sequential numbering pattern in footnotes or endnotes.	Select your required option from the list available with the **Options** button in the **Insert | Footnote** command.
Change the placement of footnotes or endnotes.	Select your required options from the list available with the **Options** button in the **Insert | Footnote** command.

Concepts summary

Use *footnotes* and *endnotes* to supply additional information about text in a document, or to cite references or sources. Footnotes typically appear at the bottom of individual pages.

Endnotes typically appear at the end of the document. You insert both types of notes with the same command: **Insert | Footnote**.

Every footnote or endnote consists of text and an indicator called a *reference mark*. This is the superscripted symbol or number that appears in the body of the document to indicate that a footnote or endnote is present. By default, Word inserts sequential numbers as reference marks. When you move, delete or relocate a numbered footnote or endnote, Word automatically updates all other footnotes or endnotes in the document accordingly. You can also use symbols as reference marks.

In Print Layout view, you edit and format footnote and endnote text just as you would text in the body of a document. In Normal view, Word does not display notes by default. To view them, choose **View | Footnotes**. Word opens a separate window at the bottom of your screen in which you can access and work with all footnotes and endnotes in your document.

Chapter 17: quick quiz

Circle the correct answer to each of the following multiple-choice questions about footnotes and endnotes in Word.

Q1	A footnote is ...
A.	Additional information or references regarding the main text that appears at the end of document.
B.	A summary of information about a document that can be displayed with the **File	Properties** command.
C.	Additional information or references regarding the main text that appears at the bottom of a page within a document.
D.	A text box positioned in a page footer with the **Insert	Text Box** command.

Q2	An endnote is ...
A.	Additional information or references regarding main text that appears at the end of document.
B.	A summary of information about a document that can be displayed with the **File	Properties** command.
C.	Additional information or references regarding the main text that appears at the bottom of a page within a document.
D.	A text box positioned in the page footer with the **Insert	Text Box** command.

Q3	In Word, which command do you choose to insert a footnote or endnote in a document?
A.	Insert | Footnote.
B.	Tools | Options | Notes.
C.	Insert | Notes | Footnote.
D.	Format | AutoNotes.

Q4	In Word, a footnote or endnote reference mark is ...
A.	A superscripted number that appears in the body of a document to indicate that a footnote or endnote is present.
B.	A symbol or number positioned in a page header.
C.	A superscripted letter 'F' or 'N' that that appears in the body of a document to indicate that a footnote or endnote is present.
D.	A superscripted symbol or number that appears in the body of a document to indicate that a footnote or endnote is present.

Q5	In which type of documents are you mostly likely to use custom symbols as reference marks for footnotes?
A.	Financial or business documents of any length.
B.	Lengthy, multi-page documents of any type.
C.	Technical documents of any length.
D.	Short or single-page documents of any type.

Q6	In which type of documents are you mostly likely to use an automatically increasing number sequence as reference marks for footnotes or endnotes?
A.	Financial or business documents of any length.
B.	Lengthy, multi-page documents of any type.
C.	Technical documents of any length.
D.	Short or single-page documents of any type.

Q.7	In which of the following Word document views can you edit footnotes or endnotes just as you would body text?
A.	Print Layout view.
B.	Outline view.
C.	Notes view.
D.	Normal view.

Q.8	In which of the following Word document views can you edit all the footnotes or endnotes in a document within a separate window?
A.	Print Layout view.
B.	Outline view.
C.	Notes view.
D.	Normal view.

Q.9	In Word, which of the following statements about footnote and endnote formatting is untrue?
A.	You can change the appearance of all footnotes or endnotes in a document with the **Format	Style** command.
B.	You can change the appearance of a selected footnote or endnote with the **Format	Footnote** command.
C.	You can change the appearance of a selected footnote or endnote with the **Format	Paragraph** command.
D.	You can change the appearance of a selected footnote or endnote by clicking the relevant buttons on the Formatting toolbar.

Answers

1: C, **2:** A, **3:** A, **4:** D, **5:** D, **6:** B, **7:** A, **8:** D, **9:** B.

18

Bookmarks and cross-references

Objectives

In this chapter you will learn how to:

- Insert a bookmark
- Display a bookmark
- Move to a bookmark
- Delete a bookmark
- Insert a cross-reference
- Navigate with cross-references
- View cross-references
- Delete a cross-reference

New words

In this chapter you will meet the following terms:

- Bookmark
- Cross-reference

Exercise files

In this chapter you will work with the following Word files:

- Chapter18_Exercise_18-1_Before.doc
- Chapter18_Exercise_18-4_Before.doc
- Chapter18_Exercise_18-5_Before.doc
- Chapter18_Exercise_18-6_Before.doc
- Chapter18_Exercise_18-9_Before.doc

Syllabus reference

In this chapter you will cover the following items from the ECDL Advanced Word Processing Syllabus:

- **AM3.3.1.1**. Add or delete a bookmark.
- **AM3.3.1.3**. Create or delete a cross-reference.

About bookmarks

Word's bookmark feature enables the reader to move quickly to a particular location in a document, without needing to remember page numbers or headings.

The Bookmark dialog box

You insert bookmarks with the *Bookmark* dialog box, displayed with the **Insert | Bookmark** command.

Bookmark names

Bookmark names must begin with a letter. They can contain numbers but not spaces. To separate words, you can use the underscore character, for example, 'Sales_Figures'. A bookmark can have up to 40 characters.

> **Bookmark**
>
> *A named mark placed on a selected item in a document that enables readers to move to that location without needing to know the relevant page number.*

About cross-references

A cross-reference is a way to direct readers to related or otherwise relevant material located elsewhere in the same document. For example, 'For more information about software solutions, see page 32.'

Word enables you to create cross-references to various document elements, including:

- Headings formatted with built-in styles
- Bookmarks
- Footnotes and endnotes

> **Cross-reference**
>
> *An entry in a document that, if clicked, takes the reader to another location in the same document. Cross-references are useful for directing readers to related or otherwise relevant material.*

The Cross-reference dialog box

You insert cross-references with the **Insert | Cross-reference** command. The associated dialog box provides all the options you need.

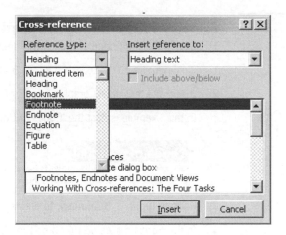

If you add or delete pages to a document that contains cross-references, you may need to update your cross-references. To do so, press **Ctrl+A** to select the entire document, and then press the **F9** key.

Working with bookmarks: the four tasks

Here are the four tasks that you need to be able to perform with bookmarks in Word:

- **Insert a bookmark**. Exercise 18.1 takes you through the steps of inserting bookmarks in a document.

- **Display all bookmarks**. Exercise 18.2 shows you how to display all bookmarks in a document.

- **Move to a bookmark**. Follow Exercise 18.3 to discover how to move to a specific bookmark in a document.

- **Delete a bookmark**. Exercise 18.4 shows you how to remove a bookmark from a document.

Working with cross-references: the four tasks

Here are the four tasks that you need to be able to perform with cross-references in Word:

- **Insert a cross-reference**. Exercises 18.5 and 18.6 take you through the steps of inserting cross-references in built-in headings and bookmarks, respectively.

- **Navigate with cross-references**. Follow Exercise 18.7 to discover how to move to material in a document by clicking cross-references.

- **Display cross-references**. Exercise 18.8 shows you how to display cross-reference field codes in a document.

- **Delete a cross-reference**. You delete a cross-reference in Exercise 18.9.

Working with bookmarks

Exercise 18.1: Inserting bookmarks

1) Start Word and open the following document:

    Chapter18_Exercise_18-1_Before.doc

2) Select the text, table, graphic or other item you want to bookmark.

    In this example, select the 'Codes of Conduct' heading on the first page.

    Codes·of·Conduct¶
    Our·staff·will·introduce·themselves·to·you·and·explain·how·they·can·help.·All·staff·
    will·wear·a·name·badge·to·enable·you·to·identify·them.¶

3) Choose **Insert | Bookmark** to display the *Bookmark* dialog box.

4) In the *Bookmark name* text box, type the following:

    Codes_of_Conduct

5) Click the **Add** button to insert the bookmark – the dialog box closes automatically.

6) Select the next heading, 'Individual Standards of Behaviour'.

7) Press **Ctrl+C** to copy the text to the Clipboard, and choose **Insert | Bookmark**.

8) Click in the *Bookmark name* box, press **Backspace** or **Delete** to remove the currently display bookmark name, and press **Ctrl+V** to paste the selected text.

9) Edit the bookmark name to read:

    Individual_Standards_of_Behaviour

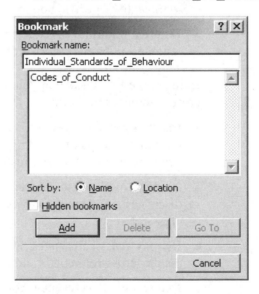

ECDL Advanced Word Processing

10) Click **Add**.

11) Move to the second page of the document, select the 'Consultant-based Services' heading, repeat steps 7 and 8, and modify the bookmark name to read:

    Consultant_based_Services

    When finished, click **Add**.

12) Save your document with the following name, and close:

    Chapter18_Exercise_18-1_After_*Your_Name*.doc

Exercise 18.2: Display all bookmarks

1) Open the Word document that you saved at the end of Exercise 18.1.

2) Choose **Tools | Options** and click the **View** tab. In the *Show* area, select the *Bookmarks* checkbox, and click **OK**.

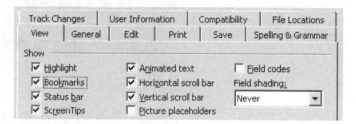

3) Scroll through your sample document. Notice that Word displays bookmarked text within dark grey or black brackets. These brackets do not appear on print-outs.

4) You can close your sample document without saving it.

Exercise 18.3: Move to a bookmark

1) Open the Word document you saved at the end of Exercise 18.1.

2) Choose **Edit | Go To** or press **F5**. Word displays the **Go To** tab of the *Find and Replace* dialog box.

3) In the *Go to what* list box, select *Bookmark*. In the *Enter bookmark name* list box, select the bookmark that you want to move to.

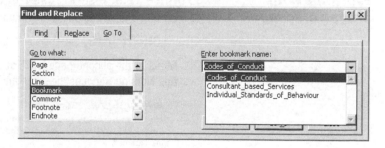

4) Click **Go To**. Word takes you to your selected location in the document. The bookmarked item is selected and the dialog box remains open.

5) You can select further bookmarks or click **Close** to close the dialog box.

6) When finished, you can close your document without saving it.

Exercise 18.4: Delete a bookmark

1) Open the following Word document:

    Chapter18_Exercise_18-4_Before.doc

2) Choose **Insert | Bookmark** and select the bookmark that you want to delete. In this example, select the 'Individual_Standards_of_Behaviour' bookmark.

3) Press **Delete**. Word removes the selected bookmark from the document. The dialog box remains open. You can remove further bookmarks or press **Close** to close the dialog box.

4) Save your document with the following name, and close:

    Chapter18_Exercise_18-4_After_*Your_Name*.doc

Working with cross-references

Exercise 18.5: Insert cross-references to built-in headings

1) Open the following Word document:

    Chapter18_Exercise_18-5_Before.doc

2) Move to the second page, click at the end of the paragraph beneath the 'Nursing Services' heading, and press **Enter**.

Nursing·Services¶

We·will·ensure·that·a·named,·qualified·nurse,·midwife·or·other·health·care· professional·takes·a·personal·responsibility·for·your·treatment·and·care·during·your· time·with·us.¶

¶

3) Type the text that you want to appear before the cross-reference. In this example, type the following, followed by a single space:

See:

4) Choose **Insert | Cross-reference**. In the *Reference type* list, select *Heading*. In the *For which heading* list, select *Individual Standards of Behaviour*.

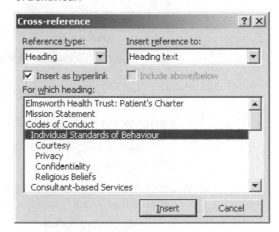

To allow readers to jump to the cross-referenced item, tick the *Insert as hyperlink* checkbox.

Click **Insert** to insert the cross-reference, and then click **Close** to close the dialog box.

5) Select the cross-reference text by dragging across it, and click the **Italics** button on the Formatting toolbar.

See: *Individual Standards of Behaviour*¶

6) Move to the first page, click at the end of the paragraph beneath the 'Codes of Conduct' heading, and press **Enter**.

• Codes·of·Conduct¶

Our·staff·will·introduce·themselves·to·you·and·explain·how·they·can·help.·All·staff· will·wear·a·name·badge·to·enable·you·to·identify·them.¶

¶

7) Type the following text, followed by a single space:

See:

8) Choose **Insert | Cross-reference**. In the *Reference type* list, select *Heading*. In the *For which heading* list, select *Standards of Service*.

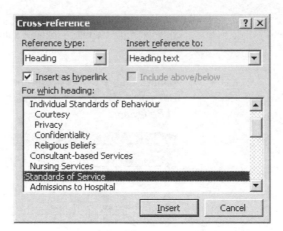

Ensure that the *Insert as hyperlink* checkbox is selected.

Click **Insert** to insert the cross-reference, and then click Close to close the dialog box.

9) Select the cross-reference text by dragging across it, and click the **Italics** button on the Formatting toolbar.

See: *Standards of Service* ¶

10) Save your document with the following name, and close:

Chapter18_Exercise_18-5_After_*Your_Name*.doc.

Exercise 18.6: Insert cross-references to bookmarks

1) Open the following Word document:

Chapter18_Exercise_18-6_Before.doc

2) On the first page, click at the end of the paragraph beneath the 'Codes of Conduct' heading and press **Enter**.

· Codes·of·Conduct¶

Our·staff·will·introduce·themselves·to·you·and·explain·how·they·can·help.·All·staff· will·wear·a·name·badge·to·enable·you·to·identify·them.¶

¶

3) Type the text that you want to appear before the cross-reference. In this example, type the following, followed by a single space:

See also:

4) Choose **Insert | Cross-reference**. In the *Reference type* list, select *Bookmark*. In the *For which bookmark* list, select *Individual_Standards_of_Behaviour*.

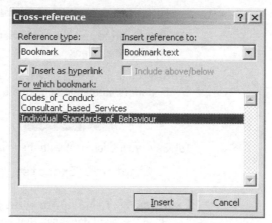

Ensure that the *Insert as hyperlink* checkbox is selected.

Click **Insert** to insert the cross-reference, and then click **Close** to close the dialog box.

5) Select the cross-reference text by dragging across it, and click the **Underline** button on the Formatting toolbar.

> See·also:·Individual·Standards·of·Behaviour¶

6) Move to the second page, click at the end of the paragraph beneath the 'Nursing Services' heading, and press **Enter**.

> *Nursing·Services*¶
> We·will·ensure·that·a·named,·qualified·nurse,·midwife·or·other·health·care·
> professional·takes·a·personal·responsibility·for·your·treatment·and·care·during·your·
> time·with·us.¶
> ¶

7) Type the following text, followed by a single space:

        See also:

8) Choose **Insert | Cross-reference**. In the *Reference type* list, select *Bookmark*. In the *For which bookmark* list, select *Codes_of_Conduct*.

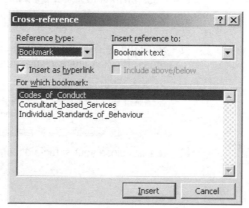

Ensure that the *Insert as hyperlink* checkbox is selected.

Click **Insert** to insert the cross-reference, and then click **Close** to close the dialog box.

9) Select the cross-reference text by dragging across it, and click the **Underline** button on the Formatting toolbar.

See·also:·Codes·of·Conduct¶

10) Save your document with the following name, and close:

Chapter18_Exercise_18-6_After_*Your_Name*.doc.

Exercise 18.7: Navigate with cross-references

1) Open the Word document that you saved at the end of Exercise 18.5.

2) Hold the cursor over the cross-reference named 'See: Standards of Service' located under the 'Codes of Conduct' heading.

Notice how the cursor changes shape to a pointing hand.

3) Click once on the cross-reference. Word moves you to the relevant location in the document. You can close the document without saving it.

4) Open the Word document that you saved at the end of Exercise 18.6.

5) Hold the cursor over the cross-reference named 'See also: Individual Standards of Behaviour' located under the 'Codes of Conduct' heading.

Notice how the cursor changes shape to a pointing hand.

6) Click once on the cross-reference. Word moves you to the relevant location in the document. You can close the document without saving it.

Exercise 18.8: Viewing cross-references

1) Open the document that you saved at the end of Exercise 18.6.

2) Press **Ctrl+A** to select the entire document.

3) Press **Alt+F9** to display all the fields in the document.

4) Scroll through the document to display the cross-reference field codes. The first one is displayed below:

·Codes·of·Conduct¶

Our·staff·will·introduce·themselves·to·you·and·explain·how·they·can·help.·All·staff·
will·wear·a·name·badge·to·enable·you·to·identify·them.¶

See·also:·{·REF·Individual_Standards_of_Behaviour·\h··*·MERGEFORMAT·}¶

5) You can close your sample document without saving it.

Exercise 18.9: Delete a cross-reference

1) Start Word and open the following document:

   `Chapter18_Exercise_18-9_Before.doc`

2) Drag across the first cross-reference to select it. It is located after the text beneath the 'Codes of Conduct' heading.

   · Codes·of·Conduct¶

   Our·staff·will·introduce·themselves·to·you·and·explain·how·they·can·help.·All·staff·
   will·wear·a·name·badge·to·enable·you·to·identify·them.¶

   See·also:·Individual·Standards·of·Behaviour¶

3) Press the **Delete** or **Backspace** key. Word removes the cross-reference. Next, select and delete the 'See also: ' text that introduced the cross-reference. Finally, delete the paragraph mark to remove the now-empty line.

4) Save your document with the following name, and close:

   `Chapter18_Exercise_18-9_After_Your_Name.doc`

Chapter 18:
quick reference

Tasks summary:
bookmarks

Task	Procedure
Insert a bookmark.	Select the text, table, graphic or other item you want to bookmark, choose **Insert | Bookmark**, type a bookmark name, and click **OK**.
Display all bookmarks in a document.	Choose **Tools | Options** and click the **View** tab. In the *Show* area, select the *Bookmarks* checkbox and click **OK**.
Move to a specific bookmark in a document.	Choose **Edit | Go To** (or press **F5**) and click the **Go To** tab. In the *Go to what* list box, select *Bookmark*. In the *Enter bookmark name* box, select the bookmark that you want to move to, and click **Go To**.
Delete a bookmark from a document.	Choose **Insert | Bookmark**, select the bookmark that you want to delete, click **Delete,** and then click **OK**.

Tasks summary: cross-references	Task	Procedure
	Insert a cross-reference.	Click where you want to insert the cross-reference, choose **Insert | Cross-reference**, select the relevant items from the *Reference type* list and in the *For which* list, ensure that the *Insert as hyperlink* checkbox is selected, and click **Insert**.
	Display all cross-references in a document.	Press **Ctrl+A** to select the entire document, and then press **Alt+F9** to display all the fields in the document.
	Delete a cross-reference from a document.	Drag across a cross-reference to select it, and press **Delete** or **Backspace**.

Concepts summary

Word's *bookmark* feature enables the reader to move quickly to a particular location in a document, without needing to remember page numbers or headings. You insert bookmarks with the *Bookmark* dialog box, displayed with the **Insert \| Bookmark** command.

Bookmark names must begin with a letter. They can contain numbers but not spaces. To separate words, you can use the underscore character, for example, 'Sales_Figures'. A bookmark can have up to 40 characters.

A *cross-reference* is a way to direct readers to related or otherwise relevant material located elsewhere in the same document. For example, 'For more information about software solutions, see page 32.'

Word enables you to create cross-references to various document elements, including headings formatted with built-in styles and bookmarks.

You insert cross-references with the **Insert \| Cross-references** command. The associated dialog box provides all the options you need.

Chapter 18: quick quiz

Circle the correct answer to each of the following multiple-choice questions about bookmarks and cross-references in Word.

Q1	A bookmark is ...
A.	Additional information or references regarding the main text that appears at the end of document.
B.	A summary of information about a document that can be displayed with the **File	Properties** command.
C.	A named mark placed in a document that enables readers to move to that location without needing to know the relevant page number.
D.	A text box positioned in a page footer with the **Insert	Text Box** command.

Q2	A cross-reference is ...
A.	A named mark placed in a document that enables readers to move to that location without needing to know the relevant page number.
B.	An entry in a document that, if clicked, takes the reader to another location in the same document.
C.	Additional information or references regarding the main text that appears at the bottom of a page within the document.
D.	A text box positioned in the page footer with the **Insert	Text Box** command.

Q3	In Word, which command do you choose to insert a bookmark in a document?
A.	**Format	Bookmarks.**
B.	**Insert	Bookmark.**
C.	**Tools	Options	Bookmarks	New.**
D.	**Insert	Marks	Bookmark.**

Q4	In Word, which command do you choose to insert a cross-reference in a document?
A.	Insert | New| Reference.
B.	Tools | Cross-references.
C.	Insert | Cross-reference.
D.	Format | Auto | Reference.

Q5	In Word, which actions do you take to display all bookmarks in a document?
A.	Choose **Tools | Options** and click the **View** tab. In the *Show* area, select the *Bookmarks* checkbox, and click **OK**.
B.	Choose **Insert | Bookmarks**, click the **Options** button, select the *View bookmarks* checkbox, and click **OK**.
C.	Click the **Book** button on the Status bar.
D.	Choose **View | Toolbars**, and select **Bookmarks**.

Q6	In Word, which actions do you take to move to a specific bookmark in a document?
A.	Click the **Find Bookmark** button on the Standard toolbar, select the bookmark that you want to move to, and click **Go To**.
B.	Choose **Edit | Find | Bookmark**, select the bookmark that you want to move to, and click **Find Now**.
C.	Press **Shift+F6**, select the bookmark that you want to move to, and click **Find Bookmark**.
D.	Choose **Edit | Go To** (or press **F5**) and click the **Go To** tab. In the *Go to what* list box, select *Bookmark*. In the *Enter bookmark name* list box, select the bookmark that you want to move to, and click **Go To**.

Q7	In Word, which actions do you take to delete a bookmark from a document?
A.	Choose **Tools | Bookmark | Delete**, select the bookmark that you want to delete, and click **OK**.
B.	Choose **Insert | Bookmark**, select the bookmark that you want to delete, click **Delete** and then click **OK**.
C.	Press **Ctrl+F8**, select the bookmark that you want delete, click **Delete** and then click **OK**.
D.	Choose **Insert | Bookmark**, select the bookmark that you want to delete, click **Remove Now** and then click **Apply**.

Q8	In Word, which actions do you take to insert a cross-reference in a document?
A.	Click where you want to insert the cross-reference, choose **Insert | Cross-reference**, type the cross-reference name, ensure that the *Insert as hyperlink* checkbox is selected, and click **Insert**.
B.	Click the **Insert Cross-reference** button on the Standard toolbar, select the relevant item from the *Reference type* list, type the cross-reference name, and click **Insert Now**.
C.	Choose **Insert | Cross-reference**, select the relevant items from the *Reference type* list and the *For which* drop-down list, ensure that the *Insert as hyperlink* checkbox is selected, and click **Insert**.
D.	Press **Ctrl+F8**, select the relevant items from the *Reference type* list and the *For which* drop-down list, and click **Insert**.

Q9	In Word, which actions do you take to displays all cross-references in a document?
A.	Press **Ctrl+A** to select the entire document, and then press **Alt+F9** to display all the fields in the document.
B.	Choose **Insert | Cross-reference**, select the *Display cross-references* checkbox, and click **OK**.
C.	Press **Ctrl+A** to select the entire document, and then display all the fields in the document by pressing **Shift+F8**.
D.	Click the **Show Cross-references** button on the Reviewing toolbar.

Q10	In Word, which actions do you take to remove a cross-reference from a document?
A.	Drag across a cross-reference to select it, and press **Delete** or **Backspace**.
B.	Choose **Tools | Cross-references | Delete**, select the cross-reference that you want to delete, and click **OK**.
C.	Choose **Insert | Cross-reference**, select the cross-reference that you want to delete, click **Remove Now** and then click **Apply**.
D.	Press **Ctrl+F8**, select the cross-reference that you want delete, click **Delete** and then click **OK**.

Q11	In Word, which of the following document elements can you not create a cross-reference to?
A.	Footnote.
B.	Footer.
C.	Built-in heading.
D.	Bookmark.

Q12	In Word, which of the following statements about bookmark names is untrue?
A.	Bookmark names can contain numbers.
B.	Bookmark names must begin with a letter.
C.	Bookmark names can have up to 40 characters.
D.	Bookmark names can contain spaces.

Answers

1: C, 2: B, 3: B, 4: C, 5: A, 6: D, 7: B, 8: C, 9: A, 10: A, 11: B, 12: D.

19 Tables of contents

Objectives

In this chapter you will learn how to:

- Create a new table of contents using default settings
- Create a new table of contents using non-default settings
- Update an existing table of contents
- Format a table of contents

New words

In this chapter you will meet the following term:

- Table of contents

Exercise files

In this chapter you will work with the following Word files:

- `Chapter19_Exercise_19-1_Before.doc`
- `Chapter19_Exercise_19-2_Before.doc`
- `Chapter19_Exercise_19-3_Before.doc`
- `Chapter19_Exercise_19-4_Before.doc`

Syllabus reference

In this chapter you will cover the following items of the ECDL Advanced Word Processing Syllabus:

- **AM3.2.2.1**. Create a table of contents.
- **AM3.2.2.2**. Update and modify an existing table of contents.
- **AM3.2.2.3**. Apply formatting options to a table of contents.

About tables of contents

Let's begin with a precise definition of a table of contents.

> **Table of contents**
>
> *A listing of a document's headings in the order in which they appear, along with the corresponding page numbers, shown at the beginning of a document. Typically, lower-level headings are indented further than higher-level ones.*

Don't confuse a table of contents with an *index*. An index (see Chapter 21) appears at the end of a document, and is generally more thorough than a table of contents. It identifies the items – topics, terms, names and places – contained in the document, and shows their corresponding page numbers.

A table of contents lists items in the order in which they appear in the document; an index lists items alphabetically by name.

Word's 30-second table of contents

If you have applied heading styles in a document, Word can generate an acceptable table of contents for you in half a minute or less. Anyone who has ever created a table of contents manually will be impressed with this feature.

A sample from an automatically generated table of contents is shown below:

Tables of contents: default settings

Word can generate a contents table very quickly because it makes a number of default choices for you. Lets look at these defaults in detail.

- **Three heading levels**. By default, Word includes paragraphs in the following styles only: Headings 1, 2 and 3. If there are more heading levels in your document, Word ignores them.

- **Progressive indentation**. As in outlines, lower heading levels are indented further from the left margin. This is a publishing convention; it results in a table of contents that is easier to read.

- **Right-aligned page numbers**. Again, Word follows the convention of aligning page numbers against the right page margin.

- **Tab leaders**. Another convention followed by Word: the insertion of dotted or continuous lines that draw the reader's eye from the left-aligned headings to the right-aligned page numbers.

- **Styles**. Word has a series of built-in styles, named TOC 1, TOC 2, and so on, that it applies to corresponding heading levels in a table of contents.

The Index and Tables *dialog box*

You insert a table of contents using the **Table of Contents** tab of the *Index and Tables* dialog box, displayed by choosing the **Insert | Index and Tables** command.

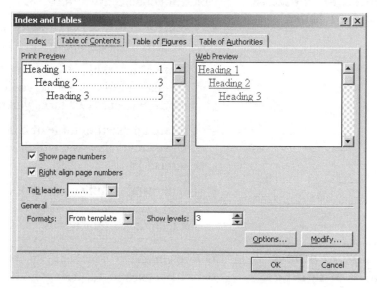

Modifying the table of contents defaults

Which default settings are you most likely to want to modify?

- **Heading levels**. The *Show levels* box enables you to override Word's default number of heading levels.

- **Styles**. It is not a good idea to apply styles other than the built-in styles to a table of contents. But, using the **Format | Style** command, you will probably want to change the attributes of these styles to something less plain.

  Another option is to select from Word's built-in gallery of formats for tables of contents. The choices include formats with names such as Classic, Distinctive and Formal.

Updating the table of contents

Typically, you will create a table of contents only once but will need to update it several times. This may be because you have added new content to your document, reordered existing content, or both.

The power of Word's automated table of contents feature is not just that it can create a new table of contents, but that it can recreate the table as often as necessary, with just a few mouse clicks.

Working with tables of contents: the four tasks

Here are the four tasks that you need to be able to perform with tables of contents in Word:

- **Create a new table of contents using default settings**. This is the fast and easy approach. See Exercise 19.1.

- **Create a new table of contents using non-default settings**. This takes a little longer, as you override Word's preset options. Exercise 19.2 takes you through the steps.

- **Update an existing table of contents**. There is more than one way to do this. You will discover your options in Exercise 19.3.

- **Formatting a table of contents**. Learn how to give your table of contents a more professional appearance by using the techniques shown in Exercise 19.4.

Creating a new table of contents

Before you start

Before you create a table of contents, ensure that the following steps have been performed:

- **Heading styles**. Check that built-in heading styles have been applied to your document's headings. You might find it easier to verify this in Outline view.

  Word's table of contents generate feature can find in a document only what you have placed in that document. Only by using paragraph styles consistently can you expect to achieve a logically organized table of contents.

- **Hidden text**. If your document uses hidden text, ensure that it is actually hidden.

- **Fields**. If your document contains fields, ensure that the fields display values rather than codes, and that the necessary fields have been updated.

Exercise 19.1: Create a table of contents with default values

In this exercise, you will generate a new table of contents for a document, based on Word's default settings.

1) Open the following file:

   ```
   Chapter19_Exercise_19-1_Before.doc
   ```

2) Position the insertion point in the blank line under the first heading.

   Elmsworth·Health·Trust:·Patients'·Charter¶
   ¶
   At·Elmsworth·Health·Trust,·we·are·committed·to·delivering·a·world-class·service.·Our·
   standards·apply·whether·you·are:¶

3) Choose **Insert | Index and Tables**, and click the **Table of Contents** tab.

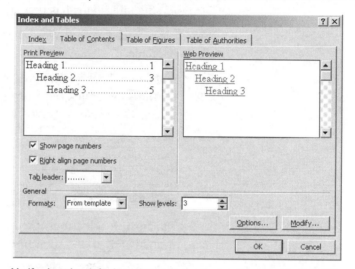

4) Verify that the default options are as shown above, and click **OK**.

   Word generates a table of contents, and positions it at the location of your insertion point. Part of the table of contents is shown below:

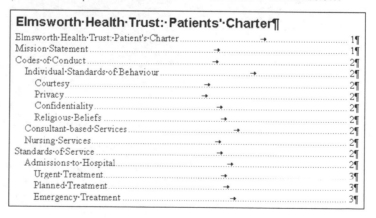

5) Save the document with the following name:

    `Chapter19_Exercise_19-1_After_Your_Name.doc`

You can now close the document.

Tables of contents and hyperlinks

When you click on a line within a Word table of contents, the line behaves like a hyperlink on a web page: it takes you to the relevant heading within the document. This feature can be a nuisance when you want to perform an action on the contents table, such as deleting a particular line or applying direct formatting to it.

To work with a Word table of contents, click in the left margin *beside* the table. This has two effects:

- **Grey background**. Word places a grey background behind the table.

  If the grey background does not appear, choose **Tools | Options**, and click the **View** tab. In the *Field shading* box, select *When selected*, and click **OK**.

  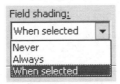

- **Paragraph selection**. Word selects the paragraph immediately to the right of the insertion point.

  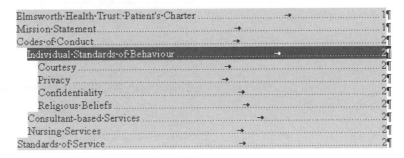

  You can now apply formatting to the paragraph, or press the **Delete** or **Backspace** key to remove it.

To select an entire table of contents, click in the left margin beside the first paragraph of the table of contents. Word then selects the entire table so that you can format it or delete it.

Exercise 19.2: Create a table of contents with non-default values

In this exercise, you will generate a new table of contents for a document based on some modifications that you make to Word's default settings.

1) Open the following file:

    `Chapter19_Exercise_19-2_Before.doc`

2) Position the insertion point in the blank line under the first heading.

3) Choose **Insert | Index and Tables**, and click the **Table of Contents** tab of the dialog box displayed.

4) In the *Tab leader* box, select the continuous line option. This replaces the default dotted line option.

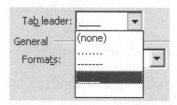

5) Change the setting of the *Show levels* box to 2. This replaces the default setting of three heading levels.

Click **OK**. Word generates and inserts the table of contents, part of which is shown below:

Elmsworth·Health·Trust:··Patients'·Charter¶

6) Save the document with the following name:

    `Chapter19_Exercise_19-2_After_Your_Name.doc`

You can now close the document.

Updating an existing table of contents

You have created a table of contents for your document, but the document has changed, with the result that the table of contents is no longer accurate. How can you update your table of contents?

Word offers two options:

- **Update page numbers only**. Select this option if you have amended, added or removed content in the document *other than* headings. If you run this option after changing your headings in any way, your heading changes will not be reflected in the updated table of contents.

  Updating only the page numbers does not affect any direct formatting that you may have applied to your table of contents.

- **Update the entire table**. Select this option if you have amended, added or removed headings in the document.

  Updating the entire table of contents removes any direct formatting that you may have applied to it.

Word generally takes a little longer to update an entire table than to update only page numbers.

Exercise 19.3: Updating a table of contents

In this exercise, you will make some changes to a table of contents, reorder text within a document, and then update the table of contents to reflect the changes.

1) Open the following file:

   `Chapter19_Exercise_19-3_Before.doc`

2) Position the insertion point in the blank line under the first heading.

   Elmsworth·Health·Trust:··Patients'·Charter¶
   ¶
   At·Elmsworth·Health·Trust,··we·are·committed·to·delivering·a·world-class·service.··Our·
   standards·apply·whether·you·are:¶

3) Choose **Insert | Index and Tables**, click the **Table of Contents** tab of the dialog box displayed, and click **OK**.

   Word generates the table of contents, and positions it at the location of your insertion point.

4) As you can see, Word includes your document's title ('Elmsworth Health Trust: Patients' Charter') as the first item in the table of contents. Let's remove this.

   If you click to the left of this first line, Word selects the entire table of contents and not just the first line. Instead, click at the paragraph mark at the end of the first line, hold down the **Shift** key, and press the left arrow key. (Before you do this, toggle the **Show/Hide** button to display paragraph marks.)

Elmsworth·Health·Trust:·Patients'·Charter¶

¶
Elmsworth·Health·Trust·Patient's·Charter ....→................................. 1¶
Mission·Statement ....→.............................. 2¶

Press **Delete** or **Backspace** to remove the selected first line from your table of contents.

5) Click at the beginning of the first paragraph of text beneath the table of contents.

Medical·Information ....→................................. 5¶
¶
|At·Elmsworth·Health·Trust,·we·are·committed·to·delivering·a·world-class·service.·Our·
standards·apply·whether·you·are:¶
•→ A·patient¶

Choose **Insert | Break**, select the *Page break* option, and click **OK**.

Show Heading 1 button

Move Up button

6) Next, you will reorder a level-1 heading within the document.

Choose **View | Outline**, and click the **Show Heading 1** button on the Outlining toolbar.

7) Click anywhere in the last paragraph ('Information and Records'), and then click the **Move Up** button.

✧ **Help·Us·To·Help·You**¶	✧ **|Information·and·Records**¶
✧ **|Information·and·Records**¶	✧ **Help·Us·To·Help·You**¶
Before	***After***

Click anywhere else on the screen to deselect the heading. You have reordered two document headings.

8) Choose **View | Print Layout**, and navigate to the page that contains the table of contents.

Hold the mouse anywhere over the contents table. Notice that the cursor changes to a 'hand' shape. (Alternatively, click anywhere in the left margin of the contents table.)

9) Right-click with the mouse. From the pop-up menu, choose the **Update Field** command. (Alternatively, press **F9**.)

10) Word displays the *Update Table of Contents* dialog box.

11) Select the *Update entire table* option and click **OK**.

Word updates the table of contents.

12) Save the document with the following name:

   Chapter19_Exercise_19-3_After_*Your_Name*.doc

13) You can now close the document.

Formatting a table of contents

Word's default table of contents formatting may not be what you want for your documents. You have three reformatting options:

- **Apply direct formatting**. You can select one or more paragraphs in the table of contents, and use the **Format | Font**, **Format | Paragraph** and **Format | Borders and Shading** commands to format them.

  All such formatting is removed when you update the table with the *Update entire table* option table of contents.

- **Apply a built-in style from the table of contents gallery**. Another option is to select from Word's built-in gallery of table of contents formats. The choices include Classic, Distinctive and Formal.

- **Change the style attributes**. This is the preferred option.

Exercise 19.4: Amending the appearance of a table of contents

In this exercise, you will use various methods to modify the appearance of a document's table of contents.

1) Open the following file:

   Chapter19_Exercise_19-4_Before.doc

2) Click in the margin to the left of the first line of the table of contents. This selects the entire table.

3) Choose **Insert | Index and Tables**, and click the **Table of Contents** tab of the dialog box displayed.

4) In the *Formats* drop-down list, select *Formal* and click **OK**.

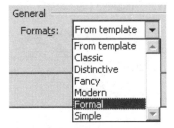

5) Word now displays the following dialog box:

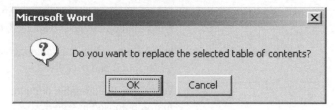

6) Click **OK**. Word now reformats the table, part of which is shown below:

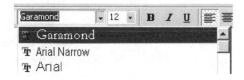

Notice that the Formal style uses upper-case letters for first- and second-level headings.

Next, you will apply some direct formatting to the table.

7) Click in the margin to the left of the first line of the table of contents. This selects the entire table.

8) On the Formatting toolbar, select the Garamond font in the *Font* box.

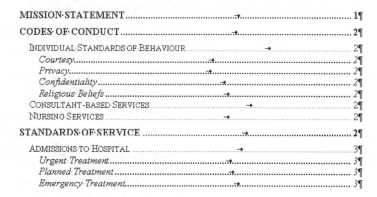

Word applies the font to the table. Click anywhere outside the table to deselect it. Your table should now look like this:

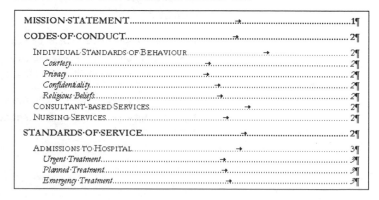

9) Hold the mouse anywhere over the table of contents and right-click. From the pop-up menu displayed, choose the **Update Field** command.

In the *Update Table of Contents* dialog box, select the *Update entire table* option and click **OK**.

Word updates the table of contents and removes the direct formatting that you applied in step 8.

10) Click in the left margin beside any heading (except the very first one) that is in the TOC 1 style.

11) Choose **Format | Style**, click **Modify**, click **Format**, and select the **Font** option. In the *Color* box, select *Dark Blue*, and click **OK**.

In the *Modify Style* dialog box, do not select either the *Add to template* or *Automatically update* checkboxes, click **OK** and click **Apply**.

Word applies the new modified style to the level-1 heading in the table. Click anywhere outside the table to deselect it.

12) Save the document with the following name:

    Chapter19_Exercise_19-4_After_*Your_Name*.doc

You can now close the document.

Chapter 19: quick reference

Tasks summary

Task	Procedure
Insert a table of contents with default settings.	Choose **Insert	Index and Tables**, click the **Table of Contents** tab of the dialog box displayed, and click **OK**.
	Word generates tables of contents, and positions it at the location of your insertion point.
Update a table of contents to reflect changes in the document.	Click to the left of the table of contents and press **F9**.
Change the appearance of a table of contents.	Select a table of contents entry in the style you want to change, choose **Format	Style**, then specify the style characteristics you want to apply.
Delete a line from a table of contents.	Click to the left of the line and press **Delete** or **Backspace**.

Concepts summary

A *table of contents* is a listing of a document's headings in the order in which they appear, along with the corresponding page numbers. You can use Word to generate a table of contents based on a document's heading styles through the **Table of Contents** tab available with the **Insert | Index and Tables** command.

Word applies the following settings by default when generating a table of contents: *three heading levels*, with lesser headings indented further from the left-margin; *right-aligned page numbers*; and *dotted lines* joining the left-aligned headings with the right-aligned page numbers.

When you click on a line within a Word table of contents, the line acts as a hyperlink: it takes you to the relevant heading within the document.

To work with a Word table of contents, click in the *left margin* beside the table. To select the entire table of contents, click in the left margin beside the first line of table of contents. Word then selects the full table so that you can format it or delete it.

You have three *reformatting* options for a table of contents: apply direct formatting, select a built-in style from the table of contents gallery, or change the table of contents style attributes.

Word provides two ways for *updating* a table of contents: *page numbers only*, or the entire *table* of headings and page numbers. The second option removes any direct formatting that you have applied to the table.

Chapter 19: quick quiz

Circle the correct answer to each of the following multiple-choice questions about tables of contents in Word.

Q1	Which of the following statements about tables of contents is not true?
A.	A table of contents appears at the beginning of a document.
B.	A table of contents can include more than one heading level.
C.	A table of contents is a listing of a document's headings in the order in which they appear, along with the corresponding page numbers.
D.	A table of contents appears at the end of a document.

Q2	Which of the following is not a publishing convention in tables of contents?
A.	Lower heading levels are indented further from the left margin.
B.	Page numbers are aligned against the right page margin.
C.	Page numbers are shown in italics.
D.	The inclusion of dotted or continuous lines from the headings to the page numbers.

Q3	Which of the following items is not a default setting within Word's table of contents feature?
A.	Three levels of headings.
B.	Dotted lines joining headings with page numbers.
C.	Right-aligned page numbers.
D.	Four levels of headings.

Q4	Which of the following actions do you perform to create a table of contents in a Word document?
A.	Choose **Insert	Index and Tables**, select the *Generate Contents* option, and click **Apply**.
B.	Select all the text in the document and click the **New** button on the Table of Contents toolbar.
C.	Choose **Insert	Index and Tables**, click the **Table of Contents** tab, and click **OK**.
D.	Select all the text in the document, and choose the **Insert	Index and Tables** command.

Q5	What happens when you click on a line within a Word table of contents?
A.	Word displays Outline view, with the relevant line selected.
B.	You are taken to the relevant heading within the document.
C.	The line is selected.
D.	Nothing.

ECDL Advanced Word Processing

Q6	How do you select an entire table of contents in Word?
A.	Click in the left margin beside the first line of the table.
B.	Click anywhere in the left margin of the table.
C.	Right-click on the first line of the table.
D.	Click in the left margin beside any level-1 heading.

Q7	What choices does Word offer you for updating a table of contents?
A.	Two options: update the entire table or just the page numbers.
B.	Three options: update the entire table, the headings only, or the page numbers only.
C.	One option: update both the headings and the page numbers.
D.	Two options: update the headings and page numbers only, or update the styles only.

Q8	What happens to a Word table of contents that contains direct formatting when you update it with the *Update entire table* option selected?
A.	Word updates the table without affecting the direct formatting.
B.	Word does not update any headings or page numbers that contain direct formatting.
C.	Word updates the table but removes headings and numbers with direct formatting.
D.	Word updates the table and removes direct formatting from headings and page numbers.

Answers

1: D, **2:** C, **3:** D, **4:** C, **5:** B, **6:** A, **7:** A, **8:** D.

20 *Captions*

Objectives

In this chapter you will learn how to:

- Insert captions and modify the default options
- Apply chapter and caption numbers
- Update caption numbers
- Activate automatic captioning

New words

In this chapter you will meet the following term:

- Caption

Exercise files

In this chapter you will work with the following files:

- Chapter20_Exercise_20-1_Before.doc
- Chapter20_Exercise_20-2_Before.doc
- Chapter20_Exercise_20-3_Before.doc
- Chapter20_Exercise_20-4_Before.doc
- Chapter20_Exercise_20-4_Worksheet.xls
- Chapter20_Exercise_20-5_Before.doc

Syllabus reference

In this chapter you will cover the following items from the ECDL Advanced Word Processing Syllabus:

- **AM3.4.6.1**: Add or update a caption to an image or table.
- **AM3.4.6.2**: Apply a numbered caption to an image, figure, table or worksheet.
- **AM3.4.6.3**: Use automatic caption options.

About captions

A caption is a numbered label, such as 'Figure 12' or 'Table 3–8', that you add to items such as pictures, tables and Excel worksheet cells in a Word document.

The components of a caption

Let's examine the various components of a caption in Word:

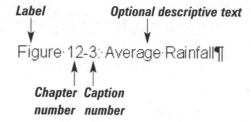

- **Label**. This is the standard text that appears in each caption. Word includes built-in labels such as 'Figure' and 'Table'.

  If required, you can create and use new labels, for example, 'Picture', 'Chart' or 'Screenshot'.

- **Caption number**. Word inserts an automatically incrementing number with each caption. For example, 'Table 1', 'Table 2', and so on.

- **Chapter number**. In multi-chapter documents, caption numbers are typically preceded by the relevant chapter number. For example, 'Table 3–5' or 'Figure 6–5'.

- **Optional text**. You can include additional text with a caption to identify or describe the item captioned. For example 'Annual Sales' or 'Average Rainfall'.

By default, captions are positioned *beneath* pictures but *above* tables or worksheet cells.

> **Caption**
>
> *A numbered label added to pictures, tables, worksheet cells or equations in a Word document. Captions can optionally include the relevant chapter number and additional descriptive text.*

The Caption dialog box

You add captions using the *Caption* dialog box, displayed by choosing the **Insert | Caption** command.

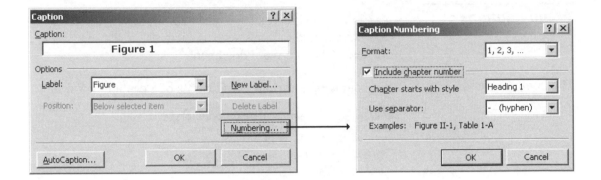

Working with captions: the five tasks

Here are the five tasks that you need to be able to perform with captions in Word:

- **Insert captions with default options**. This is the fast and easy approach. See Exercise 20.1.

- **Insert captions with non-default options**. Exercise 20.2 shows you how to take greater control over Word's captioning feature.

- **Insert captions that include chapter numbers**. Add a professional appearance to your Word documents by including the relevant chapter number with each inserted caption. See Exercise 20.3.

- **Insert captions automatically**. In Exercise 20.4, you learn how to set up automatic captioning so that Word adds a caption to every item of a particular type that you insert in your documents.

- **Update captions in a document**. Captions are fields. If you delete or move a caption, you need to update the caption numbers manually. See Exercise 20.5.

Inserting captions without chapter numbers

In the first two exercises, you will insert simple captions to accompany pictures in Word documents. The procedures for adding captions to tables and worksheet cells are similar.

Exercise 20.1: Insert captions with default options

1) Open the following file:

       Chapter20_Exercise_20-1_Before.doc

2) On the first page of your sample document, click the first picture to select it.

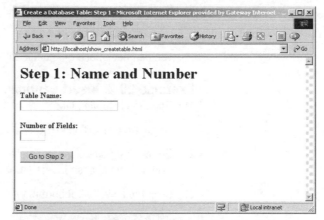

3) Choose **Insert | Caption** to display the *Caption* dialog box.

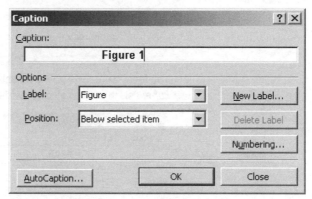

4) Accept the default options as shown above, and click **OK**.

Word inserts the caption as shown here:

Figure·1¶

5) Move to the second page of your sample document and insert captions for the three pictures on the page. Your captions should look like this:

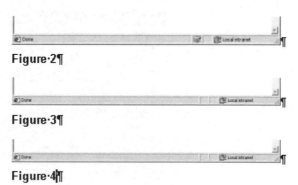

Figure·2¶

Figure·3¶

Figure·4¶

6) Save the document with the following name:

    Chapter20_Exercise_20-1_After_*Your_Name*.doc

    You can now close the document.

Exercise 20.2: Insert captions with non-default options

1) Open the following file:

    Chapter20_Exercise_20-2_Before.doc

2) On the first page of your sample document, click the first picture to select it and choose **Insert | Caption**.

3) Click the **New Label** button, type the label text 'Screen', and click **OK**.

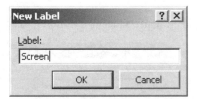

The label 'Screen' is now available as an option in the drop-down *Label* list. It is also selected by default in the *Caption* box.

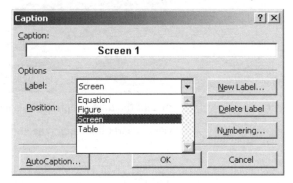

4) Click in the Caption box after the 'Screen 1' label, type the following additional text, and click **OK**:

    : Creating the Table

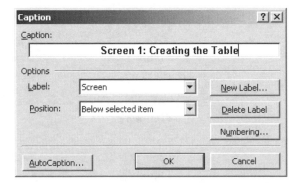

5) Move to the second page of your sample document and add the captions shown below for the three pictures on the page:

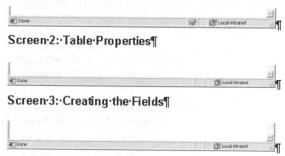

Screen·2:··Table·Properties¶

Screen·3:··Creating·the·Fields¶

Screen·4:··Field·Properties¶

6) Save the document with the following name:

    Chapter20_Exercise_20-2_After_*Your_Name*.doc

You can now close the document.

Inserting captions with chapter numbers

In multi-chapter documents, it is conventional to precede each caption number with the relevant chapter number – for example, 'Figure 1-A' or 'Table 4:6'.

Word can insert chapter numbers automatically, but only if the chapter title text is:

■ Formatted in a built-in heading style. Typically, this is Heading 1 or Heading 2.

■ Has outline numbering applied to it (see Chapter 1).

The word 'chapter' in this context simply means an individual document within a set of such documents. Chapters need not be named 'chapters'. You can name them 'Sections', 'Lessons', 'Units', or whatever you want.

Exercise 20.3: Insert captions with chapter numbers
1) Open the following file:

    Chapter20_Exercise_20-3_Before.doc

2) The headings in your sample document are formatted with the built-in heading styles Heading 1, Heading 2 and Heading 3. Your first step is to apply outline numbering to these headings. This is best done in Outline view.

Choose **View | Outline**, and click the **Show Heading 3** button on the Outlining toolbar to display heading levels 1, 2 and 3 from your document.

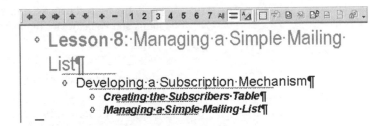

3) Position the insertion point anywhere in the level-1 heading, choose **Format | Bullets and Numbering**, click the **Outline Numbered** tab, and click to select the first of the four lower options in the dialog box.

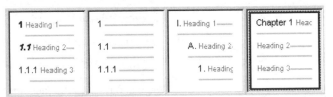

4) Click **Customize**. In the *Number format* box, change 'Chapter' to 'Lesson'. Change the *Start at* value from 1 to 8. Type a colon (:) after the number '8' in the *Number format* box.

5) Click **Font**. Set the font attributes to Arial Narrow, bold, 28 point and dark grey.

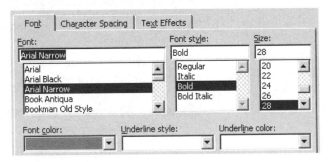

Click **OK** and **OK** to close the dialog boxes.

6) Choose **View | Print Layout**. You can see that the text 'Lesson 8:' now appears twice. The first is inserted automatically by Word's outline numbering feature.

Select the second 'Lesson 8:' and press **Delete** to remove it.

Lesson 8: Lesson 8: Managing a Simple Mailing List¶

You are now ready to insert captions that include the chapter (or, in this example, the lesson) number.

7) On the first page of your sample document, click the first picture to select it, choose **Insert | Caption**, and click **Numbering** to display the *Caption Numbering* dialog box.

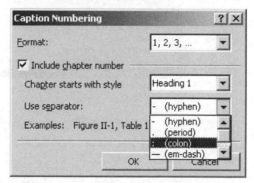

Select the *Include chapter number* checkbox. In the *Use separator* list, select the colon option. Click **OK** and **OK** to close the dialog boxes.

Word inserts the following caption beneath the selected picture:

Screen·8:1¶

8) Move to the second page of your sample document, and add the captions shown below for the three pictures on the page:

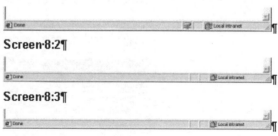

Screen·8:2¶

Screen·8:3¶

Screen·8:4¶

9) Close and save the document with the following name:

Chapter20_Exercise_20-3_After_*Your_Name*.doc

Inserting captions automatically

If you are working with a document into which you plan to insert many pictures, tables, Excel worksheet cells or equations, you can take advantage of Word's automatic captioning feature.

You can include chapter numbering with automatic captioning if the chapter title text is formatted in a built-in heading style and has outline numbering applied to it.

Word's automatic captioning options are available within the *AutoCaption* dialog box, accessed by clicking the **AutoCaption** button on the *Caption* dialog box.

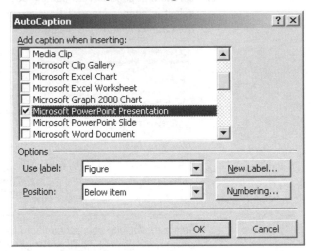

The *AutoCaption* dialog box lists a range of file types for which Word can automatically add appropriate captions. The content of the list depends on the software applications that you have installed on your PC.

Exercise 20.4: Insert captions automatically

1) Open the following file:

   Chapter20_Exercise_20-4_Before.doc

2) Your first action is to switch on automatic captions for Excel worksheet cells. Choose **Insert | Caption** and click **AutoCaption**.

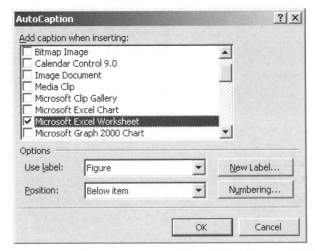

Select the checkbox for *Microsoft Excel Worksheet* and click **OK**.

3) You are now ready to insert Excel worksheet cells into your Word document.

Click at the second paragraph mark beneath the heading 'Balance Sheet for XYZ Enterprises'. This is the location at which you will insert the worksheet cells.

Choose **Insert | Object**, click the **Create from File** tab, and click the **Browse** button. Select the following sample file and click **Insert**:

Chapter20_Exercise_20_4_Worksheet.xls

Word redisplays the *Object* dialog box and shows the name of the file that you have selected for insertion.

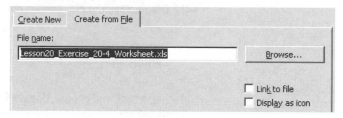

Click **OK**.

Beneath the inserted worksheet cells you can see that Word has automatically created the caption 'Figure 1'.

Figure·1¶

4) Choose **Insert | Caption**, click **AutoCaption**, deselect the *Microsoft Excel Worksheet* checkbox, and click **OK**.

5) Close and save the document with the following name:

Chapter20_Exercise_20-4_After_*Your Name*.doc

Updating caption fields

Word's captioning feature is based on fields (see Chapter 8). When you insert new captions, Word updates all other caption numbers in the document automatically. Word does this regardless of whether you insert new captions after all previous captions or *within* a series of already captioned items.

If you delete or move captions within a document, however, you need to update the caption numbers to reflect your changes. You can do this as follows:

■ Select the entire document and update all fields.

A selected caption or captions can be updated by pressing the **F9** key or by right-clicking on the selection and choosing the **Update Field** command.

- Alternatively, save and close the document, then open it again. Word will update the caption fields automatically.

Exercise 20.5: Update caption numbers

1) Open the following file:

   `Chapter20_Exercise_20-5_Before.doc`

2) Select the first picture and the caption beneath it, then press **Delete**.

3) Move to the second page. Notice that the caption numbers are now incorrect: the first caption in the document is named 'Figure 2', the second is 'Figure 3', and the third is 'Figure 4'.

4) Drag across the first caption number to select it.

5) Right-click and choose **Update Field**. Word updates your first caption as shown:

6) The two other caption numbers in your document are still incorrect. Let's update them by saving and closing the document and then opening it again.

   Save the document with the following name, then close it:

   `Chapter20_Exercise_20-5_After_Your_Name.doc`

7) Reopen your document. Notice that the second and third captions now contain the correct caption numbers. You can now close your sample document.

Chapter 20: quick reference

Tasks summary

Task	Procedure
Insert a caption.	Select the picture, table or other item for captioning, choose **Insert	Caption**, select or create a label, accept or amend the default caption position, and click **OK**.
Amend caption numbering format.	Choose **Insert	Caption**, click **Numbering**, select another numbering format, and click **OK** and **OK**.
Insert captions with chapter numbers.	Word can insert chapter numbers automatically, but only if the chapter title text is formatted in a built-in heading style and has outline numbering applied to it.
	Select the picture, table or other item for captioning, choose **Insert	Caption**, select or create a label, accept or amend the default caption position, click **Numbering**, select the *Include chapter number* checkbox, and click **OK** and **OK**.
Switch automatic captioning on or off.	Choose **Insert	Caption**, click **AutoCaption**, select or deselect the required file type(s), and click **OK** and **OK**.
Update captions.	Select a single caption or part or all of the document. Press **F9** or right-click on the selection and choose **Update Field**.
	Alternatively, close and save the document and then reopen it.

Concepts summary

A *caption* is a numbered label, such as 'Figure 12' or 'Table 3–8', that you can add to items such as pictures, tables, worksheet cells or equations in a Word document. By default, captions are positioned *beneath* pictures but *above* tables or worksheet cells.

The *caption label* is the standard text that appears in each caption. Word includes built-in labels, such as 'Figure' and 'Table'. If required, you can create and use new labels, for example, 'Picture' or 'Chart'. Optionally, you can include additional text with a caption label to identify or describe the item captioned.

Every caption includes a *caption number* field. When you insert new captions, Word updates all other caption numbers in the document automatically. Word does this regardless of whether you insert new captions after all previous captions or within a series of already captioned items. If you delete or move captions within a document, however, you need to update the caption number field to reflect your changes.

In multi-chapter documents, caption numbers are typically preceded by the relevant *chapter number*. For example, 'Table 3-5' or 'Picture 6-5'. Word can insert chapter numbers automatically, but only if the chapter title text is formatted in a built-in heading style and has outline numbering applied to it.

You add captions using the *Caption* dialog box, displayed by choosing the **Insert | Caption** command.

Chapter 20: quick quiz

Circle the correct answer to each of the following multiple-choice questions about captions in Word.

Q1	A caption is ...
A.	Additional information or references regarding the main text that appears at the end of document.
B.	A numbered label added to pictures, tables, worksheet cells or equations in a Word document.
C.	A summary of information about a document that can be displayed with the **File	Properties** command.
D.	Additional information or references regarding the main text that appears at the bottom of a page within document.

Q2	In Word, which command do you choose to insert a caption in a document?
A.	**Insert	Caption.**
B.	**Tools	Captions	Insert.**
C.	**Insert	New	Captions.**
D.	**Insert	Bookmarks or Captions.**

Q3	In Word, a caption label is ...
A.	An automatically incrementing number that Word inserts in each caption.
B.	Optional text such as 'Sales Figures' or 'Annual Rainfall' that you can add to further describe the item captioned.
C.	Standard text such as 'Figure' or 'Table' that appears in each caption.
D.	None of the above.

Q4	In Word, which of the following items can you not add a caption to?
A.	Picture.
B.	Footnote.
C.	Table.
D.	Equation.

Q5	By default, where does Word position captions for tables?
A.	Beneath the table.
B.	To the left of the table.
C.	Above the table.
D.	None of the above – you cannot add captions to tables.

Q6	By default, where does Word position captions for pictures?
A.	Beneath the picture.
B.	To the left of the picture.
C.	Above the picture.
D.	None of the above – you cannot add captions to pictures.

Q7	In Word, which action can you not perform after clicking the **Numbering** button on the *Caption* dialog box?
A.	Update the caption number fields throughout the document.
B.	Change the separator symbol between chapter and the caption number.
C.	Include the current chapter number with the caption numbers.
D.	Change the format that Word applies to the automatically incrementing caption numbers.

Q8	Which action do you take to activate automatic captioning in Word?
A.	Choose **Insert | Caption**, click **Numbering**, select the *Number all captions* checkbox, and click **Apply** and **OK**.
B.	Choose **Tools | Options**, click the **General** tab, select the *Automated captioning* checkbox, and click **OK**.
C.	Choose **Insert | Caption**, click **AutoCaption**, select the required file type(s), and click **OK** and **OK**.
D.	Choose **Format | Captions**, click the **Numbering** tab, select the *Automated captioning* checkbox, and click **OK**.

Q9	In Word, when can you automatically include chapter numbers with caption numbers?
A.	When the document is based on the Normal template (Normal.dot)
B.	When the chapter title text is formatted in a built-in heading style.
C.	When the document's headings are formatted with styles rather than with direct formatting.
D.	When the chapter title text is formatted in a built-in heading style and has outline numbering applied to it.

Answers   **1:** B, **2:** A, **3:** C, **4:** B, **5:** C, **6:** A, **7:** A, **8:** C, **9:** D.

21

Indexes

About indexes

Let's begin with a more precise definition of an index.

Index
An alphabetical listing of the main items in a document, along with the corresponding page numbers, shown at the end of a document.

Don't confuse an index with a *table of contents*. A table of contents (see Chapter 19) is generally less thorough than an index and appears at the beginning of a document.

Indexing: the two steps

Word offers a number of features to help you build and update document indexes. In Word, indexing is a two-step process:

- **Marking the index entries**. The first step in building an index is to mark all the items in your document that are to be included in the index.

  Word positions an index entry field code (XE) at each item that you mark for indexing.

- **Creating the index**. When you have marked all your index entries, you then *compile* the actual index. Word generates the page number references in the index automatically.

  This is also the stage at which you specify the index format: the number of columns, the alignment of page numbers, and which (if any) tab leaders you want to use. As with tables of contents, Word's indexing feature offers a gallery of built-in formats, with names such as Classic and Modern.

A sample Word-created index is shown below:

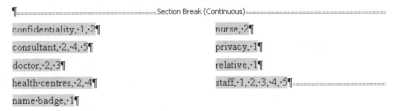

The Index and Tables dialog box

You insert an index using the **Index** tab of the *Index and Tables* dialog box, displayed by choosing the **Insert | Index and Tables** command.

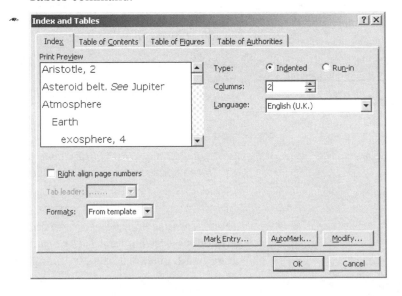

Updating the index

Typically, you compile an index only once but will need to update it several times. This may be because you have added new content to your document, reordered existing content, or both.

You can update an index by selecting it and pressing **F9**. Alternatively, right-click on the index and choose **Update Field** from the pop-up menu.

Working with indexes: the four tasks

Here are the four tasks that you need to be able to perform with indexes in Word:

- **Mark index entries**. Exercise 21.1 shows you how to mark text for inclusion in an index.

- **Compile an index**. In Exercise 21.2, you compile an index using the default options.

- **Formatting a table of contents**. Learn how to customize the appearance of your index using the techniques shown in Exercise 21.3.

- **Update an index**. Exercise 21.4 shows you how to update an index to reflect changes in the content of your document.

Working with index entries

In the first exercise, you mark items in a sample document for later inclusion in an index.

Exercise 21.1: Mark entries for indexing

1) Open the following file:

    Chapter21_Exercise_21-1_Before.doc

2) On the first page after the document's table of contents, under the heading 'Codes of Conduct', select the two words 'name badge'.

    ·Codes·of·Conduct¶
    Our·staff·will·introduce·themselves·to·you·and·explain·how·they·can·help.·All·staff·
    will·wear·a·name·badge·to·enable·you·to·identify·them.¶

3) Choose **Insert | Index and Tables**, click the **Index** tab of the dialog box, and select the **Mark Entry** button to display the *Mark Index Entry* dialog box.

    You can see the text you selected in the *Main entry* box.

Mark Index Entry

Index
Main entry: name badge
Subentry:

Options
○ Cross-reference: See
◉ Current page
○ Page range
Bookmark:

Page number format
☐ Bold
☐ Italic

This dialog box stays open so that you can mark multiple index entries.

[Mark] [Mark All] [Cancel]

4) Click the **Mark** button and then click **Close** to close the dialog box. You can see the index entry field in hidden text format. Can't see the XE field? Click the **Show/Hide** button on the Standard toolbar.

‧ **Codes·of·Conduct**¶
Our·staff·will·introduce·themselves·to·you·and·explain·how·they·can·help.·All·staff·will·wear·a·name·badge{·XE·"name·badge"·}·to·enable·you·to·identify·them.¶

5) Move to the next page of the document. Under the heading 'Nursing Services', select the word 'nurse'.

‧ *Nursing·Services*¶
We·will·ensure·that·a·named,·qualified nurse,·midwife·or·other·health·care·professional·takes·a·personal·responsibility·for·your·treatment·and·care·during·your·time·with·us.¶

6) Press the following shortcut key combination: **Alt+Shift+X**.

This displays the *Mark Index Entry* dialog box. Click the **Mark** button, and then click **Close** to close the dialog box. Your text should look like this:

‧ *Nursing·Services*¶
We·will·ensure·that·a·named,·qualified·nurse{·XE·"nurse"·}·midwife·or·other·health·care·professional·takes·a·personal·responsibility·for·your·treatment·and·care·during·your·time·with·us.¶

7) Further down the same page, under the heading 'Standards of Services', select the text 'health centres' and press **Alt+Shift+X**.

‧ **Standards·of·Service**¶
Staff·at·our·hospitals·and·health·centres·are·committed·to·achieving·specified·standards·in·the·following·areas:¶

8) Click the **Mark All** button, and then click **Close** to close the dialog box. Your text should look like this:

· Standards·of·Service¶
Staff·at·our·hospitals·and·health·centres{·XE·"health·centres"·}·are·committed·to·achieving·specified·standards·in·the·following·areas·¶

Move forward in your sample document to the heading called 'Keeping Us Informed'. You can see that other occurrences of the text 'health centres' also contain index entry marks.

• → Showing·consideration·for·other·people·in·the·hospital·and·health·centres{·XE·"health·centres"·}·and·keeping·noise·levels·to·a·minimum·¶

• → Complying·with·signs·around·the·hospital·and·health·centres{·XE·"health·centres"·}·including·those·asking·you·not·to·smoke,·not·to·use·mobile·phones,·and·our·advice·on·the·number·of·visitors·and·visiting·times.¶

9) Move back to the first page of text in your sample document. Select the word 'patient' in the first bullet point, press **Alt+Shift+X**, click **Mark All**, then click **Close**.

10) Locate occurrences of the following words in your sample document. In each case, select the word, press **Alt+Shift+X**, click **Mark All**, then click **Close**:

`relative, staff, privacy, confidentiality, consultant, doctor`

11) Save the document with the following name:

`Chapter21_Exercise_21-1_After_Your_Name`.doc

You can now close the document.

Options when marking index entries

In Exercise 21.1, you first selected each item of text that you wanted to mark as an index entry. Word displays the text that you select in the *Main entry* box of the *Mark Index Entry* dialog box.

Codes·of·Conduct¶
Our·staff·will·introduce·themselves·to·you·and·explain·how·they·can·help.·All·staff·will·wear·a·name·badge·to·enable·you·to·identify·them.¶

Word offers the following options when marking index entries:

■ Want to change the word or phrase in the *Main entry* box? Simply edit the displayed text as required.

- Want to create an index entry for a word or phrase that does not appear in your document? Do not select any text before pressing **Alt+Shift**+X. Word displays the *Mark Index Entry* dialog box without any text present in the *Main entry* box. You can then type in the text that you require.

Compiling an index

In this exercise, you will compile an index based on the index entries that you marked in Exercise 21.2.

Exercise 21.2: Compile an index

1) Open the following file:

    Chapter21_Exercise_21-2_Before.doc

2) Click at the paragraph mark on the last page of the document. This is the location at which you will create the index.

3) Choose **Insert | Index and Tables**, click the **Index** tab, verify that the default options are as shown below, and click **OK**.

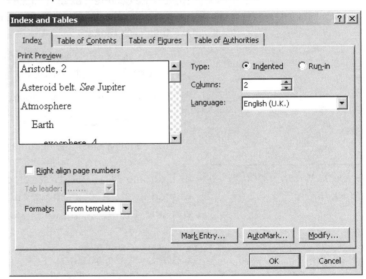

Word compiles the index as shown below:

Can't see a grey background behind each indexed item? Choose **Tools | Options**, and click the **View** tab. In the *Field shading* box, select *When selected*, and click **OK**.

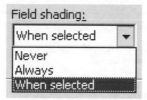

4) Save the document with the following name:

   Chapter21_Exercise_21-2_After_*Your_Name*.doc

   You can now close the document.

Index and section breaks

As you discovered in Exercise 21.2, Word places an index in a section of its own. Why? Because, by default, Word formats the index in a different number of columns to the remainder of the document. You will learn more about sections in Chapter 26.

Index formatting options

If Word's default index formatting is not to your taste, you have three reformatting options

- **Apply direct formatting**. You can select one or more paragraphs in the index, and use the **Format | Font**, **Format | Paragraph** and **Format | Borders and Shading** commands to format them.

- **Apply a built-in style from the index gallery**. Another option is to select from Word's built-in gallery of index formats. The choices include Classic, Distinctive and Formal.

- **Change the style attributes**. Word contains nine built-in styles for use in indexes, named Index Heading, Index 1, Index 2, etc. By changing the attributes of these styles with the **Format | Style** command, you can change the appearance of your index.

In Exercise 21.3, you will generate an index based on some modifications that you make to Word's default formatting settings.

Exercise 21.3: Compile an index with non-default formatting

1) Open the following file:

   Chapter21_Exercise_21-3_Before.doc

2) Click at the paragraph mark on the last page of the document, choose **Insert | Index and Tables**, and click the **Index** tab.

3) In the Formats drop-down list, select the *Classic* option, and click **OK**.

   Word generates and inserts the index like this:

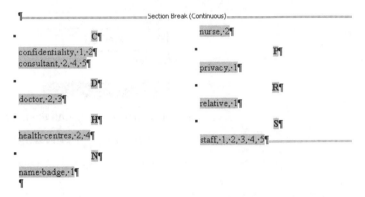

4) Click at any of the index headings (the upper-case letters that precede each alphabetic group of index entries).

5) Choose **Format | Style**, click **Modify**, then click **Format** and **Paragraph**. In the *Alignment* box, select *Left,* and click **OK**, **OK**, and **Apply**. Your index should look like this:

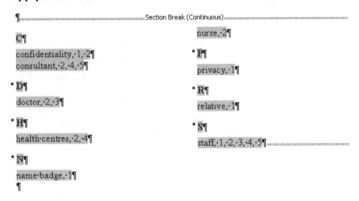

6) Save the document with the following name:

    Chapter21_Exercise_21-3_After_*Your_Name*.doc

You can now close the document.

Updating an index

You have created an index for your document – but the document has changed, with the result that the index is no longer accurate. How can you update your index?

In Exercise 21.4, you will make some changes to a document, and then update the index to reflect the changes.

Exercise 21.4: Update an index

1) Open the following file:

    Chapter21_Exercise_21-4_Before.doc

2) Move to the last page of text in your sample document, and select the first bullet point beneath the heading 'Medical Information'.

- **Medical·Information**¶
You·have·the·right·to·be·informed·of·the·nature·of·your·illness·or·condition·in· language·that·you·can·fully·understand,·and·to·be·informed·concerning··¶
- → The·results·of·your·tests·and·x-rays{·XE·"x-rays"·}·¶
- → The·purpose,·method,·likely·duration·and·expected·benefit·of·the·proposed· treatment·¶

Press **Delete** to remove it. The paragraph contained a marked index entry. You need to update your index to reflect your editing change

3) Move to the final page of the document, i.e. the page that contains the index.

Hold the mouse over any index field and either press **F9** or right-click with the mouse and choose **Update Field** from the pop-up menu.

Word updates the index. You can see that the entry for 'X-rays, 6' is removed.

4) Save the document with the following name:

    Chapter21_Exercise_21-4_After_*Your_Name*.doc

You can now close the document.

Chapter 21: quick reference

Tasks summary

Task	Procedure
Mark an index entry.	Select the text, press **Alt+Shift+X**, click **Mark** or **Mark All**, and then click **Close**.
Compile an index.	Position the insertion point where you want the index to appear, select your required format from the built-in gallery, choose **Insert | Index and Tables**, click the **Index** tab, and click **OK**.
Change the appearance of an index.	Select the index text and apply direct formatting. Or modify the attributes of the built-in indexing styles.
Update an index to reflect changes in the document.	Click on any field in the compiled index and press **F9**.

Concepts summary

An *index* is an alphabetical listing of the main items in a document, along with the corresponding page numbers, shown at the end of a document. You can use Word to *mark* text items for inclusion in an index, and to create or *compile* the index itself. The marking and compilation options are available within the **Index** tab when you choose the **Insert | Index and Tables** command.

Word places *section breaks* before and after an index because, by default, the index is formatted in a different number of columns to the remainder of the document.

You have three *formatting* options for an index: apply direct formatting, select a built-in style from the Index gallery, or change the index style attributes. You can *update* an index to reflect changes in the document content.

Chapter 21: quick quiz

Circle the correct answer to each of the following multiple-choice questions about indexes in Word.

Q1	Which of the following statements about indexes is untrue?
A.	An index lists the important items in a document.
B.	Items in an index are listed in alphabetical order.
C.	An index appears at the end of a document.
D.	Items in an index are listed in page number order.

Q2	In Word, which of the following keyboard shortcuts can you use when marking an index entry?
A.	**Alt+Ctrl+X.**
B.	**Alt+F9.**
C.	**Alt+Shift+X.**
D.	**F9.**

Q3	In Word, which of the following command actions can you perform to mark an index entry?
A.	Choose **Tools	Index**, click **Index Entry**, and then click **OK**.
B.	Choose **Insert	Index and Tables**, click the **Index** tab, click **Mark Entry**, and then click **OK**.
C.	Choose **Format	Index**, click **Mark Entry**, and then click **Apply**.
D.	Choose **Insert	Index and Tables**, click the **Index** tab, click **Mark**, and then click **Close**.

ECDL Advanced Word Processing

Q4	In Word, how can you create an index entry for a word or phrase that does not appear in your document?
A.	Do not select any text before pressing **Alt+Shift+X**, type the required text in the dialog box, and then click **Mark** and **Close**.
B.	Choose **Tools | Index**, click **Index New Entry**, type the required text in the dialog box, and then click **OK**.
C.	Click anywhere in the document left margin, press **Alt+Ctrl+X**, type the required text in the dialog box, and then click **Mark** and **Close**.
D.	None of the above – you cannot create index entries for words or phrases that do not appear in a document.

Q5	In Word, what is the effect of clicking the **Mark All** button in the *Mark Index Entry* dialog box?
A.	Word compiles an index of all commonly occurring words and phrases in the document.
B.	You are taken to the relevant index entry in the compiled index.
C.	All occurrences of the text in the *Mark entry* box within the dialogue box will be included in the compiled index.
D.	All occurrences of text formatting with built-in heading styles will be included in the compiled index.

Q6	In Word, which of the following command actions do you take to compile an index?
A.	Choose **Format | Index**, click **Compile Now**, and then click **Apply**.
B.	Choose **Insert | Index and Tables**, click the **Index** tab, and click **OK**.
C.	Right-click on any index entry field in the document, and choose **Compile Index** from the pop-up menu displayed.
D.	Choose **Insert | Index and Tables**, click the **Compile Index** tab, click **Compile**, and then click **Close**.

Q7	Which of the following breaks does Word automatically insert before and after a compiled index?
A.	Column breaks.
B.	Page breaks.
C.	Text-wrapping breaks.
D.	Section breaks.

Q8	In Word, which of the following actions do you take to update an index?
A.	Right-click on any field in the compiled index and press **Alt+Shift+X**.
B.	Select the compiled index, choose **Format | Index**, click **Update** and then click **Apply**.
C.	Click on any field in the compiled index and press **F9**.
D.	None of the above – you must recompile the index if the document content changes.

Answers

1: D, **2:** C, **3:** D, **4**: A, **5:** C, **6:** B, **7:** D, **8:** C.

22 Font and paragraph effects

Objectives

In this chapter you will learn how to:

- Apply static and animated effects to selected text
- Apply borders and shading to paragraphs
- Apply widow and orphan controls to paragraphs

New words

In this chapter you will meet the following terms:

- Widow
- Orphan

Exercise files

In this chapter you will work with the following Word files:

- Chapter22_Exercise_22-1_Before.doc
- Chapter22_Exercise_22-2_Before.doc
- Chapter22_Exercise_22-3_Before.doc
- Chapter22_Exercise_22-4_Before.doc
- Chapter22_Exercise_22-5_Before.doc

Syllabus reference

In this chapter you will cover the following items from the ECDL Advanced Word Processing Syllabus:

- **AM3.1.1.1**: Apply text effect options: strikethrough, superscript, subscript, shadow, etc.
- **AM3.1.1.2**: Apply animated text effect options.
- **AM3.1.2.1**: Use paragraph shading options.
- **AM3.1.2.2**: Usc paragraph border options.
- **AM3.1.2.3**: Apply widow and orphan controls to paragraphs.

Font and paragraph effects

Word offers the following effects that you can apply to text and paragraphs through the **Format | Font** and **Format | Paragraph** commands.

- **Font options**. These include font features such as superscript, shadow and small capitals.

- **Animated text**. You can apply animation to text that appears on the screen but not on print-outs.

- **Paragraph borders and shading**. You can place a variety of border types around paragraph. You can also insert coloured backgrounds behind paragraphs for emphasis or decorative effect.

- **Widows and orphans**. You can prevent Word from printing the first line of a paragraph alone at the bottom of a page (*orphan*) or the last line of a paragraph alone at the top of a page (*widow*).

Working with text and paragraph effects: the five tasks

Here are the five tasks that you need to be able to perform with text and paragraph effects in Word:

- **Apply font effects**. Exercise 22.1 shows you how to apply font effects.

- **Apply animated text effects**. In Exercise 22.2, you apply Word's animated text effects.

- **Apply paragraph borders**. Exercise 22.3 takes you through the steps of applying borders around paragraphs.

- **Apply paragraph shading**. You learn how to place coloured backgrounds behind paragraphs in Exercise 22.4.

- **Apply widow and orphan controls**. In Exercise 22.5 you discover how to switch off the Word feature that prevents single lines appearing at the top and bottom of pages.

Working with font effects

Word offers a wide range of font options within the **Font** tab of the **Format | Font** command.

Effects		
☐ Strikethrough	☐ Shadow	☐ Small caps
☐ Double strikethrough	☐ Outline	☐ All caps
☐ Superscript	☐ Emboss	☐ Hidden
☐ Subscript	☐ Engrave	

The table opposite lists and describes these font effects.

Name	Description	Example	Typical usage
Strikethrough	Applies a solid line through the middle of the text.	~~Coursebook~~	Revision tracking
Double strikethrough	Applies a double solid line through the middle of the text.	~~Coursebook~~	Revision tracking
Superscript	Raises the text and reduces its font size.	$x^2 + y^2$	Exponents
Subscript	Lowers the text and reduces its font size.	H_2SO_4	Chemical formulas
Shadow	Applies a shadow behind the text.	Coursebook	Decorative headings
Outline	Displays character borders only.	Coursebook	Decorative headings
Emboss	Displays text as if it were raised off the page.	Coursebook	Decorative headings
Engrave	Displays text as if were pressed into the page.	Coursebook	Decorative headings
Small caps	Displays text in upper-case characters and reduces the font size.	COURSEBOOK	Decorative headings
All caps	Displays text in upper-case characters.	COURSEBOOK	Headings
Hidden	Makes text invisible. You can use the Show/Hide button to toggle the display of the text.		Revision tracking

In the first exercise, you will apply some font effects to a sample document.

Exercise 22.1: Apply font effects

1) Start Word and open the following document:

    ```
    Chapter22_Exercise_22-1_Before.doc
    ```

2) Select the word Danger, choose **Format | Font**, click the **Font** tab, select the *Outline* and *All caps* options, and click **OK**.

3) Select the words 'Hazardous Material' and 'Handle with Extreme Caution', choose **Format | Font**, click the **Font** tab, select the *Small caps* option, and click **OK**.

4) Select the words 'Sulphuric Acid', choose **Format | Font**, click the **Font** tab, select the *Shadow* option, and click **OK**.

5) In the line containing 'H2SO4', select the '2', choose **Format | Font**, click the **Font** tab, select the *Subscript* option, and click **OK**. Repeat this action for the '4' in 'H2SO4'.

Your document should now look like this:

6) Save your sample document with the following name, and close it:

`Chapter22_Exercise_22-1_After_Your_Name.doc`

Working with animated text effects

Word offers a wide range of on-screen text animation effects within the **Animation** tab of the **Format | Font** command.

The following table lists and describes these text effects.

Name	Description
Blinking Background	Causes the text and background to alternate between black-on-white and white-on-black.
Las Vegas Lights	Surrounds the text with flashing, multi-coloured, neon-like dots.
Marching Black Ants	Surrounds the text with a dynamic, dashed, black border.
Marching Red Ants	Surrounds the text with a dynamic, dashed, red border.
Shimmer	Repeatedly blurs the text and then returns it to normal.
Sparkle Text	Displays a layer of flashing, multi-coloured sparkles over the text.

Exercise 22.2: Apply text animation effects

1) Open the following Word document:

   Chapter22_Exercise_22-2_Before.doc

2) Select the words 'Blinking Background', choose **Format | Font**, click the **Text Effects** tab, select the *Blinking Background* option, and click **OK**.

3) Select the words 'Las Vegas Lights', choose **Format | Font**, click the **Text Effects** tab, click the *Las Vegas Lights* option, and click **OK**.

4) Select the words 'Marching Black Ants', choose **Format | Font**, click the **Text Effects** tab, click the *Marching Black Ants* option, and click **OK**.

5) Select the words 'Marching Red Ants', choose **Format | Font**, click the **Text Effects** tab, click the *Marching Red Ants* option, and click **OK**.

6) Select the words 'Shimmer', choose **Format | Font**, click the **Text Effects** tab, click the *Shimmer* option, and click **OK**.

7) Select the words 'Sparkle Text', choose **Format | Font**, click the **Text Effects** tab, click the *Sparkle Text* option, and click **OK**.

8) Save your sample document with the following name, and close it:

   Chapter22_Exercise_22-2_After_*Your_Name*.doc

Working with paragraph borders and shading

You can call attention to paragraphs by adding borders (decorative boxes) and shading (coloured backgrounds) using the options available with the **Format | Borders and Shading** command.

Border options

To apply a border, select the paragraph (including its paragraph mark), choose **Format | Borders and Shading**, click the **Borders** tab, select your required options, and click **OK**.

Word offers a range of border settings. Use the *Preview* area on the right of the dialog box to select the edges that you want bordered. The default is all four edges. You can also control the border colour and width.

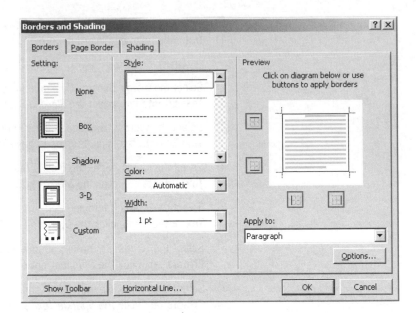

Exercise 22.3: Apply paragraph borders

1) Open the following Word document:

   ```
   Chapter22_Exercise_22-3_Before.doc
   ```

2) Select the 'Carpets Uncovered' paragraph, choose **Format | Borders and Shading**, and click the **Borders** tab.

   Click the *Shadow* setting and click **OK**.

3) Select the 'Everything Half Price' paragraph, choose **Format | Borders and Shading**, and click the **Borders** tab.

   In the *Width* box, select *3 pt*. In the *Preview* area, click the top box edge.

   In the *Width* box, select *1 pt*. In the *Preview* area, click the bottom box edge and click **OK**.

4) Select the 'Unit 42, Retail Park' paragraph, choose **Format | Borders and Shading**, and click the **Borders** tab.

   Click the *Box* setting. In the *Width* box, select $1\frac{1}{2}$ *pt* and click **OK**.

   Your document should look like this:

5) Save your sample document with the following name, and close it:

   Chapter22_Exercise_22-3_After_*Your_Name*.doc

To apply shading, select the paragraph (including its paragraph mark), choose **Format | Borders and Shading**, click the **Shading** tab, select your fill, style and colour options, and click **OK**.

- **Fill**. The text background colour. If you want to place a grey shade behind black text, use 25% or less of grey, otherwise the text will be difficult to read.

- **Style**. Allows you to apply tints (percentages of a colour) or patterns of a second colour (selected in the *Color* box) on top of the selected fill colour. Leave the *Style* box at its default value of *Clear* if you do not want to apply a second colour.

- **Colour**. If you have selected a pattern in the *Style* box, select the colour of the lines and dots in the pattern here.

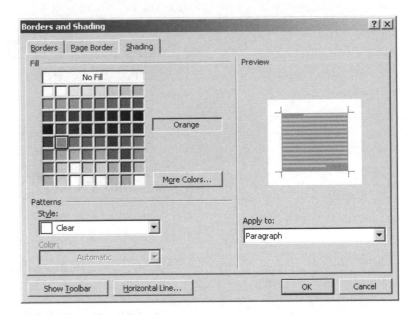

Paragraph bordering and shading options are commonly applied to the same paragraph to achieve visual effects.

Exercise 22.4: Apply paragraph shading

1) Open the following Word document:

    Chapter22_Exercise_22-4_Before.doc

2) Select the 'Carpets Uncovered' paragraph, choose **Format | Borders and Shading**, and click the **Shading** tab.

    In the *Fill* area, click *Gray-25%* and click **OK**.

3) Select the 'Everything Half Price' paragraph, choose **Format | Borders and Shading**, and click the **Shading** tab.

    In the *Fill* area, click *Black* and click **OK**.

    With the paragraph still selected, choose **Format | Font** and change the text colour to white.

4) Select the 'Unit 42, Retail Park' paragraph, choose **Format | Borders and Shading**, and click the **Borders** tab.

    Click the *Shadow* setting.

    Next, click the **Shading** tab. In the *Fill* area, click *Gray-25%* and click **OK**.

    Your document should now look like this:

ECDL Advanced Word Processing

5) Save your sample document with the following name, and close it:

Chapter22_Exercise_22-4_After_*Your_Name*.doc

Working with widows and orphans

Professional typesetters and designers follow two important rules when formatting multi-page documents:

- Never print the last line of a paragraph by itself at the top of a page. Such a line is called a *widow*.

- Never print the first line of a paragraph by itself at the bottom of a page. Such a line is called an *orphan*.

By default, Word prevents the occurrence of widows and orphans. You can switch off this setting by choosing **Format | Paragraph**, clicking the **Line and Page Breaks** tab, deselecting the *Widow/Orphan control* checkbox, and clicking **OK**.

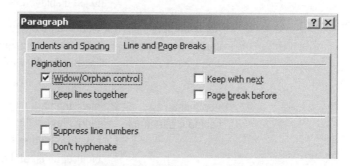

Widow
The last line of a paragraph displayed alone at the top of a page.

Orphan
The first line of a paragraph displayed alone at the bottom of a page.

Exercise 22.5: Switch off widow and orphan control

1) Open the following document:

   `Chapter22_Exercise_22-5_Before.doc`

2) Select the final paragraph of text, beginning with the words 'While it's easy ...'

   This paragraph runs from the bottom of the first page to the top of the second page.

3) Choose **Format | Paragraph**, click the **Line and Page Breaks** tab, deselect the *Widow/Orphan control* checkbox, and click **OK**.

   Notice that the last line of the paragraph now appears by itself at the top of the second page – a widow.

4) Save your sample document with the following name, and close it:

   `Chapter22_Exercise_22-5_After_Your_Name.doc`

Chapter 22: quick reference

Tasks summary

Task	Procedure
Apply font effects.	Select the text, choose **Format	Font**, click the **Font** tab, select a font effect checkbox or boxes, and click **OK**.
Apply animated text effects.	Select the text, choose **Format	Font**, click the **Text Effects** tab, select an animated effect from the list displayed, and click **OK**.
Apply borders around a paragraph.	Select the paragraph (including its paragraph mark), choose **Format	Borders and Shading**, click the **Borders** tab, select your required options, and click **OK**.
Apply shading behind a paragraph.	Select the paragraph (including its paragraph mark), choose **Format	Borders and Shading**, click the **Shading** tab, select your fill, style and colour options, and click **OK**.
Switch widow/ orphan control on/off.	Select the paragraph, choose **Format	Paragraph**, click the **Line and Page Breaks** tab, select or deselect the *Widow/Orphan control* check box, and click **OK**.

Concepts summary

Word offers a range of *font effects*, such as outline, shadow and subscript, which you can apply to selected text in documents. *Animated text effects* allow selected text to change dynamically on screen. These effects are available with the **Format | Font** command.

You can call attention to paragraphs by adding *borders* (decorative boxes) and *shading* (coloured backgrounds), using the options available with the **Format | Borders and Shading** command.

By default, Word prevents *widows* (the last line of a paragraph appearing alone at the top of a page) and *orphans* (the first line of a paragraph appearing alone at the bottom of a page). This setting is controlled within the **Line and Page Breaks** tab of the **Format | Paragraph** command.

Chapter 22: quick quiz

Circle the correct answer to each of the following multiple-choice questions about font and text effects, borders and shading, and widows and orphans in Word.

Q1	In Word, to which of the following types of text would you typically apply a subscript font effect?
A.	Chemical formulas.
B.	Exponents in mathematical text.
C.	Text that is marked for deletion.
D.	Decorative headings.

Q2	In Word, to which of the following types of text would you typically apply a small caps font effect?
A.	Body text.
B.	Decorative headings.
C.	Text that is marked for deletion.
D.	Exponents in mathematical text.

Q3	In Word, to which of the following types of text would you typically apply an outline font effect?
A.	Decorative headings.
B.	Body text.
C.	Field codes.
D.	Chemical formulas.

Q4	In Word, which of the following statements about animated text effects is untrue?
A.	Blinking Background and Shimmer are two animated text effects available with Word.
B.	Animated text effects appear both on screen and on print-outs.
C.	Animated text effects are controlled within the **Font** tab of the **Format | Font** command.
D.	Animated text effects appear on screen but not on print-outs.

Q5	In Word, which of the following statements about paragraph borders is untrue?
A.	A border can be applied selectively to one or more of the following edges of a paragraph: top, bottom, left and right.
B.	Paragraph borders are controlled within the **Borders** tab of the **Format | Borders and Shading** command.
C.	You can control the width but not the colour of paragraph borders.
D.	You can control both the width and the colour of paragraph borders.

Q6	In Word, which of the following statements about paragraph shading is untrue?
A.	Paragraph shading is controlled within the **Shading** tab of the **Format | Borders and Shading** command.
B.	Borders or shading, but not both at once, can be applied to a selected paragraph.
C.	The term 'fill' refers to the paragraph background colour.
D.	Borders and shading can be applied to the same paragraph.

Q7	In Word, which of the following statements about widows is untrue?
A.	Widow and orphan settings are controlled within the **Line and Page Breaks** tab of the **Format | Paragraph** command.
B.	A widow is the last line of a paragraph appearing alone at the top of a page.
C.	By default, Word prevents the occurrence of widows and orphans.
D.	A widow is the first line of a paragraph appearing alone at the bottom of a page.

Q8	In Word, which of the following statements about orphans is untrue?
A.	Widows and orphans settings are controlled within the **Line and Page Breaks** tab of the **Format | Paragraph** command.
B.	An orphan is the last line of a paragraph appearing alone at the top of a page.
C.	By default, Word prevents the occurrence of widows and orphans.
D.	An orphan is the first line of a paragraph appearing alone at the bottom of a page.

Answers   **1:** A, **2:** B, **3:** A, **4:** B, **5:** C, **6:** B, **7:** D, **8:** B

23

Text boxes and text orientation

- **AM3.4.3.3**. Apply border and shading options in text boxes.

- **AM3.4.3.4**. Link text boxes.

- **AM3.1.1.7**. Use text orientation options.

About text boxes

In a Word document, text flows continuously from the beginning of the document to the end, from the top left of the first page to the bottom right of the last.

Sometimes, however, you might want to insert and position text in a block or container separate from the main text of the document. In publishing, such boxes are named call-outs or sidebars. In Word, the term used is *text boxes*.

E-business·is·a·way·to·electronically·deliver·customized·information·about· organizations,·their·products·and·services.·Examples·are·internal·employee· communications,·automated·stock·control·systems,·recruiting·and· employment.¶

THE·INTERNET¶
A·global,·public·network· linked·by·computers·that· allows·users·to·share· information·and·interact.¶

What·are·we·buying·on-line?·The·most·common·purchases· are·computer·software·and·hardware,·compact·disks,· books,·travel,·entertainment,·clothing·and·shoes,· groceries,·health·and·beauty·products·and·discount· brokerage·services.¶

Analysts·predict·that·e-commerce·will·also·become·increasingly·popular·for· locating·and·buying·hard-to-find·and·unique·products.·The·Net·has·seen· phenomenal·growth·in·on-line·auction·houses·that·sell·everything·from· planes,·to·cars,·to·jewellery,·fine·art·and·collectables.·EBay.com·is·a·popular· example.¶

An example of a text box in Word

You can insert several text boxes on the same page, format the text directly or with styles, add borders and shading (coloured backgrounds), and resize, move, copy, and cut and paste text boxes, as required.

Here are some of the items that you can include in a Word text box:

- Text

- Text in a table

- Pictures

- Fields

And here are some of the items that you cannot include:

- Columns

- Comments

- Footnotes and endnotes

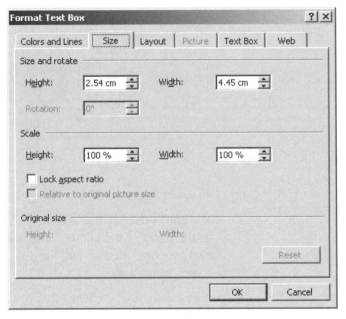

Text box

A container for text or other items that is separate from the remainder of the text in the document. Text boxes can be formatted, sized, moved, copied, and cut and pasted, as required.

Text Box button

You can create a new text box by clicking the **Text Box** button on the Drawing toolbar, or by choosing **Insert | Text Box**. You then draw the text box by dragging with the mouse.

Formatting text boxes

Want to change any aspect of a text box? Just right-click on any of its edges, and choose **Format Text Box** from the pop-up menu displayed.

Linking text boxes

You can connect or *link* a series of text boxes so that text flows forward from one text box to the next. Linked text boxes are most commonly used in magazine or newsletter layouts, where, for example, a story that begins in a text box on one page can be continued in linked text boxes on later pages.

Text orientation

A feature that text boxes share with table cells is that the text that they contain can be oriented at 90 degrees. Text that is not inside a text box or table cell cannot be reoriented in this way.

Working with text boxes and text orientation: the five tasks

Here are the five tasks that you need to be able to perform with text boxes and text orientation in Word:

- **Add and remove text boxes**. Exercise 23.1 shows you how to insert and delete text boxes.

- **Edit, resize and move text boxes**. Follow Exercise 23.2 to learn how to edit the text in a text box, amend a box's size, and change a box's position.

- **Apply borders and shading to text boxes**. Exercises 23.3 and 23.4 take you through the steps of applying borders and coloured backgrounds to text boxes.

- **Link text boxes**. You discover how to connect a series of text boxes in Exercise 23.5.

- **Orient text in text boxes and tables**. See Exercises 23.6 and 23.7 to learn how to orient text in a text box and a table cell at 90 degrees.

Working with new text boxes

Text Box button

Exercise 23.1: Add and remove text boxes

1) Start Word and open the following document:

   `Chapter23_Exercise_23-1_Before.doc`

   Is the Drawing toolbar visible? If not, use **View | Toolbars** to display it.

2) Click the **Text Box** button on the Drawing toolbar, or choose **Insert | Text Box**. Your cursor changes to a cross.

3) Drag the mouse to draw a text box to the left of the text beneath the heading 'Introduction'.

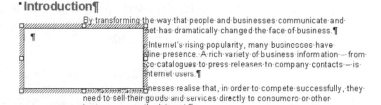

4) Click at the paragraph mark in the text box, and type the following text:

   ```
   The Internet
   A global, public network linked by computers
   that allows users to share information and
   interact.
   ```

   Your sample document should look like this:

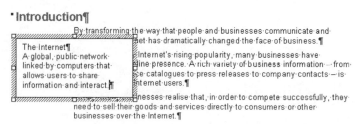

5) Select the heading 'The Internet' in the text box. Using **Format |
Font**, change it to Arial Narrow, small caps, and change the font
colour to red.

6) Click on any edge of the text box. Notice that Word changes the pattern
of the text box edges. This tells you that the text box is selected.

7) You can now copy, cut or delete the text box. Press **Delete** to remove
the text box.

8) Click the **Text Box** button on the Drawing toolbar, or choose **Insert |
Text Box**. Drag the mouse to draw a text box to the left of the text
beneath the heading ' What is ebusiness?'.

- **What·is·ebusiness?**¶

E-business·is·a·way·to·electronically·deliver·customized·information·about·
organizations,·their·products·and·services.·Examples·are·internal·employee·
communications,·automated·stock·control·systems,·recruiting·and·

ng·on-line?·The·most·common·purchases·are·computer·
ware,·compact·disks,·books,·travel,·entertainment,·clothing·
ies,·health·and·beauty·products·and·discount·brokerage·

hat·e-commerce·will·also·become·increasingly·popular·for·
g·hard-to-find·and·unique·products.·The·Net·has·seen·
phenomenal·growth·in·on-line·auction·houses·that·sell·everything·from·
planes,·to·cars,·to·jewellery,·fine·art·and·collectables.·EBay.com·is·a·popular·
example.¶

9) Repeat steps 4 and 5 for your new text box.

10) Right-click on any edge of the text box, and choose **Format Text Box**
from the pop-up menu. Click the **Layout** tab, select the *Square* option,
and click **OK**.

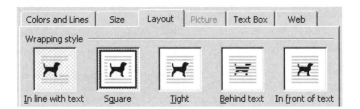

The main text of your document now flows around the text box. Click
anywhere else in your document to deselect the text box. It should
now look like this:

What·is·ebusiness?¶

E-business·is·a·way·to·electronically·deliver·customized·information·about·organizations,·their·products·and·services.·Examples·are·internal·employee·communications,·automated·stock·control·systems,·recruiting·and·employment.¶

THE·INTERNET¶
A·global,·public·network·linked·by·computers·that·allows·users·to·share·information·and·interact.¶

What·are·we·buying·on-line?·The·most·common·purchases·are·computer·software·and·hardware,·books,·travel,·compact·disks,·entertainment,·clothing·and·shoes,·health·and·beauty·products,·groceries,·and·discount·brokerage·services.¶

Analysts·predict·that·e-business·will·also·become·increasingly·popular·for·locating·and·purchasing·hard-to-find·and·unique·products.·The·Net·has·seen·huge·growth·in·on-line·auction·websites·that·sell·everything·from·cars·to·jewellery,·fine·art·and·collectables.·Perhaps·the·most·popular·and·successful·example·is·www.ebay.com.¶

Don't worry if your text box is too large for the amount of text that it contains. You will learn how to resize text boxes in Exercise 23.2.

11) Save your sample document with the following name, and close it:

Chapter23_Exercise_23-1_After_*Your_Name*.doc

Working with existing text boxes

Word allows you to perform a wide range of actions on a text box, as Exercise 23.2 shows.

Exercise 23.2: Edit, resize and move text boxes

1) Open the following Word document:

Chapter23_Exercise_23-2_Before.doc

2) Click in the text box, and edit the text 'global, public network' to read 'public, global network'.

3) Select the heading 'THE INTERNET'. Change its font size to 12 point.

4) Select the text beneath the heading in the text box, and change its font size to 12 point, bold.

THE·INTERNET¶
A·public,·global·network·linked·by·computers·that·allows·users·to·share·

5) You need to increase the size of your text box. Click on the middle sizing handle on the lower edge of the text box, and drag downwards with the mouse until all the text in the text box is visible.

To size a text box more precisely, right-click on any of its edges, choose **Format Text Box**, click the **Size** tab, enter the dimensions you require, and click **OK**.

6) Click on any edge of the text box to select it, and drag with the mouse downwards until its lower edge is in line with the final paragraph above the heading 'What's in it for the consumer?'.

> **THE INTERNET¶**
> **A·global,·public·
> network·linked·by·
> computers·that·allows·
> users·to·share·
> information·and·
> interact.¶**

Analysts·predict·that·e-business·will·also·become·increasingly·popular·for·locating·and·purchasing·hard-to-find·and·unique·products.·The·Net·has·seen·huge·growth·in·on-line·auction·websites·that·sell·everything·from·cars·to·jewellery,·fine·art·and·collectables.·Perhaps·the·most·popular·and·successful·example·is·www.ebay.com.¶

Another·sector·that·has·mushroomed·is·on-line·investing.·Investors·can·buy·and·sell·stocks·and·shares,·keep·up-to-date·with·news·headlines·and·market·quotes·(delayed·or·real-time),·and·review·their·account·information.¶

To make small, precise movements in a text box's position, select the text box, hold down the **Ctrl** key and press the arrow keys.

7) Save your sample document with the following name, and close it:

`Chapter23_Exercise_23-2_After_Your_Name`.doc

Working with borders and shading

You can call attention to text boxes by adding borders (decorative boxes). Word allows you to apply borders to a selected text box in two ways:

- Using the **Colors and Lines** tab of the *Format Text Box* dialog box, displayed by right-clicking on any edge of the text box and choosing the **Format Text Box** command from the pop-up menu.

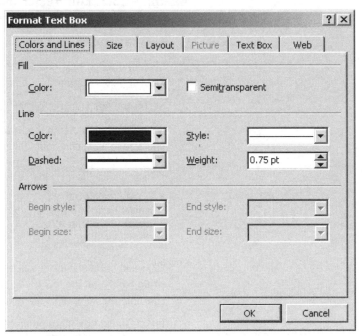

By default, Word applies a 0.75 pt continuous black border around all four sides of every new text box that you create. The default fill colour (background colour) is white.

- Using the options available with the **Format | Borders and Shading** command.

The second method is better because it offers more options and provides greater control. Before applying borders with **Format | Borders and Shading**, however, first *turn off the default border*. Exercise 23.3 takes you through the steps.

Exercise 23.3: Apply borders to a text box

1) Open the following Word document:

   `Chapter23_Exercise_23-3_Before.doc`

2) Right-click on any edge of the text box, choose the **Format Text Box** command, click the **Colors and Lines** tab, select *No Line* from the *Line Color* drop-down list, and click **OK**.

   You have removed the default text box border.

3) Select the text box, choose **Format | Borders and Shading**, and click the **Borders** tab.

   In the *Setting* area, click *None*. In the *Color* drop-down list, select *Red*.

   In the *Width* box, select *3 pt* in the *Preview* area, click the top box edge.

   In the *Width* box, select *1 pt*. In the *Preview* area, click the bottom box edge and click **OK**.

   If you cannot see the lower border of the text box, click the middle sizing handle on the lower edge of the text box, and drag downwards with the mouse until the lower border is visible. Click anywhere outside the text box to deselect it. Your text box should now look like this:

   THE INTERNET¶
   A·global,·public·
   network·linked·by·
   computers·that·allows·
   users·to·share·
   information·and·
   interact.¶

   Analysts·predict·that·e-business·will·also·become· increasingly·popular·for·locating·and·purchasing·hard-to-find· and·unique·products.·The·Net·has·seen·huge·growth·in·on- line·auction·websites·that·sell·everything·from·cars·to· jewellery,·fine·art·and·collectables.·Perhaps·the·most·popular· and·successful·example·is·www.ebay.com.¶

   Another·sector·that·has·mushroomed·is·on-line·investing.· Investors·can·buy·and·sell·stocks·and·shares,·keep·up-to- date·with·news·headlines·and·market·quotes·(delayed·or· real-time),·and·review·their·account·information.¶

4) Save your sample document with the following name, and close it:

   `Chapter23_Exercise_23-3_After_Your_Name.doc`

Exercise 23.4: Apply shading to a text box

1) Open the following Word document:

    `Chapter23_Exercise_23-4_Before.doc`

2) Right-click on any edge of the text box, choose the **Format Text Box** command, click the **Colors and Lines** tab, and select *No Line* from the *Line Color* dropdown list.

You have removed the default text box border.

3) In the *Fill Color* area, select a dark colour. Click **OK**.

4) Select the text in the text box and, using **Format | Font**, change the font colour to white. Your text box should now look like this:

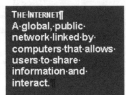

Analysts·predict·that·e-business·will·also·become· increasingly·popular·for·locating·and·purchasing·hard-to-find· and·unique·products.·The·Net·has·seen·huge·growth·in·on-line·auction·websites·that·sell·everything·from·cars·to· jewellery,·fine·art·and·collectables.·Perhaps·the·most·popular· and·successful·example·is·www.ebay.com.¶

Another·sector·that·has·mushroomed·is·on-line·investing.· Investors·can·buy·and·sell·stocks·and·shares,·keep·up-to-date·with·news·headlines·and·market·quotes·(delayed·or· real-time),·and·review·their·account·information.¶

5) Save your sample document with the following name, and close it:

    `Chapter23_Exercise_23-4_After_Your_Name.doc`

Linking text boxes

Word enables you to link a series of text boxes so that text flows forward from one text box to the next. Here are the main points that you need to know about linked text boxes:

- Linked text boxes do not need to be on the same page. However, they must all be contained in a single document.

- You may have more than one series of linked text boxes in the same document.

- As you edit text in any box to make it shorter or longer, the text in the next linked text box moves backward or forward.

- If there is not enough text to fill all the linked boxes, the final box or boxes remain empty.

- If there is too much text to fit within the linked chain of boxes, the text runs below the lower edge of the final box.

- You can edit, resize, move and reformat linked text boxes in the same way that you would work with unlinked text boxes.

- In practice, you will want to add a line such as 'continued on page 2' for your linked text boxes. The best way to do so is to create a separate text box below the linked box, and type the 'continued ...' text in that separate box.

You link text boxes two at a time. Simply select the first box, click the **Create Text Box Link** button on the Text Box toolbar, and then select the second text box.

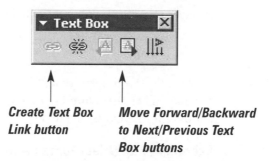

Create Text Box
Link button

Move Forward/Backward
to Next/Previous Text
Box buttons

You can then link the second text box to a third box, and so on.

Linked text boxes

Two or more text boxes in a document that are connected such that text flows forward from the first to the second, and so on.

Exercise 23.5: Link text boxes

1) Open the following document:

   Chapter23_Exercise_23-5_Before.doc

2) Click any edge of the text box on the first page to select it. If the Text Box toolbar does not appear, use the **View | Toolbars** command to display it.

3) Click the **Create Text Box Link** button on the Text Box toolbar.

4) Move forward to the second page, and click any edge of the second text box to select it. The two text boxes in your sample document are now linked.

Create Text Box
Link button

5) Select the final paragraph of text in the document, beginning with the words 'A rich variety of ...' and press **Ctrl+X** to cut it.

6) Click at the paragraph mark in the first of the two linked text boxes and press **Ctrl+V** to paste the text.

7) Move to the second page of your sample document. Notice that the text has flowed forward to this second text box.

As·with·any·other·
business·activity,·it's·
always·a·good·idea·
to·see·what·your·
competition·is·doing.·
If·they·have·a·web·

Continued·on·next·page

presence·and·seem·
to·be·benefiting·from·
it,·your·company·
might·want·to·follow·
their·example.¶

Continued·from·previous·page

8) Save your sample document with the following name, and close it:

```
Chapter23_Exercise_23-5_After_Your_Name.doc
```

Working with text orientation

By default, Word displays text horizontally. You can use the **Format | Text Direction** command to display text vertically – but only if the text is in a text box or a table.

Exercise 23.6: Orient text in a text box

1) Open the following document:

```
Chapter23_Exercise_23-6_Before.doc
```

Text Box button

2) Click the **Text Box** button on the Drawing toolbar, or choose **Insert | Text Box**. Your cursor changes to a cross.

3) Drag the mouse to draw a text box to the left of the heading 'Introduction'.

> *Introduction*¶
> By·transforming·the·way·that·people·and·businesses·communicate·and·
> interact,·the·Internet·has·dramatically·changed·the·face·of·business.¶
>
> Impressed·by·the·Internet's·rising·popularity,·many·businesses·have·
> established·an·online·presence.·A·rich·variety·of·business·information—

4) Right-click on any edge of the text box to select it. Choose **Format | Text Box**, click the **Size** tab, change the height to 14 cm, and click **OK**.

5) Select the document heading, 'The New Era of e-Business', and press **Ctrl+X** to cut it.

6) Click at the paragraph mark in the text box and press **Ctrl+V** to paste the heading text in it.

7) With the cursor positioned anywhere in the text box, choose **Format | Text Direction**, click the bottom-to-top orientation option, and click **OK**.

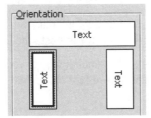

8) Click anywhere in the text box, and then click the **Align Top** button on the Formatting toolbar.

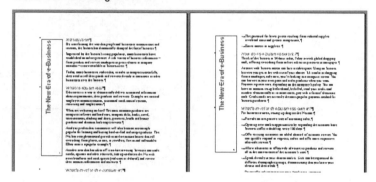

9) Click on the top edge of the text box to select it. Move to the second page of your sample document, click anywhere on the second page, and press **Ctrl+V** to paste the text box. Finally, drag the text box to reposition it at the top left of the page.

10) Both pages should now contain a vertical heading positioned just inside the left margin.

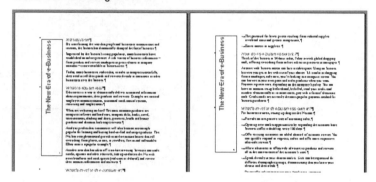

11) Save your sample document with the following name, and close it:

Chapter23_Exercise_23-6_After_*Your_Name*.doc

Exercise 23.7: Orient text in a table

1) Open the following document:

Chapter23_Exercise_23-7_Before.doc

2) Click just to the left of the first row of the table to select that row.

3) Choose **Format | Text Direction**, click the top-to-bottom orientation option, and click **OK.**

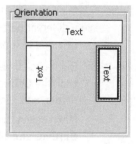

4) Click anywhere in the table, and then click the **Align Top** button on the Formatting toolbar.

5) With the top row still selected, choose **Table | Table Properties**, click the **Cell** tab, select the *Vertical alignment Center* option, and click **OK**.

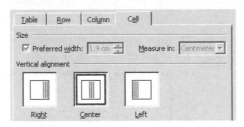

6) Click anywhere outside the top row to deselect it. The top row should now look like this:

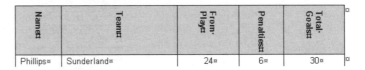

7) Save your sample document with the following name, and close it:

    Chapter23_Exercise_23-7_After_*Your_Name*.doc

Chapter 23: quick reference

Tasks summary

Task	Procedure
Create a text box.	Click the **Text Box** button on the Drawing toolbar, or choose **Insert	Text Box**. Then draw the text box by dragging with the mouse.
Resize a text box.	Click on any sizing handle and drag. Or right-click on any edge, choose **Format Text Box**, click the **Size** tab, enter the dimensions, and click **OK**.
Move a text box.	Click on any edge to select the text box and drag to a different part of the same page. Or cut the selected text box and paste it to another page.
Add borders to a text box.	Right-click on any edge, choose **Format Text Box** click the **Colors and Lines** tab, remove the default border, and click **OK**.
	Next, select the text box, choose **Format	Borders and Shading**, click the **Borders** tab, select your required border options, and click **OK**.

ECDL Advanced Word Processing

Add a background colour to a text box.	Right-click on any edge, choose **Format Text Box**, click the **Colors and Lines** tab, select the required fill options, and click **OK**.
Link two text boxes.	Select the first text box, click the **Create Text Box Link** button on the Text Box toolbar, and then select the second text box.
Orient text at 90° in a text box or table cell.	Click anywhere in the text box or cell, choose **Format	Text Direction**, select your required orientation option, and click **OK**.

Concepts summary

In Word, *text boxes* hold text and other items that are positioned separately from the main text of the document. You can insert several text boxes on the same page, format the text directly or with styles, add borders and shading (coloured backgrounds), and resize, move, copy, and cut and paste text boxes, as required.

You can connect or *link* a series of text boxes so that text flows forward from one text box to the next. Text located in text boxes or table cells can be *oriented* at 90 degrees to the remainder of the document.

Chapter 23:
quick quiz

Circle the correct answer to each of the following multiple-choice questions about text boxes and text orientation in Word.

Q1	In Word, a text box is …
A.	Text formatted with Word's built-in Text Box paragraph style.
B.	A container for holding text or other items that is separate from the main text in the document.
C.	Text surrounded by a solid border applied with the **Format	Borders and Shading** command.
D.	A storage area for holding commonly-used text for convenient insertion in multiple documents.

Q2	In Word, which of the following actions would you perform to create a text box?
A.	Choose **Insert	Picture	Text Box**, enter the box's dimensions, and click **Insert**.
B.	Click the **Text Box** button on the Drawing toolbar and drag with the mouse.
C.	Choose **File	New	Text Box**, select the required template, and click **Create**.
D.	Click the **New Text Box** button on the Formatting toolbar and drag with the mouse.

Q3	In Word, which of the following actions would you perform to resize a text box?
A.	Click anywhere in the box, choose **Resize**, and then drag with the mouse.
B.	Right-click on any sizing handle and drag with the mouse.
C.	Right-click on any edge, choose **Resize Text Box**, click the **Dimensions** tab, enter the dimensions, and click **OK**.
D.	Click on any sizing handle and drag with the mouse.

Q4	In Word, which of the following actions requires that you first select the text box by clicking on one of its edges?
A.	Deleting the text box.
B.	Editing the text contained in the text box.
C.	Applying direct formatting to the text in the text box.
D.	Pasting new text into the text box.

Q5	In Word, which of the following items cannot be included in a text box?
A.	Columns.
B.	Fields.
C.	Pictures.
D.	Tables.

Q6	In Word, which of the following statements about text boxes is untrue?
A.	By default, text boxes have a black, 0.75 pt border.
B.	You can insert several text boxes on the same page of a document.
C.	You can apply paragraph styles to text in a text boxes.
D.	A text box can have borders or shading, but not both.

Q7	In Word, which of the following statements about linked text boxes is untrue?
A.	Text flows forward from the first linked text box to the second, and so on.
B.	A document may contain several different and separate chains of linked text boxes.
C.	Text boxes in different documents may be linked together.
D.	If there is not enough text to fill all linked boxes, the final box or boxes remain empty.

Q8	In Word, which of the following actions do you perform to link two text boxes?
A.	Select all the text in the document, and choose **Format | Text Boxes | Link All**.
B.	Select the first text box, click the **Create Text Box Link** button on the Text Box toolbar, and then select the second text box.
C.	Select both text boxes, then click the **Create Text Box Link** button on the Text Box toolbar.
D.	Select both text boxes, choose **Insert | Text Box**, click the **Links** tab, select the *Create link* checkbox, and click **OK**.

Q9	In Word, which of these text types can you orient at 90 degrees with the Format | Text Direction command?
A.	Text in table cells only.
B.	Text in text boxes, table cells, and built-in heading styles only.
C.	Text formatted with built-in heading styles only.
D.	Text in table cells and text boxes only.

Answers

1: B, **2:** B, **3:** D, **4:** A, **5:** A, **6:** D, **7:** C, **8:** B, **9:** D.

Graphics in Word

Objectives

In this chapter you will learn how to:

- Create drawing objects with the drawing tools and AutoShapes
- Stack and group AutoShapes
- Create WordArt objects
- Change picture and ClipArt borders
- Wrap text around graphics
- Insert watermarks

New words

In this chapter you will meet the following terms:

- AutoShape
- WordArt
- ClipArt
- Watermark

Exercise files

In this chapter you will work with the following Word files:

- Chapter24_Exercise_24-1_Before.doc
- Chapter24_Exercise_24-3_Before.doc
- Chapter24_Exercise_24-4_Before.doc
- Chapter24_Exercise_24-5_Before.doc
- Chapter24_Exercise_24-6_Before.doc
- Chapter24_Exercise_24-7_Before.doc
- Chapter24_Exercise_24-8_Before.doc
- Chapter24_Exercise_24-9_Before.doc

In this chapter you will cover the following items from the ECDL Advanced Word Processing Syllabus:

- **AM3.4.5.1**: Modify image borders.

- **AM3.4.5.2:** Create a simple drawing using the drawing options.

- **AM3.4.5.3**: Use predefined shapes options.

- **AM3.4.5.4**: Send predefined shapes to the back or front.

- **AM3.4.5.5**: Send predefined shapes in front of or behind text.

- **AM3.4.5.6**: Group or ungroup predefined shapes.

- **AM3.4.5.7**: Add a watermark to a document.

- **AM3.1.1.6**: Use text-wrapping options.

- **AM3.1.1.8**: Use available text design gallery options.

About graphics in Word

In Word, the term *graphics* includes:

- **User-drawn shapes**. Examples include lines, rectangles and circles. You create these using the buttons available on Word's Drawing toolbar, which is positioned along the bottom of your screen.

Can't see the Drawing Toolbar? Use the **View | Toolbars** command to display it.

- **AutoShapes**. These are Word's built-in, ready-to-insert shapes that are divided into categories such as flowchart elements, stars and banners, and call-outs. You can modify AutoShapes to your own needs.

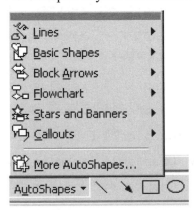

- **Pictures**. You can insert two types of picture into Word documents: ClipArt pictures from Word's built-in ClipArt library, and picture files created in other applications, such as Paintbrush, Photoshop and PaintShop Pro.

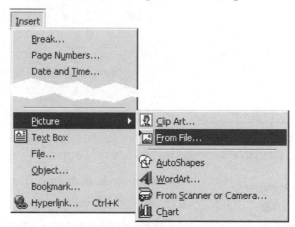

- **WordArt**. These are special effects that you can apply to selected text. You work with WordArt text in Word documents in the same way that you work with inserted pictures.

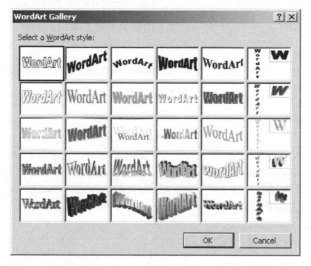

- **Watermarks**. These are graphics or text that appear either behind or on top of the document's main text. For example, you might want your company logo or the word 'Confidential' to appear in light print in the background of every page of a document.

Graphics and text flow

Typically, you will combine graphics with text on the same page. Word's **Format | AutoShape, Format | Picture** and **Format | WordArt** commands give you total control of how the text flows around graphics.

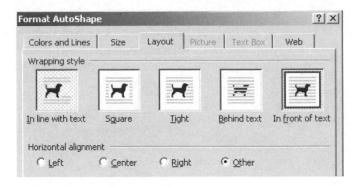

Working with drawings, pictures, WordArt, watermarks and text flow: the seven tasks

Here are the seven tasks that you need to be able to perform with graphics in Word:

- **Create basic drawings**. Learn how to draw some basic shapes in Exercise 24.1.

- **Create drawings with AutoShapes**. Exercise 24.2 shows you how to use Word's AutoShapes feature.

- **Stack and group AutoShapes**. Exercises 24.3 and 24.4 take you through the steps of stacking and grouping AutoShapes.

- **Create WordArt objects**. Apply decorative text effects in Exercise 24.5.

- **Change picture and ClipArt borders**. See Exercise 24.6.

- **Wrap text around graphics**. Explore Word text flow options in Exercise 24.7.

- **Insert watermarks**. Exercises 24.8 and 24.9 show you how to insert a watermark on one or all pages of a document.

Working with drawing objects

There are a number of common operations that you can perform on *drawing objects*, whether user-drawn shapes or AutoShapes.

Moving drawing objects

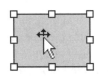

To move a drawing object within the same page, first select it by clicking anywhere on it. A cross appears at the tip of the cursor arrow. Then drag the object to its new position.

To move a drawing object between pages, select it and then cut and paste it.

Changing drawing object size and shape

You can change the size and shape of a drawing object by selecting it and clicking on any of its sizing handles. The cursor appears as a double arrow. Next, drag a sizing handle until the drawing object forms the new shape that you require.

Deleting drawing objects

To delete a drawing object, click on it and press **Delete**. You can always reverse a deletion by clicking the **Undo** button on Word's Standard toolbar.

Working with Word's drawing tools

Line and arrow tools

Line button

Arrow button

Arrow Style button

To draw a line, click the **Line** button on the Drawing toolbar, place the cursor where you want the line to begin, click and drag to where you want the line to end, and release the mouse button.

- To draw a perfectly horizontal or vertical line, hold down the **Shift** key while dragging.

- To draw a line ending in an arrow, click on the **Arrow** button and draw it in the same way.

- To change the style of the arrowhead, or the direction of the arrow, click the arrow to select it, click the **Arrow Style** button, and select a different style.

Rectangle and square tools

Rectangle button

To draw a rectangle, click the **Rectangle** button on the Drawing toolbar, place the cursor where you want one corner of the rectangle, click and drag diagonally to where you want the opposite corner of the rectangle, and release the mouse button.

To draw a perfect square, hold down the **Shift** key as you drag with the mouse.

Ellipse and circle tools

Oval button

To draw an ellipse (oval), click the **Oval** button, place the cursor where you want the shape to begin, click and drag until the shape is the size you want, and release the mouse button.

To draw a perfect circle, hold down the **Shift** key as you drag with the mouse.

Line colour and style

Line Color button

Line Style button

Dash Style button

In the case of lines, arrows and closed shapes (such as rectangles and circles), you can specify the colour and thickness of the line or shape border. Click the **Line Color** button and select a colour, either before you draw the line or closed shape, or, with the line or shape selected, after you have drawn it.

To delete a border around a closed shape, select *No Line* in the *Line Color* pop-up menu.

Change the thickness of a line or border by clicking the **Line Style** button.

Make a line or border a dashed line (in a choice of dash styles) by clicking the **Dash Style** button.

Fill colour

Fill Color button

Use the arrow to the right of the **Fill Color** button to select the colour with which the inside of the closed shape (such as a square or ellipse) should be filled.

You can choose the fill colour before you draw the shape, or you can select an existing shape and then choose a fill colour.

To make a closed object transparent, select *No Fill* in the *Fill Color* pop-up menu.

Shadow effects

Shadow button

To place a shadow behind a selected object, click the **Shadow** button and choose from the shadow styles available on the pop-up menu.

Exercise 24.1: Create basic drawings

1) Start Word and open the following document:

   Chapter24_Exercise_24-1_Before.doc

2) Click the **Rectangle** button on the Drawing toolbar, and draw a rectangle around the words 'First Aid Kit'.

   With the rectangle still selected, click the **Fill Color** button on the Drawing toolbar and choose *No Fill*. Click the **Line Color** button and select *Red*. Click the **Line Style** button and select *3 pt*. Your graphic should look like this

3) Click the **Oval** button on the Drawing toolbar and draw an oval around the word '£100'.

   With the oval still selected, click the **Fill Color** button on the Drawing toolbar and choose *No Fill*. Click the **Line Style** button and select *3 pt*. Your graphic should look like this:

4) Click the **Arrow** button on the Drawing Toolbar and draw an arrow to the left of the word '£100'.

   With the arrow still selected, click the **Line Style** button and select *6 pt*. Press **Ctrl+C** to copy the arrow, press **Ctrl+V** to paste it, and move the arrow to the right of the word '£100'. The pasted arrow is now selected. Click the **Arrow Style** button, and select the left-pointing arrow. Your graphic should now look like this:

5) Save your sample document with the following name, and close it:

   `Chapter24_Exercise_24-1_After_Your_Name.doc`

Working with AutoShapes

AutoShapes are ready-made shapes that you can insert in your documents. AutoShape categories include lines, basic shapes, flowchart elements, stars and banners, and call-outs.

To select an AutoShape, click the **AutoShapes** button on the Drawing toolbar and choose from the options offered by the pop-up menu.

AutoShapes

Ready-made shapes, including lines, geometric shapes and flowchart elements, that you can insert and modify in your Word documents.

Exercise 24.2: Create a drawing with AutoShapes

1) Open the following document:

   `Chapter24_Exercise_24-2_Before.doc`

2) Click at a paragraph mark after 'Carpets Unlimited' and before 'Everything Half Price'.

3) Click the **AutoShapes** button on the Drawing toolbar, click **Stars and Banners**, and click the first option, called 'Explosion 1'.

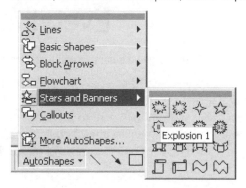

4) Draw the AutoShape under the 'Carpets Unlimited' heading as shown below:

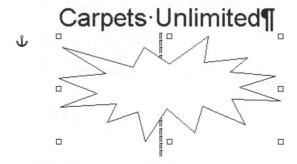

5) Right-click on the AutoShape, and choose the **Add Text** command from the pop-up menu.

6) At the paragraph mark that appears in the AutoShape, type the word 'SALE' in upper-case characters.

7) Select the word 'SALE'. Change it to Arial, 48 point, bold, and centre-aligned.

8) On the Drawing toolbar, click the arrow to the right of the **Fill Color** button.

Select *Gray-50%*.

Fill Color button

9) Select the word 'SALE' and change the font colour to white. The top of your sample document should look like this:

10) Save your sample document with the following name, and close it:

`Chapter24_Exercise_24-2_After_`*`Your_Name`*`.doc`

AutoShapes and stacks

Word allows you to layer or *stack* AutoShapes so that they overlap each other. You arrange AutoShapes in a stack using the **Draw | Order** command on the Drawing toolbar. You can bring an object to the front or send it to the back of a stack, or bring forward or send backward one level in a stack. You can also stack an AutoShape so that it appears behind the text in a document.

Exercise 24.3: Stacking AutoShapes

1) Open the following document:

    Chapter24_Exercise_24-3_Before.doc

2) Click anywhere in the first AutoShape, the one containing the words 'Lowest Prices'. Next, right-click on any of its borders. From the pop-up menu displayed, choose **Order | Send to Back**.

3) Click anywhere in the third AutoShape, the one containing the words 'Expert Service'. Next, right-click on any of its borders. From the pop-up menu displayed, choose **Order | Bring to Front**.

    Your AutoShapes should look like this:

4) Save your sample document with the following name, and close it:

    Chapter24_Exercise_24-3_After_*Your_Name*.doc

AutoShapes and text

Typically, an AutoShape drawn in a document that contains text is *stacked* in front of the text.

To display an AutoShape behind the text, right-click on the AutoShape and choose **Order | Send Behind Text** from the pop-up menu displayed.

If·you·require·accident·and·emergency·treatment,·and·arrive·at·your·Casualty· Department,·you·will·be·assessed·immediately·by·a·professional·and·your·needs· identified.·Eme   tment·will·always·take·priority·over·minor·injuries.· However,·we·   ·the·patients·within·45·minutes·of·their·assessment.·If·this· is·not·possible,·   nation·will·be·given·to·you·by·a·member·of·staff.¶

If·you·need·to·be·admitted·to·hospital·from·the·Casualty·Department,·we·guarantee·to· admit·you·to·a·ward·as·soon·as·possible.·In·the·vast·majority·of·cases·this·should·be· within·one·hour·of·a·decision·being·taken·to·admit·you.¶

AutoShapes stacked in front of and behind text

AutoShapes and groups

You can group AutoShapes or other drawing objects so that you can move, format, stack or work with them as if they were a single object.

- **Grouping**. To group objects, hold down the **Shift** key and click on each of the objects in turn. Next, click the **Draw** button on the Drawing toolbar and choose **Group**. You can now work with them as if there were a single object.

- **Ungrouping**. To ungroup a selected group of objects, click the **Draw** button on the Drawing Toolbar and choose the **Ungroup** command.

Exercise 24.4: Grouping and ungrouping AutoShapes

1) Open the following document:

   Chapter24_Exercise_24-4_Before.doc

2) Hold down the **Shift** key, click anywhere in the first AutoShape, then in the second AutoShape, and finally in the third AutoShape.

3) Click the Draw button at the left of the Drawing toolbar. From the pop-up menu displayed, choose **Group**.

   Notice that one set of eight sizing handles now appears around the three AutoShapes. You can now work with the three AutoShapes as if they were a single drawing object.

4) Drag the grouped AutoShapes down to the bottom of the page.

5) Click on any of the grouped AutoShapes, click the **Draw** button at the left of the Drawing toolbar. From the pop-up menu displayed, choose **Ungroup**.

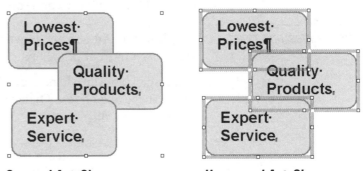

Grouped AutoShapes   **Ungrouped AutoShapes**

6) Save your sample document with the following name, and close it:

   Chapter24_Exercise_24-4_After_Your_Name.doc

Working with WordArt

WordArt enables you to apply special effects to selected text.

> **WordArt**
>
> *A Word feature that enables you to apply decorative effects –
> such as colours, shadows, rotation and depth – to selected text.
> WordArt objects can be manipulated in a similar way to inserted
> pictures.*

Exercise 24.5: Create text effects with WordArt

1) Open the following document:

    Chapter24_Exercise_24-5_Before.doc

Insert WordArt button

2) Click at the first paragraph mark in the document, and click the **Insert WordArt** button on the Drawing toolbar.

3) Word displays the *WordArt Gallery* dialog box. Click the first style at the top left of the dialog box and click **OK**.

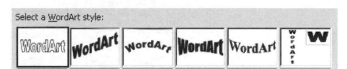

4) Word displays the *Edit WordArt Text* dialog box. In the *Text* box is the sample text 'Your Text Here'.

   Delete this text, type the words 'Carpets Uncovered', and click **OK**.

   Word displays your WordArt text. Drag it up to the top of your document, and make it about 20% larger by dragging one of its corner handles.

5) Word displays the WordArt toolbar.

   Click the Format WordArt button. On the **Colors and Lines** tab, change the fill colour to red and click **OK**.

   The top of your sample document should look like this:

6) Save your sample document with the following name, and close it:

`Chapter24_Exercise_24-5_After_Your_Name.doc`

Working with pictures

You can illustrate your documents by inserting pictures created in other software applications, scanned photographs or ClipArt.

ClipArt pictures

Word includes a gallery of ClipArt pictures that you can use in different documents. They are grouped in categories, ranging from Academic to Food and Travel.

To insert a ClipArt picture in a Word document, choose **Insert | Picture | ClipArt**, click a picture category to select it, right-click your required picture, and choose **Insert** from the pop-up menu displayed. Finally, click the **Close** box at the top-right of the *Insert ClipArt* dialog box.

> **ClipArt**
>
> *Built-in standard or 'stock' pictures that can be used and reused in Word documents.*

Non-ClipArt pictures

To insert a picture of your own – your company logo, for example – in a document, choose **Insert | Picture | From File**, select the required picture file, and choose **Insert**. Word accepts pictures in most common picture file formats.

In ECDL Advanced Word Processing, you only need to know how to add a border to ClipArt and other pictures, and how to modify existing borders.

Exercise 24.6: Change borders around ClipArt and pictures

1) Open the following Word document

    Chapter24_Exercise_24-6_Before.doc

2) Right-click anywhere on the arrow, choose **Format AutoShape** from the pop-up menu displayed, and click the **Colors and Lines** tab.

3) In the *Line Color* drop-down list, select *Red*. In the *Weight* box, select *8 pt*.

    When finished, click **OK**.

4) Right-click anywhere on the ClipArt picture at the bottom of the page, choose **Borders and Shading** from the pop-up menu displayed, and click the **Borders** tab.

5) In the *Settings* area, click *Shadow*. In the *Color* drop-down list, select *Green*. In the *Width* drop-down list, select *3 pt*.

    When finished, click **OK**.

6) Save your sample document with the following name, and close it:

    Chapter24_Exercise_24-6_After_*Your_Name*.doc

Working with text wrapping

Wrapping is the way in which text *flows* around a graphic, whether a drawing object, a picture or a WordArt object. Word offers the following options:

Text wrapping	Description	Example
In line with text	Positions the object in the document on the line that contains the insertion point. This is the default setting for pictures and WordArt. It is not available for AutoShapes.	
Square	Wraps text around an outer square or rectangular boundary of the object.	
Tight	Wraps text closely around the edges of the object.	

Text wrapping	Description	Example
Behind text	Places or *stacks* the object behind text in the document.	
In front of text	Places or *stacks* the object in front of text in the document. This is the default option for AutoShapes.	

To modify text wrapping for a selected object, right-click on it, select **Format AutoShape, Format WordArt** or **Format Picture** from the popup menu displayed, click the **Layout** tab, select your required wrapping option, and click **OK**.

Exercise 24.7: Wrap text around a picture

1) Open the following Word document:

   Chapter24_Exercise_24-7_Before.doc

2) Click at the beginning of the second paragraph of body text.

   By·transforming·the·way·that·people·and·businesses·communicate·and·
   interact,·the·Internet·has·dramatically·changed·the·face·of·business.¶

3) Choose **Insert | Picture | Clip Art**, click the **Business** category to select it, right-click the 'three desks' picture, and choose **Insert** from the pop-up menu.

4) Click **Close** to close the *Insert Clip Art* dialog box.

5) Reduce the inserted picture by 50% by dragging its lower right-hand corner handle. Your picture should look as shown. Notice that it is in line with Text, the default positioning option.

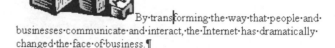

By·transforming·the·way·that·people·and· businesses·communicate·and·interact,·the·Internet·has·dramatically· changed·the·face·of·business.¶

6) Right-click the picture, choose **Format Picture**, click the **Layout** tab, click the **Square** option, and click **OK**. Your picture should now look like this:

From·a·base·of·40·million·users·in·1996,·the·number·of·online·users·is· predicted·to·reach·1·billion·in·2005.¶

By·transforming·the·way·that·people·and· businesses·communicate·and·interact,·the· Internet·has·dramatically·changed·the·face·of· business.¶

Impressed·by·the·Internet's·rising·popularity,· many·businesses·have·established·an·online· presence.·A·rich·variety·of·business· information·—·from·service·and·product· catalogues·to·press·releases·to·company·

contacts·—·is·now·available·to·Internet·users.¶

7) Right-click the picture, choose **Format Picture**, click the **Layout** tab, click the **Tight** option, and click **OK**. Your picture should look like this:

By· transforming·the·way·that·people·and·businesses· communicate·and·interact,·the·Internet·has·dramatically· changed·the·face·of·business.¶

Impressed·by·the·Internet's·rising·popularity,·many· businesses·have·established·an·online·presence.·A· rich·variety·of·business·information·—·from· service·and·product·catalogues·to·press· releases·to·company·contacts·—·is·now· available·to·Internet·users.¶

8) Save your sample document with the following name, and close it:

Chapter24_Exercise_24-7_After_*Your_Name*.doc

Working with watermarks

A watermark is a picture, drawing object or text box that is:

- displayed *behind* the main text of page;

- of light or *feint* colour, so that it does not impair the legibility of the main text on the page.

Examples of text watermarks would be the words 'First draft' or 'Confidential'. Company logos are the most common examples of picture watermark. Usually, you will want to insert a watermark on either *one* or *all pages* of a document.

- **Single-page watermark**. If the watermark is a a picture, right-click on it, choose **Format Picture**, select the **Picture** tab, and select *Watermark* from the *Color* drop-down list. Click the **Layout** tab, select the *Behind text* option, and click **OK**.

  If the watermark is an AutoShape or WordArt object, right-click on it, choose **Format AutoShape** or **Format WordArt**, click the **Layout** tab, select the *Behind text* option, and click **OK**.

- **All-page watermark**. Choose **View | Header and Footer**. Insert the picture, or create the AutoShape or WordArt, in the header or footer. Right-click on the object, and use the **Format** command to stack the object behind the text. If using a picture, you can apply a watermark effect with the **Format** command.

  To apply a text watermark, insert a text box in the header or footer, type your watermark text in it, and format the text.

  If using odd and even page headers and footers, remember to insert your watermark into both the odd and even headers or footers.

Watermark

A picture, drawing or text box that appears behind the text on one or all pages of a document. Watermarks are typically of feint colour so that they do not impair the legibility of the main text on the page.

Exercise 24.8: Insert a picture watermark on a single page

1) Open the following Word document:

   Chapter24_Exercise_24-8_Before.doc

2) Click at the start of the paragraph containing the words 'Everything Half Price'.

3) Choose **Insert | Picture | Clip Art**, click the **Household** category to select it, right-click the 'furniture' picture, and choose **Insert** from the pop-up menu. Click **Close** to close the *Insert Clip Art* dialog box.

4) Click the picture to select it, then right-click it, choose **Format Picture**, click the **Picture** tab, select *Watermark* from the *Color* drop-down list, click the **Layout** tab, click the *Behind text* option, click the *Center horizontal alignment* option, and click **OK**. Your picture should look like this:

5) Save your sample document with the following name, and close it:

Chapter24_Exercise_24-8_After_*Your_Name*.doc

Exercise 24.9: Insert a text box watermark on every page

1) Open the following Word document:

Chapter24_Exercise_24-9_After_*Your_Name*.doc

2) Choose **View | Header and Footer**. Word displays the insertion point in the header of the first page.

You may find it helpful to reduce the page display to 50%.

3) Choose **Insert | Text Box**, draw the text box, and type in the words 'Draft Copy Only'.

4) Select the text in the text box, format it in Arial, bold, 36 point, and change the font colour to light grey. If necessary, increase the size of the text box to accommodate the text.

5) Drag the text box to the centre of the page.

6) Right-click the border of the text box, choose **Format Text Box** and click the **Colors and Lines** tab. In the *Line Color* drop-down list, click *No Line*, and click **OK**.

7) Click the **Close** button on the Header and Footer toolbar. Scroll through your document to verify that the watermark appears on every page.

8) Save your sample document with the following name, and close it:

Chapter24_Exercise_24-9_After_*Your_Name*.doc

Chapter 24: quick reference

Drawing toolbar buttons

Button	Description
＼	Draws a straight line. To draw a perfectly horizontal or vertical line, hold down the **Shift** key as you drag with the mouse.
＼	Draws a line ending in an arrow.
▢	Draws a rectangle. To draw a perfect square, hold down the **Shift** key as you drag with the mouse.
◯	Draws an ellipse (oval). To draw a perfect circle, hold down the **Shift** key as you drag with the mouse.
◀	Applies WordArt – decorative effects such as colours, shadows, rotation and depth – to selected text.
🎨	Specifies the colour with which the inside of a closed shape (such as a square or ellipse) should be filled.
🖌	Specifies the colour and thickness of the line or shape border.
≡	Specifies the thickness of a line or a shape border.
⠿	Specifies the style of a line or shape border.
⇄	Specifies the arrow line style.

Tasks summary: drawing basic shapes	Task	Procedure
	Draw a line.	Click the **Line** button on the Drawing toolbar, place the cursor where you want the line to begin, click and drag to where you want the line to end, and release the mouse button.
		To draw a perfectly horizontal or vertical line, hold down the **Shift** key as you drag with the mouse.
	Draw a rectangle or square.	Click the **Rectangle** button on the Drawing toolbar, place the cursor where you want one corner of the rectangle, click and drag diagonally to where you want the opposite corner of the rectangle, and release the mouse button.
		To draw a perfect square, hold down the **Shift** key as you drag with the mouse.
	Draw an oval or circle.	Click the **Oval** button on the Drawing toolbar, place the cursor where you want the shape to begin, click and drag until the shape is the size you want, and release the mouse button.
		To draw a perfect circle, hold down the **Shift** key as you drag with the mouse.

Tasks summary: lines, borders and fills	Task	Procedure
	Change line or border colour.	Click the **Line Color** button on the Drawing toolbar, select a colour, either before you draw the line or closed shape, or, with the line or shape selected, after you have drawn it.
		To delete a border around a closed shape, select *No Line* in the **Line Color** pop-up menu.
	Change fill colour.	Use the arrow to the right of the **Fill Color** button to select the colour with which the inside of the closed shape (such as a square or ellipse) should be filled. You can choose the fill colour before you draw the shape, or you can select an existing shape and then choose a fill colour.
		To make a closed object transparent, select *No Fill* in the **Fill Color** pop-up menu.

Tasks summary: *AutoShapes*	

Task	Procedure
Insert an AutoShape.	Click the **AutoShapes** button on the Drawing toolbar, and select the AutoShape category and the individual AutoShape.
Stack AutoShapes.	Select an AutoShape, choose the **Draw | Order** command on the Drawing toolbar, and select your required option, such as **Bring to Front**, **Send to Back** or **Send Behind Text**.
Group/ungroup AutoShapes.	To group objects, hold down the **Shift** key and click on each of the objects in turn. Next, click the **Draw** button on the Drawing toolbar and choose **Group**.
	To ungroup a selected group of objects, click the **Draw** button on the Drawing Toolbar and choose **Ungroup**.

Tasks summary: WordArt,
pictures and watermarks

Task	Procedure
Insert WordArt.	Place the cursor where you want the WordArt to appear, click the **WordArt** button on the Drawing toolbar, select your required style, click **OK**, type your text, select a font and font size, and click **OK**.
Change picture borders.	Right-click the picture, choose **Format Picture**, click the **Colors and Lines** tab, select your required options, and click **OK**.
Create a watermark on a single page.	If you want to use a picture object, right-click on it, choose **Format Picture**, select the **Picture** tab, select *Watermark* from the *Color* drop-down list, click the **Layout** tab, select the *Behind text* option, and click **OK**.
	If you are using an AutoShape or WordArt object, right-click on it, choose **Format AutoShape or Format WordArt**, click the **Layout** tab, select the *Behind text* option, and click **OK**.
Insert a watermark on all pages of a document.	Choose **View | Header and Footer**, and insert the picture, or create the AutoShape, WordArt or text box in the header or footer. Right-click on the object, and use the **Format** command to stack the object behind the text. If using a picture you can also apply a watermark effect with the **Format** command.

ECDL Advanced Word Processing

	Task	Procedure
Tasks summary: *text wrapping*	**Task**	**Procedure**
	Control text wrapping.	Right-click on the object, choose **Format**, click the **Layout** tab, select your required text flow option, and click **OK**.

Concepts summary

Word's Drawing toolbar, which is positioned along the bottom of your screen, enables you to draw a wide range of graphic objects.

Lines, rectangles and circles are examples of *user-drawn shapes*. *AutoShapes* are Word's built-in, ready-to-insert shapes that are divided into categories such as flowchart elements, stars and banners, and call-outs. You can modify AutoShapes to your needs.

You can layer or *stack* AutoShapes so that they overlap each other. You can bring an object to the front or send it to the back of a stack, or bring it forward or send it backward one level in a stack. You can also stack an AutoShape so that is appears behind the text in a document. A collection of AutoShapes can be *grouped* together and manipulated as if they were a single object.

You can insert two types of *pictures* into Word documents: ClipArt pictures from Word's built-in ClipArt library, and picture files created in other applications. You can add a *border* to ClipArt and other pictures, and modify existing borders.

WordArt is a feature that enables you to apply decorative effects – such as colours, shadows, rotation and depth – to selected text. WordArt objects can be manipulated in a similar way to inserted pictures.

Text wrapping is the way in which text *flows* around a drawing graphic, whether a user-drawn shape, an AutoShape, a picture or a WordArt object.

A *watermark* is a picture, drawing object or text box that is displayed behind the main text of a page. Watermarks are coloured lightly so that they do not impair the legibility of the main text on the page. You can insert a watermark on a single page or, using the header or footer area, on all pages of a document.

Circle the correct answer to each of the following multiple-choice questions about user-created drawings, AutoShapes, WordArt, pictures, text flow and watermarks in Word.

Q1	To draw a perfectly horizontal or vertical line in Word, you ...
A.	Click the **Line** button on the Drawing toolbar and hold down the **Shift** key as you drag with the mouse.
B.	Click the **Straight Horizontal Line** button on the Drawing toolbar and drag with the mouse.
C.	Click the **Line** button on the Drawing toolbar and hold down the **Ctrl** key as you drag with the mouse.
D.	Click the **Straight Line** button on the Drawing toolbar and hold down the **Ctrl** key as you drag with the mouse.

Q2	On Word's Drawing toolbar, which of the following buttons do you click to draw a line with an arrow?
A.	
B.	
C.	
D.	

Q3	To draw a perfect square in Word, you ...
A.	Click the **Square Box** button on the Drawing toolbar and hold down the **Ctrl** key as you drag with the mouse.
B.	Click the **Perfect Square** button on the Drawing toolbar and drag with the mouse.
C.	Click the **Rectangle** button on the Drawing toolbar and hold down the **Shift** key as you drag with the mouse.
D.	Click the **Rectangle** button on the Drawing toolbar and hold down the **Ctrl** key as you drag with the mouse.

Q4	In which part of the Word window is the Drawing toolbar displayed by default?
A.	In the top left of the Word window.
B.	Along the bottom of the Word window.
C.	As part of the Formatting toolbar.
D.	Along the top of the Word window.

Q5	To draw a perfect circle in Word, you ...
A.	Click the **Perfect Circle** button on the Drawing toolbar and drag with the mouse.
B.	Click the **Oval** button on the Drawing toolbar and hold down the **Shift** key as you drag with the mouse.
C.	Click the **Oval** button on the Drawing toolbar and hold down the **Ctrl** key as you drag with the mouse.
D.	Click the **Circle** button on the Drawing toolbar and hold down the **Ctrl** key as you drag with the mouse.

Q6	On Word's Drawing toolbar, which of the following buttons do you click to change the colour of a line or border?
A.	
B.	
C.	
D.	

Q7	On Word's Drawing toolbar, which of the following buttons do you click to change the inside colour of a closed shape?
A.	
B.	
C.	
D.	

Q8	In Word, which of the following actions do you perform to insert an AutoShape?
A.	Choose **Insert	AutoShape**.
B.	Choose **Format	AutoShapes**.
C.	Choose **Insert	Pictures	AutoShapes**.
D.	Click the **AutoShapes** button on the Drawing toolbar.

Q9	In Word, which of the following is not an AutoShape category?
A.	Stars and Banners.
B.	Academic.
C.	Flowchart.
D.	Callouts.

Q10	In Word, which of the following statements about AutoShapes is untrue?
A.	AutoShapes can be stacked so that they overlap each other.
B.	AutoShapes are not displayed in Normal view.
C.	A collection of AutoShapes can be grouped so that they can be manipulated as a single object.
D.	AutoShapes cannot be stacked behind the main text in a document.

Q11	In Word, the term WordArt refers to ...
A.	Built-in standard or stock pictures that can be used and reused in Word documents.
B.	Pictures stored in AutoText.
C.	A feature that enables decorative effects – such as colours, shadows, rotation and depth – to be applied to selected text.
D.	Word's built-in gallery of ready-to-insert drawing objects.

Q12	In Word, which of the following statements about WordArt is untrue?
A.	You apply WordArt effects by clicking the **WordArt** button on the Drawing toolbar.
B.	You can amend the default font and font size when applying WordArt effects to selected text.
C.	You apply WordArt effects by choosing the **Insert	Picture	WordArt** button on the Drawing toolbar.
D.	WordArt objects cannot be manipulated in a similar way to inserted pictures.

Q13	In Word, which of the following statements about text wrapping is untrue?
A.	You apply text wrapping to a graphic by selecting it, choosing **Format	Text Flow**, selecting the required text flow option, and clicking **OK**.
B.	In front of text is the default text wrapping option for AutoShapes.
C.	You apply text wrapping to an object by right-clicking on it, choosing **Format**, clicking the **Layout** tab, selecting the required text flow option, and clicking **OK**.
D.	In line with text is the default text wrapping option for pictures and WordArt. It is not available for AutoShapes.

Q14	In Word, which of the following statements about watermarks is untrue?
A.	Watermarks are typically of feint colour so that they do not impair the legibility of the main text on the page.
B.	Pictures, drawings, WordArt objects and text boxes can be used as watermarks.
C.	The **Picture** tab of the **Format Picture** command includes an option to prepare a picture for use as a watermark.
D.	Only pictures, drawings and WordArt objects can be used as watermarks.

Q15	In Word, which of these methods do you follow to insert a watermark on every page of a document?
A.	Insert the graphic in the header or footer of the document.
B.	Add the graphic to AutoText, and then insert from AutoText into the first page of the document.
C.	Insert the graphic in the document template.
D.	Choose the **Insert	All Pages** command when inserting the graphic.

Answers

1: A, **2:** D, **3:** C, **4:** B, **5:** B, **6:** A, **7:** C, **8:** D, **9:** B, **10:** D, **11:** C, **12:** D, **13:** A, **14:** D, **15:** A.

25

Many columns, one document

Objectives

In this chapter you will learn how to:

- Apply a multi-column layout to a Word document
- Modify column widths and interline spacing
- Change the number of columns
- Insert vertical lines between columns
- Prevent paragraphs from breaking across columns
- Insert and remove column breaks

New words

In this chapter you will meet the following term:

- Multi-column layout

Exercise files

In this chapter you will work with the following Word files:

- Chapter25_Exercise_25-1_Before.doc
- Chapter25_Exercise_25-2_Before.doc
- Chapter25_Exercise_25-3_Before.doc
- Chapter25_Exercise_25-4_Before.doc
- Chapter25_Exercise_25-5_Before.doc

Syllabus reference

In this chapter you will cover the following items from the ECDL Advanced Word Processing Syllabus:

- **AM3.2.4.1**. Create multiple-column layouts.
- **AM3.2.4.2**. Modify column layouts.
- **AM3.2.4.3**. Modify column width and spacing.
- **AM3.2.4.4**. Insert a column break.
- **AM3.2.4.5**. Delete a column break.

Multi-column layouts

Like tables, columns enable you to position text, tables and graphics side by side on a page. Unlike tables, however, columns allow text to flow from the bottom of one column to the top of the next column.

Columns: the benefits to you

What are the advantages of using multi-column layouts?

- **Professional-looking newsletters**. Word's column features enable you to produce stylish newsletters quickly and easily.

- **Easier-to-read text**. Text line length within columns is shortened, with the result that the text is easier to read.

- **More content in less space**. You can generally fit more text and graphics into a multi-column layout than in a page-wide, single-column layout.

Columns: toolbar button or menu command?

You can create columns in either of two ways:

- **Toolbar button**. Click the **Columns** button on the Standard toolbar, drag with the mouse to select a layout of up to four columns, and then click.

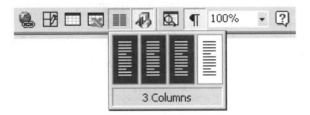

- **Menu command**. Choose **Format | Columns** to display the *Columns* dialog box, select your required options, and click **OK**.

Using the toolbar button is the fast and easy approach. The menu command, however, offers more options and gives you greater control over the layout.

In this chapter, you will apply columns to entire documents only. Applying columns to selected parts of a document is covered in Chapter 26 because this requires the use of section breaks.

Columns and document views

Word displays multi-column layouts on screen only in Print Layout view.

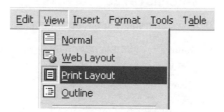

In Normal view, multiple columns are not displayed side by side but appear as a single column. Before performing the exercises in this chapter, check that Print Layout view is selected.

Multi-column layout

A layout in which text, tables and graphics are positioned side by side in such a way that text flows from the bottom of one column to the top of the next column. Multi-column layouts are commonly used in newsletters.

Working with columns: the four tasks

Here are the four tasks that you need to be able to perform with columns in Word:

- **Create multiple-column layouts**. Learn how to apply a simple, multi-column layout in Exercise 25.1 using both the Standard toolbar button and the **Format | Columns** command.

- **Change column width and spacing**. Exercise 25.2 shows you how to make your columns wider or narrower, and intercolumn spacing narrower or wider.

- **Modify multiple-column layouts**. In Exercise 25.3, you discover how to change the number of columns, add a vertical line between columns, and prevent a paragraph of text from breaking across two columns.

- **Insert and remove column breaks**. Column breaks are added and removed automatically by Word as you apply and modify column layouts. However, you can also insert and remove column breaks directly, as Exercises 25.4 and 25.5 demonstrate.

Working with new columns

In Exercise 25.1, you will apply a basic, two-column layout using Word's default options. You apply the columns first with the toolbar button and then with the menu command.

Exercise 25.1: Create a simple multi-column layout

1) Open the following document:

   `Chapter25_Exercise_25-1_Before.doc`

2) Click anywhere in the document.

3) Click the **Columns** button on the Standard Toolbar, and then choose the two-column layout.

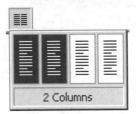

Word applies the two-column layout to your entire document.

Choose **Edit | Undo Columns**. You will now reapply the columns with the **Format | Columns** command.

4) With the insertion point positioned anywhere in the document, choose **Format | Columns** to display the *Columns* dialog box.

5) In the *Presets* area, click *Two*. Accept the default values of the other options, and click **OK**.

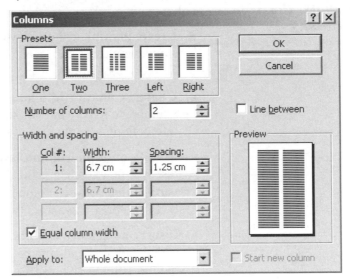

6) Word applies the two-column layout. The upper part of your document should look like this:

·The·New·Era·of· eBusiness¶

Introduction¶

By·transforming·the·way·that·people·and· businesses·communicate·and·interact,·the· Internet·has·dramatically·changed·the·face· of·business.¶

Impressed·by·the·Internet's·rising· popularity,·many·businesses·have· established·an·online·presence.·A·rich· variety·of·business·information·—·from· service·and·product·catalogues·to·press· releases·to·company·contacts·—·is·now· available·to·Internet·users.¶

that·not·all·consumers·want·to·shop·on· line.·Some·people·prefer·shopping·in·the· traditional·manner:·talking·to·sales·staff,· lingering·in·the·aisles,·'touching'·products,· and·interacting·with·other·customers.· Although·it·may·not·be·for·everyone·at·all· times,·e-business·does·offer·certain· benefits:¶

● → Opportunities·to·browse,·comparison· shop·and·make·purchases·from·the· comfort·of·their·desktop;¶

● → Convenience·—·shops·are·always·open· for·business·on·the·Net;¶

● → An·expanded·marketplace.·The·Net·is· a·global·shopping·mall.·Purchase·from· a·company·in·Paris,·Tokyo·or·San· Francisco;¶

7) Save your sample document with the following name, and close it:

Chapter25_Exercise_25-1_After_*Your_Name*.doc

Modifying column layouts

Column width and spacing

Word provides a range of features that you can use to modify your columns to make them appear precisely as you want.

In Exercise 25.2, you will learn how to adjust column width and intercolumn spacing. The two settings are inversely related:

- If you make your columns *wider*, Word automatically makes your intercolumn spacing *narrower*.

- If you make your columns *narrower*, Word automatically makes your intercolumn spacing *wider*.

Exercise 25.2: Change column width and spacing

1) Open the following three-column document:

Chapter25_Exercise_25-2_Before.doc

2) Choose **Format | Columns** to display the *Columns* dialog box. Notice that all three columns are 4.5 cm wide, and that the intercolumn spacing is 1.25 cm. Click **Cancel** to close the dialog box.

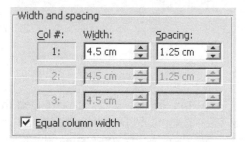

3) Choose **File | Page Setup**. On the *Margins* tab, you can see that the left and right page margins are both 2.5 cm.

Change the two margins to 3 cm, and click **OK**. You have now reduced the distance between the two margins – the area available to the text – by 1 cm.

4) Choose **Format | Columns** to display the *Columns* dialog box. Notice that Word has automatically adjusted the column width as a result of the change in page margins. The intercolumn spacing remains unaffected.

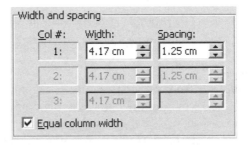

5) Click in the *Width* box for the first column, and change the value from 4.17 to 4 cm. Click **OK**.

Because the *Equal column width* checkbox is selected, the other two columns will be affected by your change to the first column Click **OK**.

6) Choose **Format | Columns** to display the *Columns* dialog box. Because you reduced the column widths from 4.17 cm to 4 cm, Word increased the column spacing from 1.25 cm to 1.5 cm.

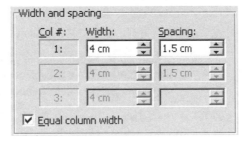

7) Save your sample document with the following name, and close it:

Chapter25_Exercise_25-2_After_*Your_Name*.doc

In Exercise 25.2, you changed the column width and Word responded by adjusting the intercolumn spacing. The opposite is also true: if you change the intercolumn spacing, Word adjusts the column width accordingly.

Other layout options available with columns in Word include the ability to:

- change the number of columns, say from two to three, or three to four;

- insert a vertical line between columns;

- prevent a paragraph of text from breaking across two columns.

Exercise 25.3 provides examples of each feature.

Exercise 25.3: Change column layout

1) Open the following document:

    Chapter25_Exercise_25-3_Before.doc

2) Choose **Format | Columns** to display the *Columns* dialog box.

    In the *Number of columns* box, replace 3 with 2, and click **OK**. You have now converted a three-column layout to a two-column layout.

3) Choose **Format | Columns** to display the *Columns* dialog box.

4) Select the *Line between* checkbox and click **OK**.

Word inserts a vertical line between your two columns.

5) Notice that the paragraph of body text beginning with the word 'Another area that has taken off' begins at the bottom of the first column and ends at the top of the second column.

6) Click anywhere in this paragraph, choose **Format | Paragraph**, click the **Line and Page Breaks** tab, select the *Keep lines together* checkbox, and click **OK**.

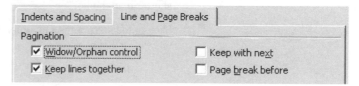

Word now positions this paragraph in its entirety at the top of the second column. The upper part of your document should now look like this:

·|The·New·Era·of·
eBusiness¶

Introduction¶

By·transforming·the·way·that·people·and·
businesses·communicate·and·interact,·the·
Internet·has·dramatically·changed·the·face·
of·business.¶

Impressed·by·the·Internet's·rising·
popularity,·many·businesses·have·
established·an·online·presence.·A·rich·
variety·of·business·information·—·from·
service·and·product·catalogues·to·press·
releases·to·company·contacts·—·is·now·
available·to·Internet·users.¶

Some·people·prefer·shopping·in·the·
traditional·manner:·talking·to·sales·staff,·
lingering·in·the·aisles,·'touching'·products,·
and·interacting·with·other·customers.·
Although·it·may·not·be·for·everyone·at·all·
times,·e-business·does·offer·certain·
benefits:¶

● → Opportunities·to·browse,·comparison·
shop·and·make·purchases·from·the·
comfort·of·their·desktop;¶

● → Convenience·—·shops·are·always·open·
for·business·on·the·Net;¶

● → An·expanded·marketplace.·The·Net·is·a·
global·shopping·mall.·Purchase·from·a·
company·in·Paris,·Tokyo·or·San·
Francisco;¶

7) Save your sample document with the following name, and close it:

Chapter25_Exercise_25-3_After_*Your_Name*.doc

Working with column breaks

As you apply and modify multi-column layouts in a document, Word automatically inserts column breaks at the appropriate locations. Sometimes, however, you will want to insert or remove such breaks directly.

Typically, there are two reasons why you might want to force the end of a column and the beginning of another:

- **Highlight headings and introductions**. You might want a document heading and perhaps some introductory text or graphic to appear on their own in the first column on a page.

- **Balance column length**. Text in the final column is often shorter than that in preceding columns. By inserting a column break, you can give your multi-column page a more even appearance.

Exercise 25.4: Insert a column break

1) Open the following document:

Chapter·25_Exercise_25-4_Before.doc

2) Move to the bottom of the page. You can see that the right column is shorter than the left.

Click at the start of the paragraph beginning with the words 'Deciding whether to have'.

3) Choose **Insert | Break** to display the *Break* dialog box.

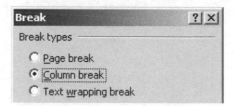

Select *Column break* and click **OK**.

Word inserts the column break at your selected location.

● → Depending·on·the·type·of·business,·
your·website·can·be·used·to·link·with·
suppliers,·order·raw·materials,·check·
stock·levels·and·conduct·sales. ¶

································Column Break································

4) Save your sample document with the following name, and close it:

    Chapter25_Exercise_25-4_After_*Your_Name*.doc

Exercise 25.5: Remove a column break

1) Open the following document:

    Chapter25_Exercise_25-5_Before.doc

2) Move to the bottom of the page. Click just to the left of the column break at the bottom of the left column.

● → Depending·on·the·type·of·business,·
your·website·can·be·used·to·link·with·
suppliers,·order·raw·materials,·check·
stock·levels·and·conduct·sales. ¶

3) Press the **Delete** key. Word removes the column break.

4) Save your sample document with the following name, and close it:

    Chapter25_Exercise_25-5_After_*Your_Name*.doc

Removing multi-column layouts

Want to remove a multi-column layout from a document? Click anywhere in the document, click the **Column** button on the Standard toolbar, and choose the single column layout. Word removes the multi-column layout.

Alternatively, with the cursor anywhere in the document, choose **Format | Columns**. In the *Number of columns* box, type 1. Finally, click **OK**.

Chapter 25: quick reference

Tasks summary

Task	Procedure
Apply a multi-column layout to a document.	Click the **Columns** button on the Standard toolbar and choose a layout of up to four columns.
	Alternatively, choose **Format	Columns**, select the required number of columns, specify any other layout options, and click **OK.**
Change column width.	Choose **Format	Columns**, type a new width for the column(s) or intercolumn spacing(s), and click **OK**.
Change the number of columns.	Choose **Format	Columns**. In the *Presets* area, type the number of columns you require, and click **OK**.
Insert or remove vertical lines between columns.	Choose **Format	Columns**. Select or deselect the *Line between* checkbox, and click **OK**.
Control paragraph breaks across columns.	Click anywhere in the text paragraph, choose **Format	Paragraph**, select or deselect the *Keep lines together* checkbox, and click **OK**.
Insert a column break.	Click in the text where you want the break to appear, choose **Insert	Break**, select the *Column break* option, and click **OK**.
Remove a column break.	Select the column break and press **Delete**.

Concepts summary

Word's *columns* feature enables you to position text, tables and graphics side by side on a page so that text flows from the bottom of one column to the top of the next column. Multi-column layouts are commonly used for *newsletters*.

You can generally fit *more content* into a multi-column layout than in a page-wide, single-column layout. Also, because text line length within columns is shorter, the resulting text can be *easier to read*.

ECDL Advanced Word Processing

You can create columns before or after you type text. Word gives you complete control of multi-column layouts, including the ability to change column width and intercolumn spacing, change the number of columns, add or remove vertical lines between columns, and insert or delete column breaks directly. You can also prevent particular paragraphs from breaking across columns.

Chapter 25: quick quiz

Circle the correct answer to each of the following multiple-choice questions about columns in Word.

Q1	In Word, which of the following statements about multi-column layouts is untrue?
A.	You cannot change the number of columns in an existing multi-column layout.
B.	Columns allow text to flow from the bottom of one column to the top of the next column.
C.	You can insert vertical lines between columns.
D.	You can insert and remove column breaks directly.

Q2	In Word, which of the following buttons on the Standard toolbar can you click to begin inserting columns?
A.	
B.	
C.	
D.	

Q3	In Word, which of the following menu commands can you click to begin inserting columns?
A.	Tools | Options | Columns.
B.	Format | Columns.
C.	Table | New Columns.
D.	Insert | Columns.

Q4	In Word, which of the following statements about column width and intercolumn spacing is untrue?
A.	The wider the columns, the narrower the intercolumn spacing.
B.	When you change column width, Word adjusts the intercolumn spacing automatically.
C.	The narrower the columns, the wider the intercolumn spacing.
D.	When you decrease intercolumn spacing, Word reduces the column widths automatically.

Q5	To insert vertical lines between columns in a Word document, you …
A.	Right-click in the intercolumn gap, and choose **Insert Vertical Line** command from the pop-up menu displayed.
B.	Choose **Format	Columns**, select the *Line between* checkbox, and click **OK**.
C.	Right-click in the intercolumn gap, and choose the **Lines	Vertical** command from the pop-up menu displayed.
D.	Choose **Insert	Columns**, select the *Vertical line* checkbox, and click **OK**.

Q6	To change the number of columns in a Word document, you …
A.	Choose **Format	Columns**, select a different preset value, and click **OK**.
B.	Right-click on any column, choose **Change Columns**, type the number of columns, and click **OK**.
C.	Choose **Insert	Columns**, select a different number of columns from the drop-down list, and click **OK**.
D.	Right-click on any column, choose **Column Number**, type the number of columns, and click **OK**.

Q7	In Word, how do you prevent a particular paragraph from breaking across two columns?
A.	Click anywhere in the text paragraph, choose **Format | Paragraph**, select the *Keep with next* checkbox, and click **OK**.
B.	Click anywhere in the text paragraph, choose **Format | Columns**, deselect the *Break paragraph* checkbox, and click **OK**.
C.	Right-click on the paragraph, choose **Breaks**, deselect the *Paragraph break* checkbox, and click **OK**.
D.	Click anywhere in the text paragraph, choose **Format | Paragraph**, select the *Keep lines together* checkbox, and click **OK**.

Q8	In a Word document, which of the following actions do you take to insert a column break?
A.	Choose **Format | Columns | Break**, select the *New column break* checkbox, and click **OK**.
B.	Right-click where you want to break to appear, and choose **Breaks | Column**.
C.	Choose **Insert | Break**, select the *Column break* option, and click **OK**.
D.	None of the above – you cannot insert a column break directly

Q9	In Word, which of the following actions do you take to remove a column break?
A.	Click at the column break to select it and press **Delete**.
B.	Right-click on the column break, and choose **Cut** from the pop-up menu displayed.
C.	Click at the column break to select it and press **Ctrl+V**.
D.	None of the above – you cannot remove a column break directly

Answers

1: A, **2:** D, **3:** B, **4:** D, **5:** B, **6:** A, **7:** A, **8:** C, **9:** A.

26

Many sections, one document

Objectives

In this chapter you will learn how to:

- Insert section breaks
- Delete section breaks
- Print the following parts of a document: odd-numbered pages, even-numbered pages, and selected text
- Print multiple copies of a document of part or a document

New words

In this chapter you will meet the following term:

- Section

Exercise files

In this chapter you will work with the following Word files:

- `Chapter26_Exercise_26-1_Before.doc`
- `Chapter26_Exercise_26-3_Before.doc`
- `Chapter26_Exercise_26-4_Before.doc`
- `Chapter26_Exercise_26-5_Before.doc`
- `Chapter26_Exercise_26-6_Before.doc`

Syllabus reference

In this chapter you will cover the following items from the ECDL Advanced Word Processing Syllabus:

- **AM3.2.3.1**. Create sections in a document.
- **AM3.2.3.2**. Delete section breaks in a document.
- **AM3.6.1.1**. Print odd-numbered pages only.
- **AM3.6.1.2**. Print even-numbered pages only.
- **AM3.6.1.3**. Print a defined selection.
- **AM3.6.1.4**. Print a defined number of pages per sheet.

About sections

The section break feature in Word enables you to split a document into two or more parts or *sections*, and to apply different layout settings to each section. A section may consist of a single paragraph or can be several pages long. Inserting a single section break in a document creates *two* sections: the section before the section break and the section after it.

Varying the layout between sections in a document

Here are some of the layout elements that can differ between sections of the same document:

- Options within the **File | Page Setup** command – for example, page margins, paper size or orientation, and paper source for a printer.

  This command also controls header and footer settings, such as whether headers or footers are displayed on the first page, or are different on left and right pages.

- Text and numbering in headers and footers, and any other options available with the **View | Headers and Footers** command.

- Page border and shading features applied with the **Format | Borders and Shading** command.

- Footnotes and endnotes inserted and formatted with the **Insert | Footnote** command.

- Multi-column layouts.

To change the layout of a section, move the insertion point to somewhere within it, and apply your layout changes to that section.

> **Section**
>
> *A part of a Word document that can have layout settings – such as page margins, headers and footers, and columns – that are different from the rest of the document. Sections are bounded by sections breaks, and can range in length from a single paragraph to several pages.*

Multiple sections: the benefits to you

You are most likely to use section breaks to perform the following two layout actions in Word documents:

- **Column layouts**. Vary the number of columns on a single page or in a single document.

- **Tables of contents**. Interrupt page numbering between a table of contents and the text that follows. As a result, the pages on which the table of contents appears are not counted by the table of contents.

About section breaks

By default, Word documents consist of only one section. To divide the document into sections you need to:

- **Insert section breaks directly**. You do this by positioning the insertion point where you want your new section to start, choosing the **Insert | Break** command, selecting your required section break type, and clicking **OK**.

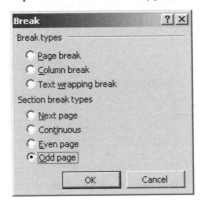

- **Use a Word feature that inserts section breaks for you**. An example is multi-column layout. If you select part of a document and apply columns, Word inserts section breaks automatically *before* and *after* the text that you selected.

Working with sections in Word: the two tasks

Here are the two tasks that you need to be able to perform with section breaks in Word:

- **Create sections in a document**. Exercises 26.1 and 26.3 take you through the steps of inserting sections breaks in Word documents. In Exercise 26.2, you discover how Word inserts section breaks automatically whenever you apply a multi-column layout to part of a document.

- **Delete sections from a document**. In Exercise 26.4, you remove section breaks from a Word document and learn how this affects a document's formatting.

Working with section breaks and multi-column layouts

In Exercise 26.1, you will create a page layout that consists of a heading that runs left to right across the top of the page with two columns of text beneath it.

ECDL Advanced Word Processing

Exercise 26.1: Multiple columns and directly inserted section breaks

1) Start Word and open the following document:

   `Chapter26_Exercise_26-1_Before.doc`

2) Click at the start of the heading 'Introduction'. This is where you want the new section to begin.

.The·New·Era·of·ebusiness¶

Introduction¶
By·transforming·the·way·that·people·and·businesses·communicate·and·interact,·the·Internet·has·dramatically·changed·the·face·of·business.¶

3) Choose **Insert | Break** to display the *Break* dialog box. Select the *Continuous* option and click **OK**.

.The·New·Era·of·ebusiness¶ ············ Section Break (Continuous) ············

Introduction¶
By·transforming·the·way·that·people·and·businesses·communicate·and·interact,·the·Internet·has·dramatically·changed·the·face·of·business.¶

4) Click anywhere in the text beneath the section break and choose **Format | Columns**.

5) In the *Presets* area, select *Two*. Select the *Line between* option.

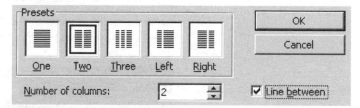

   Click **OK**.

6) Click just to the left of the page heading 'The New Era of eBusiness' to select it, and click the **Center** button on the Formatting toolbar.

   The upper part of your page should look like this:

The·New·Era·of·ebusiness ····· Section Break (Continuous) ·····

Introduction¶
By·transforming·the·way·that·people·and·businesses·communicate·and·interact,·the·Internet·has·dramatically·changed·the·face·of·business.¶

Impressed·by·the·Internet's·rising·popularity,·many·businesses·have·established·an·online·presence.·A·rich·variety·of·business·

What's·In·It·for·the·consumer?¶
While·it's·easy·to·get·caught·up·in·the·hype·surrounding·e-commerce,·not·all·consumers·want·to·shop·on·line.·Some·people·prefer·shopping·in·traditional·ways,·talking·to·sales·staff·and·"touching"·a·product.·Although·e-commerce·may·not·be·for·everyone,·it·does·offer·certain·benefits.¶

7) Save your sample document with the following name, and close it:

   `Chapter26_Exercise_26-1_After_Your_Name.doc`

Section breaks: more than one type

In Exercise 26.1, you inserted a section break of the continuous (same page) type. Word provides four section break types:

Section break type	Description
Continuous	Starts the new section on the same page.
Next page	Starts the new section on the next page.
Even page	Starts the new section on the next even-numbered page. Typically, this is a left-hand page.
Odd page	Starts the new section on the next odd-numbered page. Typically, this is a right-hand page.

In Exercise 26.2, you will select part of a document, apply a two-column layout, and observe that Word inserts section breaks automatically before and after your selected text.

Exercise 26.2: Multiple columns and automatically inserted section breaks

1) Open the following document:

   Chapter26_Exercise_26-2_Before.doc

2) Go to the heading 'Introduction' and select it and the three paragraphs beneath it, as far as, but not including, the 'What is ebusiness?' heading.

Introduction¶
By·transforming·the·way·that·people·and·businesses·communicate·and·interact,·the·Internet·has·dramatically·changed·the·face·of·business.¶

Impressed·by·the·Internet's·rising·popularity,·many·businesses·have·established·an·online·presence.·A·rich·variety·of·business·information—from·product·and·service·catalogues·to·press·releases·to·company·contacts—is·now·available·to·Internet·users.¶

Today,·many·businesses·realise·that,·in·order·to·compete·successfully,·they·need·to·sell·their·goods·and·services·directly·to·consumers·or·other·businesses·over·the·Internet.¶

3) Choose **Format | Columns**.

4) In the *Presets* area, select *Two*. Click **OK**.

   The upper part of your page should look like this:

Notice the continuous (same-page) section breaks inserted automatically before and after the text that you selected for conversion to columns. Click anywhere outside the text to deselect it.

5) Save your sample document with the following name, and close it:

    `Chapter26_Exercise_26-2_After_Your_Name.doc`

Working with section breaks and tables of contents

There is a Zen saying that an ideal list is one that includes itself. A table of contents, however, should *not* include itself.

In Exercise 26.3, you will insert an odd-page section break in a document after a table of contents and before the main text. You will then update the page numbering in the footers, and regenerate the table of contents to reflect the new page numbering.

Exercise 26.3: Section breaks and tables of contents

1) Open the following Word document:

    `Chapter26_Exercise_26-3_Before.doc`

2) Move through the seven pages of the document, noting the page numbers at the bottom of each page. You can see that the cover page and the table of contents page are numbered '1' and '2', respectively.

    You want to change this so that:

    - the cover and contents pages do not display page numbers;
    - the first page of text (currently 3) remains a right-hand page, and is numbered 1.

3) Click the page break at the bottom of the table of contents page to select it, and press **Delete** to remove the page breaks.

4) Click at the beginning of the first paragraph of text, which starts with the words 'At Elmsworth Health Trust'.

    KEEPING·US·INFORMED .... → .... 7¶
    SUBMITTING·FEEDBACK .... → .... 7¶
    MAKING·A·COMPLAINT .... → .... 7¶
    ¶
    |At·Elmsworth·Health·Trust,·we·are·committed·to·delivering·a·world-class·service.·Our·
    standards·apply·whether·you·are:¶

5) Choose **Insert | Break** to display the *Break* dialog box. Select the *Odd page* option and click **OK**.

6) Click anywhere in the text after the section break, choose **View | Header and Footer**, and click the **Switch Between Header and Footer** button on the Header and Footer toolbar.

Switch Between Header and Footer button

7) Notice that the **Same as Previous** button on the Header and Footer toolbar is selected by default. Click it to deselect it.

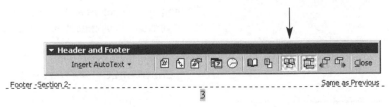

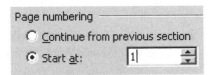

8) Click on the '3' in the footer, and click the **Format Page Number** button on the Header and Footer toolbar.

9) In the *Page numbering* area of the *Page Number Format* dialog box, click the *Start at* option. Word inserts a '1' in the associated text box. Click **OK**.

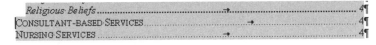

10) Click the **Show Next** button on the Header and Footer toolbar. Notice that the **Same as Previous** button on the Header and Footer toolbar is again selected by default. Click it to deselect it. Click the **Close Header and Footer** button.

11) Click anywhere on the first page of your sample document, choose **View | Header and Footer**, and click the **Switch Between Header and Footer** button on the Header and Footer toolbar.

12) Delete the page number '1' from the footer, click the **Show Next** button on the Header and Footer toolbar, and delete the page number '2' from the footer. Click the **Close Header and Footer** button.

13) Inspect the page numbers in your document. You can see that you have achieved your desired result: the cover and contents pages have no page numbers, and the pages of text are numbered from 1 to 5.

14) Your final task is to update the page numbering in the table of contents. Click just to the left of any line of the table of contents.

15) Press **F9**. Word displays the *Update Table of Contents* dialog box. Accept the default *Update page numbers only* option and click **OK**.

16) Word updates your table of contents to reflect the new page numbering. Save your sample document with the following name, and close it:

> Chapter26_Exercise_26-3_After_*Your_Name*.doc

Removing section breaks

Section breaks and formatting

Want to remove a section break? Click at the start of the section break and press the **Delete** key.

A section break controls text formatting in the section that precedes it. When you delete a section break, Word:

- removes section-specific formatting from the text that was before the section break; and

- applies to that text the formatting of the text *after* the deleted section break.

Exercise 26.4 demonstrates the effects on document formatting of deleting section breaks.

Exercise 26.4: Remove section breaks

1) Open the following Word document:

> Chapter26_Exercise_26-4_Before.doc

2) Click at the beginning of the second section break, which marks the end of the two-column layout.

> Today, many businesses realise that, in order
> to compete successfully, they need to sell
> their goods and services directly to
> consumers or other businesses over the
> Internet.⎯⎯⎯⎯Section Break (Continuous)⎯⎯⎯⎯

3) Press the **Delete** key to remove the section break. Notice that Word removes the two-column formatting with the deleted section break.

4) Click at the beginning of the first section break and press **Delete**. No formatting change is applied, because the text before and after the deleted section break had single-column formatting.

The upper part of your page should look ike this:

. The·New·Era·of·eBusiness¶

Introduction¶

By transforming the way that people and businesses communicate and interact, the Internet has dramatically changed the face of business.¶

Impressed by the Internet's rising popularity, many businesses have established an online presence. A rich variety of business information—from product and service catalogues to press releases to company contacts—is now available to Internet users.¶

Today, many businesses realise that, in order to compete successfully, they need to sell their goods and services directly to consumers or other businesses over the Internet.¶

5) Save your sample document with the following name, and close it:

`Chapter26_Exercise_26-4_After_`*`Your_Name`*`.doc`

Working with Word's print options

In Word, you are not limited to printing a document in its entirety. Nor are you confined to printing just a single copy in one print operation. Follow Exercise 25.6 to discover the range of print options available to you.

Exercise 26.5: Print document parts and multiple copies

1) Open the following Word document:

`Chapter26_Exercise_26-5_Before.doc`

2) Choose **File | Print**. From the *Print* drop-down list, select *Odd pages*, and click **OK**.

Word should print only the following pages: the cover, page 1, page 3 and page 5.

3) Choose **File | Print**. From the *Print* drop-down list, select *Even pages*, and click **OK**.

Word should print only the following pages: the table of contents, page 2, and page 4.

4) Go to the first page of text in your sample document – the page that follows the table of contents page. Select the 'Mission Statement' heading and the eight lines of text beneath that heading.

> **Mission·Statement¶**
> The·purpose·of·the·Elmsworth·Health·Trust·is·to:¶
> ·→ Promote·good·health¶
> ·→ Diagnose·and·treat·those·who·are·ill¶
> ·→ Provide·health·care·for·those·with·continuing·needs.¶
> Elmsworth·Health·Trust·is·committed·to·these·objectives:¶
> ·→ Irrespective·of·the·individual's·ability·to·pay¶
> ·→ In·partnership·with·people·and·other·organisations¶
> ·→ Within·the·resources·that·are·made·available.¶

5) Choose **File | Print**. In the *Page range* area, select the *Selection* option, and click **OK**.

Word should print only the selected text from the document. Click anywhere outside the selected text to deselect it.

6) Choose **File | Print**. In the *Pages per sheet* box, select *4 pages*, and click **OK**.

Word should print two pages of paper. The first should contain the cover, the contents page, page 1 and page 2. The second should contain pages 3, 4 and 5.

7) You can close your sample document without saving it.

Chapter 26: quick reference

Task	Procedure
Insert a section break directly.	Position the insertion point where you want the new section to begin, choose **Insert | Break**, select your required section break type, and click **OK**.
Remove a section break.	Click at the start of the section break and press the **Delete** key.

Tasks summary: printing

Task	Procedure
Print odd- or even-numbered pages only.	Choose **File | Print**. From the *Print* drop-down list, select *Odd pages* or *Even pages*, and click **OK**.
Print the currently selected part of a document.	Choose **File | Print**. In the *Page range* area, select the *Selection* option, and click **OK**.
Print multiple pages of a document on a single sheet of paper.	Choose **File | Print**. In the *Pages per sheet* box, select 1 to 16 pages, and click **OK**.

Concepts summary

A *section* is a part of a Word document that can have layout settings – such as page margins, headers and footers, and columns – that are different from the rest of the document. Sections are bounded by *section breaks*.

You are most likely to use section breaks to vary the number of columns on a single page or in a single document, and to interrupt page numbering between a table of contents and the text that follows.

Word provides four section break types: *continuous* (starts the new section on the same page), *next page* (starts the new section on the next page), *even page* (starts the new section on the next even-numbered page), and *odd page* (starts the new section on the next odd-numbered page).

Word's *print options* include the ability to print odd- or even-numbered pages or selections only, and to output multiple copies.

Chapter 26: quick quiz

Circle the correct answer to each of the following multiple-choice questions about sections and print options in Word.

Q1	A section in a Word document is …
A.	The part of a document that contains the cover page and the table of contents.
B.	The part of the document that contains preset formatting and standard content supplied by the document's template.
C.	Any part of the document that can have layout settings that are different from the rest of the document.
D.	Any part of the document that uses text, graphics or other content inserted by the AutoText feature.

Q2	Which of the following actions do you take to insert a section break in a Word document?
A.	Choose **Insert | Break**, select your required section break type, and click **OK**.
B.	Right-click where you want the break to appear, and choose the **New Break** command from the pop-up menu.
C.	Choose **Insert | Section Break**, and click **OK**.
D.	Click the **Insert Section Break** button on the Formatting toolbar, select your required section break type, and click **OK**.

Q3	Which of the following Word features inserts one or more section breaks in a document automatically?
A.	A table of contents.
B.	A multiple column layout applied only to a selected part of a document.
C.	Any table.
D.	None of the above – you must insert section breaks directly.

Q4	In Word, which of the following is not a section break type?
A.	First page.
B.	Odd page.
C.	Next page.
D.	Continuous.

Q5	Which of the following formatting features requires the division of a Word document into sections?
A.	The Chapter heading built-in paragraph style applied to the first paragraph of a document.
B.	Multiple column layouts applied only to a selected part of a document.
C.	A table of contents.
D.	An index.

Q6	Which of the following formatting features, applied to only part of a document, does not require the division of a Word document into sections?
A.	Page border and shading features.
B.	Text and numbering in headers and footers.
C.	Footnotes and endnotes.
D.	An index.

Q7	Which of the following actions do you take to remove a section break from a Word document?
A.	Click anywhere on the section break and choose **Breaks | Delete**.
B.	Switch to Outline view, click the **View Breaks** button, select the section break, and press the **Backspace** or **Delete** key.
C.	Click at the start of the section break and press the **Delete** key.
D.	Right-click on the section break and choose **Breaks | Delete** from the pop-up menu.

Q8	In Word, how does the removal of a section break affect the formatting of the text before the deleted section break?
A.	The formatting after the deleted section break is applied to the text that was before the deleted section break.
B.	The formatting before the deleted section break is applied to the text that was after the deleted section break.
C.	The text reverts to the paragraph styles in the associated document template. Any directly applied formatting is removed.
D.	None of the above – the removal of a section break does not affect document formatting.

Q9	In Word, which of the following is not a print option?
A.	Print odd-numbered pages only.
B.	Print the document template only.
C.	Print even-numbered pages only.
D.	Print the selected part of the document only.

Answers

1: C, **2:** A, **3:** B, **4:** A, **5:** B, **6:** D, **7:** C, **8:** A, **9:** B.

27

Mail merge

About mail merge elements

Word's mail merge feature enables you to generate letters containing personalized details, such as names and addresses, for sending to large numbers of people. Three elements are required for the production of mail merge letters: the form letter, the data source and the merge fields. Let's review each element in turn.

Form letters

A form letter holds the text that remains the same in every letter, plus punctuation, spaces and perhaps graphics. You don't type the personalized details in the form letter, because these will be different on each copy of the final, merged letter.

> **Form letter**
>
> *A Word document containing information (text, spaces, punctuation and graphics) that remains the same in each copy of the merged letter.*

Data sources

A data source holds the information that changes for each copy of the final, merged letter – the names and addresses of the people that you want to send the merged letters to.

Data sources can be created in Word, or in a spreadsheet (such as Excel) or database (such as Access).

> **Data source**
>
> *A file containing information (such as names and addresses) that will be different in each merged copy of the final letter.*

Merge fields

Merge fields are special instructions that you insert in your form letter. They tell Word which details you want to merge from your data source, and where Word is to position them in your merged letter.

«FirstName»¶

«Title»·«LastName»,¶

«Company».¶

Merge fields have names such as Job Title, First Name and Town, and are enclosed within double angle brackets. When you merge the form letter and the data source, Word replaces the merge fields in the form letter with the associated details from the data source. For example, Word might replace the merge field called Town with Bristol, Carlisle or Derby on different copies of the merged letter.

> **Merge field**
>
> *An instruction to Word to insert a particular type of information, such as job title or a line of an address, in a specified location on the form letter.*

About mail merge procedures

You perform mail merge actions with Word's *Mail Merge Helper* dialog box, which is displayed by choosing the **Tools | Mail Merge** command, and with the various buttons on the Mail Merge toolbar.

The Mail Merge Helper *dialog box*

You use this dialog box chiefly for creating new form letters and data sources, or for selecting already-created ones.

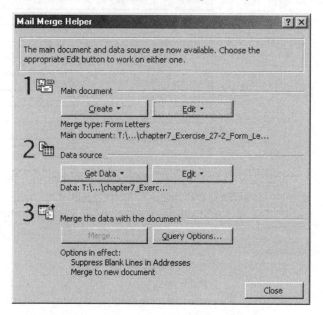

The Mail Merge toolbar

Word displays this toolbar after you create or open a form letter and select a data source. You can use its buttons to insert the merge fields, perform sort and query operations on the data source, and preview merge letters before printing them.

What's advanced about advanced mail merge?

ECDL Advanced Word Processing introduces two new mail merge features, both of which relate to the data source. These are *sorting* and *querying*.

Whichever file type you use as a data source for a mail merge, two conditions apply:

- The data source contents must be arranged in a table, with horizontal rows and vertical coloumns.

- The top row must contain titles identifying the information categories in the columns underneath, such as LastName or PostCode.

Spreadsheets and databases, by nature, can display information in this way. When using a Word document as a data source, you must enter the information in a table, similar to that shown below.

FirstName¤	LastName¤	StreetAddress¤	District¤	PostCode¤	¤
Pamela¤	Connors¤	59·High·Road¤	Santry¤	Dublin·9¤	¤
Margaret¤	Conroy¤	12·Crescent·Gardens¤	Tenenure¤	Dublin·6¤	¤
Ismail¤	Corboy¤	17·Laurel·Avenue¤	Sanymount¤	Dublin·4¤	¤
Denis¤	Collins¤	29·Sandhills·Road¤	Tallaght¤	Dublin·24¤	¤
Derek¤	Corcoran¤	33·Beechwood·Heights¤	Drumcondra¤	Dublin·9¤	¤
Maurice¤	Shelbourne¤	Health·Centre¤	Drumcondra¤	Dublin·9¤	¤
Deborah¤	Cosgrave¤	The·Park·Clinic¤	Santry¤	Dublin·9¤	¤
Mary¤	Costello¤	63·The·Vaults¤	Thomas·Street¤	Dublin·8¤	¤
James¤	Pearce¤	12·Road¤	Raheny¤	Dublin·5¤	¤
Edward¤	Lawson¤	87·Booterstown·Avenue¤	Booterstown¤	Dublin·4¤	¤

Each horizontal row, whether in a Word table, a spreadsheet or a database, is referred to as a *record*, and holds details of an individual person. Each vertical column is called a *field*, and holds information of the same type about each person.

Sorting the data source

The order in which records were originally typed into a data source may not be the order in which, later on, you would prefer to generate mail merge letters. The act of rearranging one or more records into a different sequence is called *sorting*.

For example, you could sort records by the LastName field, so that Adams is displayed first, followed by Brown, then Callaghan, Dickens, and so on.

It is particularly useful in mail merges to be able to sort records by postal district, because you can then collate the printed letters in a manner most helpful to your distribution system.

Rearranging records in a data source based on the values in one or more fields, with the result that the mail merge letters are printed according to postal district or some other user-chosen sequence.

You learn how to sort a data source in Exercise 27.3.

Querying the data source

Sometimes, you may want to generate mail merge letters for only *some* people in your data source: only those in a certain postal district, for example. Or, if your data source also holds financial information, only for those people with unpaid bills. This is called *querying* the data source.

Selecting from a data source only those records that meet your chosen criteria, with the result that mail merge letters are generated only for the relevant people.

You learn how to query a data source in Exercise 27.4.

Working with advanced mail merge: the three tasks

Here are the three tasks that you need to be able to perform with mail merge in Word:

- **Edit a mail merge data source**. Exercise 27.1 takes you through the steps of amending a mail merge data source file. The file is a Word document containing a table.

- **Sort records in a data source**. In Exercise 27.3, you sort a data file before generating a mail merge.

- **Merge a form letter with a queried data source**. Exercise 27.4 shows you how to query a data source for printing mail merge letters for selected people only.

Editing a mail merge source

In Exercise 27.1, you will open a mail merge data source file and amend it in the following ways: edit a record, add a new record, and finally delete a record.

Exercise 27.1: Amend a mail merge data source file

1) Start Word and open the following document:

```
Chapter27_Exercise_27-1_Before.doc
```

Your document consists of names and addresses arranged in a table. Each table row corresponds to a record of an individual person's details.

Your first task is to edit a record.

2) Locate the record containing the details for 'Dennis Collins', and click in the cell containing the first name 'Dennis'. Edit the text to 'Derek'.

Your next task is to add a new record, i.e. a new row, to the Word table.

3) Click anywhere in the bottom row of the table, and choose **Table | Insert I Rows** Below.

In the new row, type the following details:

FirstName	Anne
SecondName	Byrne
StreetAddress	54 Baggot Street
District	Grand Canal
PostCode	Dublin 2

Finally, you will delete a record from the table.

4) Click just to the left of the row containing the name 'EM Gallagher' to select the row. Choose **Table | Delete | Rows**.

5) Save your sample document with the following name, and close it:

Chapter27_Exercise_27-1_After_*Your_Name*.doc

Mail merge: an overview

In Word, mail merging is a five-step process. Let's review each step before continuing further. All steps are available within the **Tools | Mail Merge** command:

1. **Prepare your form letter**. You can open an already-typed letter to use as your form letter, or you can create a new letter as part of the mail merge operation.

2. **Select your data source**. You can select a Word file containing a table or a file created in another software application, such as Microsoft Access or Excel.

3. **Insert merge fields in your form letter**. Using the **Insert Merge Field** button on the Mail Merge toolbar, you can select and then position the merge fields in your form letter.

4. **Preview your merged letters**. Before you produce your merged letters, click on the **View Merged Data** toolbar button to preview the first one or two merged letters.

5. **Print your merged letters**. Happy with the preview? Click the **Mail Merge** toolbar button to perform the complete merge operation. Select the *Merge to printer* option to output copies of your merged letters.

ECDL Advanced Word Processing

In Exercise 27.2, you will perform a basic mail merge operation. You will use the form letter created and its associated data source as the basis for performing the sorting and querying tasks in Exercises 27.3 and 27.4

Exercise 27.2: Perform a simple mail merge

1) Open the following Word document:

    Chapter27_Exercise_27-2_Form_Letter_Before

    This will be the form letter for your mail merge operation.

2) Choose **Tools | Mail Merge**. In the *Main document* area of the *Mail Merge Helper* dialog box, click **Create** and then choose **Form Letters**.

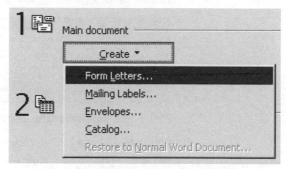

3) In the next dialog box displayed, click **Active Window**.

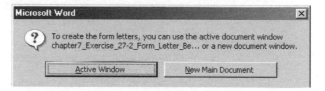

    Word redisplays the *Mail Merge Helper* dialog box.

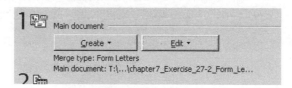

4) In the *Data source* area of the dialog box, click **Get Data**, and then choose **Open Data Source**.

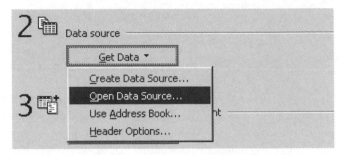

5) Select the following Word document as your data source, and click **Open**:

    Chapter27_Exercise_27-2_Data_Source

6) Word now displays the following dialog box.

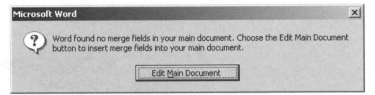

Click **Edit Main Document**, as directed.

7) On the Mail Merge toolbar, click the Insert Merge Field button to view the fields available for merging to your form letter.

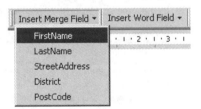

8) For each merge field, place the cursor in the appropriate position in your form letter, click the **Insert Merge Field** button, and click the relevant field title from the drop-down list. Continue until your form letter looks like this:

```
¶
To:  →  «FirstName» «LastName»,¶
 →   →  «StreetAddress»,¶
 →   →  «District»,¶
 →   →  «PostCode» ¶
¶
¶
¶
¶
¶
 →   →   →   →   →   →   →   →   →   →  20/11/2001¶
¶
¶
Dear «FirstName»,¶
¶
```

Do not forget to type spaces between merge fields just as you would between ordinary text.

Now everything is in place for the mail merge operation.

**View Merged
Data button**

9) Click the **View Merged Data** button on the Mail Merge toolbar. Word displays the first merged letter. It should look like this:

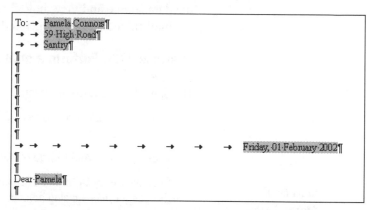

10) You can move forwards and backwards through the merged letters by clicking the **Next Record** and **Previous Record** buttons on the Mail Merge toolbar.

You are now ready to perform the mail merge.

**Start Mail
Merge button**

11) Click the **Start Mail Merge** button on the Mail Merge toolbar to display the *Merge* dialog box.

Select the options as shown below and click **Merge**.

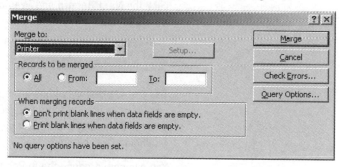

12) Word now displays the *Printer* dialog box. Click **OK** to print your merged letters – or click **Close** to exit from the merge operation without printing.

13) Save your form letter with the following name, and close it:

```
Chapter27_Exercise_27-2_Form_Letter_
After_Your_Name.doc
```

Working with a sorted data source

In Exercise 27.3, you will open a form letter similar to the one that you saved in Exercise 27.2. Like the form letter in the previous exercise, the form letter in Exercise 27.3 is linked to a data source. As a result, Word displays the Mail Merge toolbar when you open the form letter. You will then sort the records in the data source and view how this affects the sequence in which the mail merge letters are printed.

Exercise 27.3: Perform a mail merge from sorted data source

1) Open the following document:

   ```
   Chapter27_Exercise_27-3_Form_Letter_
   Before.doc
   ```

Start Mail Merge button

2) Click the **Start Mail Merge** button on the Mail Merge toolbar.

3) Click the **Query Options** button on the *Merge* dialog box to display the *Query Options* dialog box, and then click the **Sort Records** tab.

4) Select the *LastName* field in the *Sort by* drop-down list. Accept the default sort order of *Ascending*. Click **OK**.

5) Word redisplays the *Merge* dialog box. Click **Close** to close it and return to your form letter.

View Merged Data button

6) Let's inspect the effect of your sort on your mail merge letters. Click the **View Merged Data** button on the Mail Merge toolbar, and then click the **Next Record** and **Previous Record** buttons on the Mail Merge toolbar.

You can see that Word has arranged the letters in a new, alphabetic sequence according to the recipient's last name. For example, the letter to Anne Byrne will be printed first, and that to Maurice Shelbourne will be printed last.

7) You can now produce the merged letters by clicking the **Start Mail Merge** button on the Mail Merge toolbar to display the *Merge* dialog box, selecting your required options, and, when Word displays the *Printer* dialog box, clicking **OK**.

ECDL Advanced Word Processing

8) Save your form letter with the following name, and close it:

> Chapter27_Exercise_27-3_Form_Letter_
> After_*Your_Name*.doc

Working with a queried data source

In Exercise 27.4, you will open a form letter that is linked to a data source. As a result, Word displays the Mail Merge toolbar when you open the form letter. You will then query the records in the data source and view how your query limits the number of mail merge letters that will be printed.

Exercise 27.4: Perform a mail merge from a queried data source

1) Open the following Word document:

> Chapter27_Exercise_27-4_Form_Letter_
> Before.doc

**Start Mail
Merge button**

2) Click the **Start Mail Merge** button on the Mail Merge toolbar.

3) Click the **Query Options** button on the *Merge* dialog box to display the **Filter Records** tab.

4) In the *Field* drop-down list, select *LastName*. In the *Comparison* drop-down list, select *Equal to*. In the *Compare to* box, type the name Byrne.

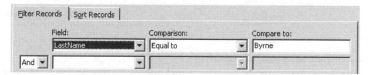

Click **OK** and then **Close** to return to your form letter.

**View Merged
Data button**

5) Let's inspect the effect of your sort on your mail merge letters. Click the **View Merged Data** button on the Mail Merge toolbar, and then click the **Next Record** and **Previous Record** buttons on the Mail Merge toolbar.

6) You can see that Word has created just a single mail merge letter – the letter to Anne Byrne.

7) You can now produce the merged letter by clicking the **Start Mail Merge** button on the Mail Merge toolbar to display the *Merge* dialog box, selecting your required options, and, when Word displays the *Printer* dialog box, clicking **OK**.

8) Save your form letter with the following name, and close it:

> Chapter27_Exercise_27-4_Form_Letter_
> After_*Your_Name*.doc

Chapter 27:
quick reference

Tasks summary

Task	Procedure
Perform a mail merge from a sorted data source.	Open a form letter that has a data source associated with it.
	Click the **Start Mail Merge** button on the Mail Merge toolbar and click the **Sort Records** tab.
	Select your required field in the *Sort by* drop-down list, accept or amend the sort order, and click **OK** and then **Close**.
Perform a mail merge from a queried source.	Open a form letter that has a data source associated with it.
	Click the **Start Mail Merge** button on the Mail Merge toolbar.
	On the **Filter Records** tab, select your required field in the *Field* drop-down list and your required operator in the *Comparison* drop-down list. Type the query text in the *Compare to* box, and click **OK** and then **Close**.

Concepts summary

Mail merge is the process of combining a *form letter* (which holds the unchanging letter text) and a *data source* (which holds the names, addresses and other details that are different in every merged letter).

The data source can be created in Word, in a spreadsheet or in a database. Whichever file type is used, its contents must be arranged in a table, with the top row containing the field titles. *Merge fields* in the form letter indicate which details are taken from the data source, and where they are positioned on the final, merged letter.

You can *sort* the records in a data source to print the mail merge letters in a particular sequence, such as according to postcode. You can also *query* the data source so that Word prints mail merge letters only for selected people.

Chapter 27: quick quiz

Circle the correct answer to each of the following multiple-choice questions about mail merge in Word.

Q1	In Word, which of the following elements is not required to generate mail merge letters?
A.	Merge fields.
B.	Form letter.
C.	Mail merge template.
D.	Data source.

Q2	In Word, which of the following statements about form letters is true?
A.	They may contain text but not graphics.
B.	They can be created in a spreadsheet or database.
C.	They are limited to a single page of text.
D.	They hold the content that remains the same in every letter

Q3	In Word, which of the following statements about mail merge fields is untrue?
A.	They are stored in the mail merge template.
B.	They are enclosed within double angle brackets.
C.	They have names such as JobTitle, FirstName and Town.
D.	They tell Word which details to merge from the data source.

Q4	In Word, which of the following statements about data sources is untrue?
A.	Their contents must be arranged in a table.
B.	A spreadsheet or database file can be used as a data source.
C.	They contain records regarding the people who are to receive the merged letters.
D.	They are enclosed within double angle brackets.

Q5	In a mail merge operation in Word, which of the following tasks would you perform first?
A.	Select the data source.
B.	Open an already-typed letter to use as your form letter.
C.	Sort and/or query the data source.
D.	Insert the merge fields.

Q6	Which of the following toolbar buttons would you click to preview mail merge letters before printing them?
A.	Merge...
B.	« » ABC
C.	
D.	

Q7	In Word, what effect does sorting records in the data source have on the mail merge letters?
A.	It enables more than one data source to be used in printing the letters.
B.	It restricts the number of letters printed according to the user-selected sort criteria.
C.	It changes the sequence in which the letters are produced by the printer.
D.	None of the above.

Q8	In Word, what effect does querying the records in the data source have on the mail merge letters?
A.	It restricts the number of letters printed according to the user-specified query criteria.
B.	It changes the sequence in which the letters are produced by the printer.
C.	It enables multiple data sources to be used in printing the letters.
D.	None of the above.

Answers

1: C, **2:** D, **3:** A, **4:** D, **5:** B, **6:** B, **7:** C, **8:** A.

Index

pictures
    inserted into documents 64, 369, 378–9, 386–7
    surrounded by text 380–1
pie charts 252
plot area 242, 257
print options 414
promotion of headings 3–4, 7, 12–13
Protect Document dialog box 193–4
protection
    for documents 146, 150–5
    for forms 187, 192–5, 203–6
    for subdocuments 178

quotes, straight or curly 94–5, 102

read-only documents 150–1, 155, 178
records for mail merge 422
rectangles, drawing of 371, 384–5
reference marks 262, 276
reformatting of multiple documents 49
Remove Subdocuments button 179
reordering of numbered headings 11–12
reorganization of documents 7–9
Replace text as you type checkbox 77–9, 85
reviewers of documents, identification of 148–9
Reviewing toolbar 145, 147, 149, 153, 161, 164, 166
revision marks 161, 163, 166–7
rows in tables, sorting of 219–21, 225

section breaks 407–16
    and formatting 413–14
    insertion of 408, 415
    in multi-column layouts 409–11
    removal of 413–15
    in tables of contents 411–13
    types of 410
sections of documents, layout differences between
        407, 415
separator characters 214
separator lines
    above endnotes 274
    above footnotes 269–70
shading
    behind field results 112
    behind paragraphs 338, 341, 343–7, 407
shadow effects 339, 372
shapes, user-drawn 368, 387
Shimmer effect 340–1

shortcut keys
    for document navigation 136–7
    for styles 27–9
    for text selection 136–7
Show Heading buttons 8–9, 12–13, 174–5
signatures, scanned images of 64
small caps 339
sort orders 221, 226
sorting
    of records for mail merge 422–3, 428–30
    of rows in tables 219–21, 225
    two-level and three-level types of 221–3
spaces between words, missing 74
Sparkle Text effect 340–1
spellchecking 74, 76–80, 85
splitting of cells 216–19, 225–6
squares, drawing of 371, 385
strikethrough 160, 166, 339
structure of documents 5
Style Area 23
Style Box 21–2, 30
style modifications
    stored in individual documents or in templates
        52–3, 56, 60
    updating document formats for 60
style sheets 21, 49; *see also* templates
styles 19–32, 48, 122
    amendment of 24–5, 32
    application and reapplication of 28–30
    applied with AutoFormat 57–60
    automatically defined on the basis of user's
        formatting 101–2
    built into Word 19, 32
    creation of 25–9, 32
    display of information on 22–3, 32
    in endnotes 274
    in footnotes 269
    short-cut keys for 27–9
    storage of 48–9
    in tables of contents 297, 304
subdocuments 171–2
    addition to or removal from master document
        178–80
    displayed within master document 177
    headings or heading levels converted into 172–6,
        180–1
    inserted in outlines 180
    insertion of existing documents as 176–7, 181

Licensing Agreement

This book comes with a CD software package. By opening this package, you are agreeing to be bound by the following:

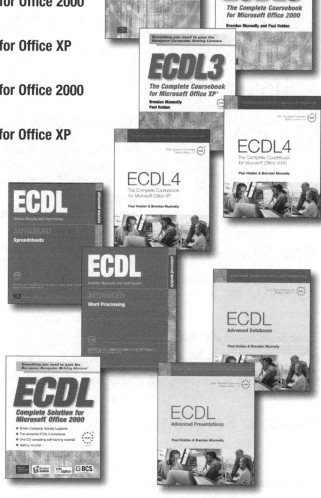